ARTHUR SCHNITZLER

UNIVERSITY OF NORTH CAROLINA
STUDIES IN THE GERMANIC LANGUAGES
AND LITERATURES

Publication Committee

FREDERIC E. COENEN, EDITOR

WERNER P. FRIEDERICH   GEORGE S. LANE

JOHN G. KUNSTMANN   HERBERT W. REICHERT

For other volumes in this series see page 151.

NUMBER FIFTY-SIX

UNIVERSITY
OF NORTH CAROLINA
STUDIES IN
THE GERMANIC LANGUAGES
AND LITERATURES

Left to Right, Top to Bottom: K3., C13.3, C29.3, B31.2, B41.4, C4.10, X102.

AN ANNOTATED ARTHUR SCHNITZLER BIBLIOGRAPHY

Editions and Criticism in German, French, and English
1879-1965

RICHARD H. ALLEN

With a Foreword by Robert O. Weiss
President of the International Arthur Schnitzler Research Association

CHAPEL HILL
THE UNIVERSITY OF NORTH CAROLINA PRESS

Printed in the Netherlands by Royal VanGorcum Ltd., Assen

For Schnitzler Scholars, Collectors, and Friends

FOREWORD

The appearance of a thorough and competently assembled bibliography is always a welcome event in the world of literature. The present volume, however, will be greeted with special enthusiasm by Schnitzler-scholars everywhere because the lack of such a reference work has long been a source of difficulties and frustrations to them. Moreover, this compilation is not only a fine investigative aid, it is also a meritorious scholarly contribution. To produce it, years of careful, conscientious, and sometimes discouraging work were required, but the result justifies the effort. Even a cursory inspection of these pages will show that they contain all the information one could desire in a bibliography. (The only missing item of importance is Schnitzler's *Nachlass*, but since it has neither been published nor even exhaustively inventoried, it could not be included here. Of course, such excerpts from the posthumous papers as did appear in print are duly registered.)

There is, then, no need to discuss further a work that can speak so clearly for itself. Instead, I should like to express on this occasion my deep satisfaction at the part which the *International Arthur Schnitzler Research Association* (IASRA) was able to play in aiding Professor Allen's realization of his project by furnishing financial assistance to facilitate publication.

While the IASRA has many times in the past provided scholars engaged in appropriate research with needed materials from the *Schnitzler Archive*, microfilms, information, and advice, it has never before been in a position to make funds available for a specific project. I sincerely believe that the Association has done well to sponsor Professor Allen's work and that its Executive Council could hardly have made a better choice for their first venture in awarding research grants.

Spring 1966

Robert O. Weiss
President, IASRA

PREFACE

The present undertaking is an attempt to record chronologically and systematically all of the German editions of Arthur Schnitzler's works, the English and French translations, and all criticism on the author (including reviews) appearing in German, French, and English. (In the case of the latter, items appearing in newspapers, literary histories, and standard works of reference are, in general, excluded.) Descriptive or evaluative annotations are added when deemed appropriate. The period of coverage is from the publication of Schnitzler's first work in 1879 through 1965. The bibliography is as complete as I have been able to make it, using American library resources and helpful European correspondents. At the beginning of his work the bibliographer is apt to proclaim "comprehensive and exhaustive," only to end wearily with "selective." I hope that this is not the case here; for any instances of "selectivity" I assume sole responsibility.

A word on the antecedents and genesis of this work. A number of incomplete bibliographies of Schnitzler's works, translations, and criticism have appeared in the past. Several of the early monographs on the author contained brief listings of the published works and major criticism; the first formal attempt at a Schnitzler-bibliography was all of five pages, appearing in 1913 with the title "Arthur Schnitzler: A Bibliography; Translation, Production and Criticism in English" by Archibald Henderson. Master's theses by Beatrice M. Schrumpf and Lawrence E. Gemeinhart, done in the early 1930's under the direction of America's first Schnitzler scholar, Otto P. Schinnerer of Columbia University, dealt with American criticism and translations, and criticism appearing in certain Berlin literary periodicals. The greatest contribution to Schnitzler bibliographical scholarship was made by Schinnerer himself with the publication of his "Systematisches Verzeichnis der Werke von Arthur Schnitzler" in 1932. This monumental undertaking was planned in nine parts and was to include all of the literary works, the medical writings, the aphorisms and philosophical writings, "Verschiedenes," as well as the translations into all foreign languages. Unfortunately, only the sections covering the literary works were completed. These have become the starting point for all bibliographical investigations and the 1961-1962 edition of the *Gesammelte Werke* was based on them. The present bibliography is no exception and owes much to Schinnerer's compilation. Schinnerer, however, made no attempt to treat Schnitzler criticism and there have been no earlier efforts *per se* to do this. Doctoral dissertations written on the author have, as a matter of course, contained partial bibliographies of the works and criticism (those found in the dissertations by Georgette Boner in 1930 and Herbert Lederer in 1953 have been more complete than most), but in no instance have these listings been annotated.

The bibliography presented here is an outgrowth of my doctoral dissertation done at the University of Michigan in 1964: "Arthur Schnitzler's Works and their Reception: An Annotated Bibliography." The second half of this work consisted of a Schnitzler bibliography in chronological form with 1007 entries. The present bibliography is essentially a reorganization and expansion of this material. I have recast the whole into a systematic form, bringing together editions, translations, and criticism for each individual work; the number of entries is now over 2000. It is hoped that these changes and additions (I have also added an index of Schnitzler-titles) will enhance the usefulness of the work.

My greatest debt in this undertaking is to Professor Walter Reichart of the University of Michigan; it is he who first suggested the need for an annotated Schnitzler bibliography and it was under his direction that I completed my dissertation in 1964. He has been a constant source of encouragement and his suggestions have to a great degree made the present work possible. I would mention too my indebtedness to Professor Robert O. Weiss for permission to consult the microfilmed Schnitzler archive and for his interest in the project; hardly less is my debt of gratitude to the International Arthur Schnitzler Research Association and its individual members for support and cooperation in the undertaking (I would mention in particular Mr. Leonard Simons of Detroit). I thank Madame Dominique Auclères and Madame Françoise Derré in France, and Frau Gerda Niedieck of the S. Fischer Verlag for many bibliographical favors; and I am grateful to Professor Heinrich Schnitzler of Vienna for his interest in the completion of the work. Finally, without the cooperation of many reference librarians, Schnitzler scholars, and wifely patience this labor could never have been ended.

Albion College   Richard H. Allen
Albion, Michigan   December, 1965

TABLE OF CONTENTS

ARTHUR SCHNITZLER'S LIFE AND WORKS:
A SURVEY

Our knowledge of Schnitzler's life is at best fragmentary. The author's reluctance to answer questions about his personal life or to submit biographical sketches has left us with relatively little autobiographical information. Frida Ilmer commented on this in 1933, two years after the author's death:

> Schnitzlers Einstellung gegenüber den Versuchen, biographische Daten von ihm zu erlangen, verdient übrigens bemerkt zu werden. Ausser den Tatsachen, dass er am 15. Mai 1862 geboren wurde, sich ursprünglich der Medizin widmete und am 21. Oktober 1931 daselbst starb, besitzen wir nur sehr spärliche Daten über sein Leben, die meistens auf Aussagen seiner Freunde beruhen. Über sein Privatleben wissen wir so gut wie nichts. Der Grund dafür liegt darin, dass Schnitzler sich entschieden – und scheinbar auch erfolgreich – gegen angehende Biographen wehrte.[1]

Sol Liptzin begins his monograph on Schnitzler of 1932:

> Always frank in answering questions about his literary work, he resented all written references to his personal life. When asked for complete biographical data, he submitted the following: "I was born in 1862 and was a physician."[2]

It is of course true that we now know more about the author than was the case in the first years after his death. Several volumes of published correspondence (as well as periodical articles containing correspondence), the memoirs of his wife, and numerous special studies have contributed to our store of biographical information. But we shall have to await the publication of Schnitzler's autobiography, *Leben und Nachklang, Werk und Widerhall*, covering the first twenty-seven years of his life, and the numerous *Tagebücher*, kept for fifty years of his life, for a complete biographical portrait. In the meantime we shall have to remain content with a biographical sketch drawn primarily from external sources.

Arthur Schnitzler was born of upper middle-class Jewish parents in Vienna on May 15, 1862. The father, Johann Schnitzler, physician and university professor, was born in Gross-Kanissa (Hungary) and his native tongue was Hungarian. His own father too had been a physician, and so the medical tradition was well-established in the

Schnitzler family. The original family name "Zimmermann" was changed for some unknown reason by the father to "Schnitzler." The author's father, Johann Schnitzler, was a prominent laryngologist, who counted a number of well-known theatrical people among his patients (such as Adolf Sonnenthal and Charlotte Wolter). It is interesting to note that in his youth he had written a few dramas himself, but had given up his literary activities when he entered the medical school of the University of Vienna. According to a recent biographical study Schnitzler regarded his father as a "superficial, friendly man without a deep knowledge of people."[3] The mother, Louise Markbreiter, had also been born in Hungary, but came from the Burgenland area, where German was always spoken. Her brother was a well-known lawyer in Vienna. Arthur was the oldest of two brothers; Julius, his younger brother, later became an outstanding surgeon and director of the Vienna City Hospital.

The Schnitzler house was located in the Jägerzeile, now the Praterstrasse, in Vienna. The importance of *Ort* and *Zeit* for the author has often been cited: cosmopolitan Vienna before the First World War with its intricate class structure and highly heterogeneous population. Of equal importance in his development was his Jewishness; Schnitzler himself was keenly aware of his Jewish origins. Whether his parental faith was a burden to him or not we can only surmise on the basis of his writings. Robert O. Weiss concludes that it was:

> There can be no doubt that Arthur Schnitzler tasted the bitter dregs of anti-Semitism. Only a member of an actively persecuted minority could have written a novel like *Der Weg ins Freie* . . . and only a man who had gained much inner stature through suffering hatred and injustice could have replied with the moderation and, above all, the analytical understanding demonstrated in the drama "Professor Bernhardi."[4]

Yet, the house in the Jägerzeile, by virtue of the father's profession, constituted a gathering place for theatrical people and artists. The character Irsil might well speak for the young Schnitzler in "Alkandi's Lied":

> Mein Vater war ein kunstbefliss'ner Mann
> In uns'rem Hause, jedem Edlen offen,
> Hat man der Künstler beste angetroffen.[5]

The father often received complimentary tickets to the opera and the Burgtheater. Arthur frequently accompanied him, seeing at the age of six or seven his first theatrical performance, *Orpheus*, at the Carltheater. At the age of ten the boy witnessed a performance of Gounod's *Faust*, during the course of which one of the actors bowed in the direction of Professor Schnitzler's box. The great astonishment of the young boy at the impropriety of such behavior would seem to foreshadow his later artistic preoccupation with the problem of reality and illusion epitomized in "Der grüne Kakadu."

Perhaps stimulated by his artistic environment, Schnitzler began writing at the early age of nine. In a letter to Georg Brandes, the established writer recalls his early efforts:

> Früher einmal, von meinem 9. bis zu meinem 20. Lebensjahr hab' ich geschrieben "wie der Vogel singt" – – ich muss damals sehr glücklich gewesen sein; denn ich erinnere mich gar nicht, wie ichs eigentlich gemacht habe. Ich habe noch manches, Trauerspiele und Fastnachtsspiele und komische Romane; nahezu durchaus blödsinnig. Aber ich habe selbst zu der Zeit, da ich diese Dinge schrieb, nie das Bedürfnis gehabt, es irgendwem zu zeigen.[6]

His first major dramatic attempt came in 1872 and was called "Aristokrat und Demokrat," probably influenced by Schiller's *Sturm und Drang* plays. Prior to the publication of "Anatol" in 1893, Schnitzler had written about thirty plays, fifteen dramatic fragments, and a large number of poems. Schinnerer, in commenting on the early works, discerns in them a definitely hedonistic, epicurean philosophy.[7]

From 1871 to 1879 he attended the Akademische Gymnasium in Vienna, at the same time continuing his youthful writing efforts. According to Herbert Lederer the major literary influences at this time were Tieck, Immermann, and E. T. A. Hoffmann; one might surmise that it was from the last of these that he acquired his tendency towards exotic names.[8] In 1878 Schnitzler began his most ambitious pre-*Anatol* work, the Grillparzer-like drama "Aegidius," which he completed two years later.

In 1879 he entered the University of Vienna as a student in the *medizinische Fakultät*, graduating with the M. D. degree in 1885. From 1885 to 1888 he was *Aspirant* and *Sekundärarzt* in Vienna. His internship was under Professor Standhardtner for internal medicine, under Professor Isidor Neumann for dermatology and syphilology, and under Professor Meynert for psychiatry. His literary interests and wide readings never diminished; he occupied himself with Kant, Schopenhauer, Nietzsche, Hebbel, Georg and Ludwig Büchner, Ernst Mach (his old friend Hermann Bahr was a Mach-disciple) and Hermann von Helmholtz. Schnitzler's first published work, observations on a medical conference in Amsterdam, appeared in 1879 in a medical journal edited by his father. His first published literary work (the poem "Liebeslied der Balledrine") appeared the following year in a Munich literary journal. Six years later, in 1886, a number of aphorisms and his first narrative work appeared in the Viennese weekly, *Die Deutsche Wochenschrift*. In the same year his first contribution was accepted by the Viennese literary periodical, *An der schönen blauen Donau*, edited by Paul Goldmann. Some of these early contributions appeared under the pseudonym "Anatol."

In the summer of 1888 Schnitzler undertook a study trip to London

3

(investigating medical conditions and clinics under Felix Simon), Paris, and Copenhagen. Upon his return he took up the position of *Assistent* at the Allgemeine Poliklinik, where he worked under his father as a resident in laryngology. Simultaneously he served from 1887 to 1894 as editor of the *Internationale Klinische Rundschau*, to which he also contributed a number of medical book reviews. In spite of his activity in laryngology it soon became evident that his real medical interest was psychiatry. In 1887 he had reviewed a book by Charcot, translated from the French by Sigmund Freud, and he soon gained some competence in hypnosis. His medical dissertation in 1889 was entitled "Behandlung der funktionellen Aphonie durch Hypnose." (Hypnosis plays a rôle in several of the early works.) At this time he conducted many hypnotic experiments, keeping careful notes of the results. At least one critic has affirmed that Schnitzler's decision to give up these experiments was the result of malicious rumors circulating among the uneducated public.

Hermann Bahr, upon his return from Paris, had gathered around himself a group of the young "moderns" in the Café Griensteidl, a group that became known as "Jung Österreich" and later as "Jung Wien." The group included, among others, in addition to Bahr himself, Beer-Hofmann, Hofmannsthal, Felix Dörmann, Karl Kraus, Richard Specht, Felix Salten, Peter Altenberg, and Schnitzler. Here many a literary conversation was held and here many a literary work was read aloud by its author, discussed, and criticized. But Schnitzler, as much as he might have appeared at this time to his contemporaries as the living embodiment of Anatol, soon broke away from café society with its literary associations, thereby revealing an inclination towards aloofness. In April, 1892, he wrote to Richard Beer-Hofmann: "Das Café Griensteidl existiert für mich nicht mehr . . . Ich will versuchen, ein Virtuose der Einsamkeit zu werden."[9]

Turning again to Schnitzler's literary activities, the stage manuscript of "Das Märchen," a problem play showing the strong influence of Ibsen, was printed at the author's own expense in 1891. The play was subsequently performed in 1893 at Das Deutsche Volkstheater in Vienna. The same year saw the publication of the complete "Anatol"-cycle, again at the author's own expense. His literary reputation was not secured, however, until 1894 when "Sterben" appeared in *Die Neue Deutsche Rundschau*. Even greater was the applause for "Liebelei," when it was performed the following year under the direction of Max Burckhard in the Burgtheater. Olga Schnitzler writes of this production in her memoirs:

> Auf der vierten Galerie des Burgtheaters hatte ich bittere Tränen geweint um Christinens Schicksal, und etwas erstaunlich Neues, Schönes war geschehen: Da standen sie nicht wie sonst auf der Bühne in einer heroischen Dekoration, in farbigem Kostüm, grosse Verse rollend, nein, ein junges

Mädchen aus dem Volk klagte im wienerischen Dialekt ihre Liebe und ihre Verzweiflung, einfache Menschen, nah und vertraut, waren in die Sphäre der Dichtung gehoben worden. Konnte man ihnen nicht in jedem Augenblick begegnen, waren es nicht Worte echter, väterlicher Einsicht, die der alte Musiker, Christinens Vater, da oben sprach? Wusste hier einer von unserer nur zögernd und schamhaft eingestandenen Bedrängnis, wagte er es auszusprechen, dass die unbegreiflich festgerammten Begriffe unserer Eltern keine Geltung mehr hatten für uns, die wir nun heranwuchsen? Man war also nicht im Unrecht, nicht allein – – welche Befreiung![10]

"Liebelei" was published in book form in 1896 by the S. Fischer Verlag in Berlin, a firm that was soon to become the author's regular publisher.

Schnitzler's decision to turn "professional" as a writer was made in 1893-1894; until then he had had some misgivings about his literary ability and was also concerned about his father's reaction. The death of Johann Schnitzler in 1893 and his son's leaving the Allgemeine Poliklinik in the same year to establish himself as a general practitioner in Vienna seem to mark a turning point in his life. It was possibly his disillusionment with his medicical colleagues, coupled with the feeling that he had chosen the wrong speciality (laryngology), that turned Schnitzler from a medical career. Though he continued to practice medicine, and in a brief outline of his life stresses that he never officially gave up his medical practice, his dominant interest became writing.

In 1895 Schnitzler met Marie Reinhard, who, until her death four years later, held his affection. Olga Schnitzler reveals that the character Anna in *Der Weg ins Freie* is modeled after her, and that, in fact, the whole novel is highly autobiographical. In a letter to Georg Brandes dated May 8, 1899, Schnitzler wrote:

Vor sieben Wochen ist das Geschöpf begraben worden, das ich von allen Menschen der Erde am liebsten gehabt habe, meine Geliebte, Freundin und Braut – die durch mehr als vier Jahre meinem Leben seinen ganzen Sinn und seine ganze Freude gegeben hat – und seither dämmere ich hin, aber existiere kaum mehr. Aus der Fülle der Gesundheit und Jugend hat sie eine blödsinnige und tückische Krankheit innerhalb zweier Tage ins Grab gerissen, und ich habe sie sterben gesehen, bei vollem Bewusstsein sterben gesehen.[11]

In 1903 Schnitzler married Olga Gussmann and that same year a son was born, Heinrich, who later followed a theatrical career and for several years was Professor of Speech and Drama at the University of California.[12] A daughter committed suicide in 1928 because of her husband's infidelity. Since 1909 the Schnitzlers lived in a newly purchased house in the Sternwarte Strasse.

1893 saw the publication of shorter narrative works, *Die Frau des Weisen*, as well as his second problem play, "Freiwild". "Reigen" appeared in 1900 in manuscript form to be distributed among a small circle of the author's friends. (When Olga Gussmann, soon to become his wife, asked him if she might see this much-discussed work, he replied that it might not be appropriate for a young lady.) The same year "Leutnant Gustl" was published in the *Neue Freie Presse* (Vienna) and soon Schnitzler, who was *Oberarzt* in the Reserves, heard of a military investigation concerning his satire. The following judgment was rendered:

> Der Ehrenrat für Landwehroffiziere und Kadetten Wien hat über die wider den Oberarzt Dr. Arthur Schnitzler im Verhältnis der Evidenz des k. k. Landw. J. R. Klagenfurt Nr. 4 erhobene Anschuldigung, dass er als dem Offiziersstande angehörig eine Novelle verfasste und in einem Weltblatte veröffentlichte, durch deren Inhalt die Ehre und das Ansehen der k. k. österr. u. ung. Armee herabgesetzt wurde, sowie dass er gegen die persönlichen Angriffe der Zeitung *Reichswehr* keinerlei Schritte unternommen hat nach der am 26. April stattgehabten Schlussverhandlung erkannt – der beschuldigte Oberarzt hat die Standesehre... verletzt... [Schnitzler had not answered a denunciatory article in the *Reichswehr*.][13]

In consequence he was demoted to *Sanitätssoldat*.

In 1901 "Der Schleier der Beatrice" was brought out by S. Fischer, to be followed in 1902 by the cycle *Lebendige Stunden*. Many critics have designated the publication of "Der einsame Weg" in 1904 as the beginning of the author's "second period," a moving away from impassioned youthful cynicism to a greater reflective maturity. Other major dramatic works to follow were "Der Ruf des Lebens" and "Zwischenspiel" in 1906, "Komtesse Mizzi" in 1908, "Der junge Medardus" and "Das weite Land" in 1910. With the publication of "Professor Bernhardi" in 1912 the second period draws to a close. A number o narrative works were published during these years, "Der blinde Geronimo und sein Bruder" appeared in 1900, and the author's only novel, *Der Weg ins Freie*, in 1908.

The fact that Otto Brahm, the gifted theater director and close friend of Schnitzler, died in 1912 has been suggested as an important factor in the author's turning more and more to the narrative form. Schnitzler's fiftieth birthday in the same year was celebrated by the German press, a number of special *Hefte* appeared in his honor, and several critical studies on him were published. Three of his dramas earned him literary prizes: for "Zwischenspiel" he received the Grillparzerpreis in 1908; for "Der junge Medardus" the Raimundpreis in 1910; and for "Professor Bernhardi" the Wiener Volkstheaterpreis in 1914.

Up to the outbreak of the first World War Schnitzler traveled extensively in Europe, frequently spending his summers in Switzerland or on the Danish coast (the third act of "Komödie der Verführung" is laid here). His reaction to the senselessness of war is found in his correspondence with Georg Brandes and in the posthumously published work "Über Krieg und Frieden." After the war he finally agreed to a performance of "Reigen;" the première took place in

Berlin in 1920, leading to demonstrations and riots, in consequence of which a court trial was held on the morality of the work. In the final verdict the drama was vindicated and designated a "moral deed" in the interest of the preservation of public morality.

In 1921 Schnitzler and his wife separated. In a letter to Brandes he writes:

> Von meiner Frau bin ich geschieden – aber wir sind gute Freunde geblieben – ja in der letzten Zeit wieder geworden, könnte man besser sagen.[14]

The death of his daughter in 1928 was a heavy blow. Schnitzler's loneliness, so often mentioned by critics as a central problem in his works, increased as he grew older. One recalls Baron Diebl and Anatol's exchange in "Anatols Grössenwahn:"

> Baron: Also Eremit geworden?
> Anatol: Eremit geblieben.[15]

Invited to visit America, Schnitzler declined, saying that he was becoming "menschenmüde." He died of a heart attack on October 21, 1931, while still attempting to give to his most elusive drama, "Der Ruf des Lebens," its final form.

Schnitzler's third literary period, beginning in 1912 and extending up to his death, has often been called "retrospective" by critics, and it is perhaps true that the author felt most at home in pre-1914 Vienna; indeed, the tributes accorded to him in 1922 speak of him and his works as if already belonging to the past. His greatest literary achievements were narrative in form, although the cycle *Komödie der Worte*, published in 1915, and the dramas "Fink und Fliederbusch," "Die Schwestern," "Komödie der Verführung," "Der Gang zum Weiher," and "Im Spiel der Sommerlüfte" fall into this last period. Among his masterpieces in narrative form during these years were "Frau Beate und ihr Sohn" in 1913, "Doktor Gräsler, Badearzt"(1917), "Casanovas Heimfahrt" (1918), "Fräulein Else" (1924), "Traumnovelle" (1925), and finally "Flucht in die Finsternis" (1931). A number of works have been published since the author's death, but an even greater amount of material remains in the *Nachlass*, awaiting editing and publication.

In this brief sketch too little has been said of the variety in form and content of the Schnitzlerian world. It is hoped that the bibliography which follows will better display this richness and contribute in some small measure to a better understanding of an author whose permanent position in the history of German literature is now secure.

NOTES

[1] Frida Ilmer, "Die Gestalt des Künstlers bei Schnitzler"(unpublished Ph.D. dissertation, Johns Hopkins University, 1933), p. 177-178 (note).

[2] Sol Liptzin, *Arthur Schnitzler* (New York: Prentice-Hall, 1932), p. 1.

[3] Herbert I. Kupper and Hilda S. Rollman-Branch, "Freud and Schnitzler – 'Doppelgänger'," *Journal of the American Psychoanalytical Association*, VII (1959), 112.

[4] Robert O. Weiss, "A Study of Arthur Schnitzler (With Special Consideration of the Problem of Psychosis in 'Flight into Darkness')" (unpublished Ph. D. dissertation, Stanford University, 1955), p. 34-35.

[5] Arthur Schnitzler, *Die dramatischen Werke* (Frankfurt a.M.: S. Fischer, 1962), Bd. I, S. 10.

[6] Kurt Bergel (ed.), *Georg Brandes und Arthur Schnitzler: Ein Briefwechsel* (Bern: Francke), S. 71-72.

[7] See Otto P. Schinnerer, "The Early Works of Arthur Schnitzler," *Germanic Review*, IV (1929), 153-197, and "The Literary Apprenticeship of Arthur Schnitzler," *Germanic Review*, V (1930), 58-82.

[8] See Herbert Lederer, "The Problem of Ethics in the Works of Arthur Schnitzler" (unpublished Ph. D. dissertation, University of Chicago, 1953), especially Chapter III, "Arthur Schnitzler's Literary Background."

[9] Lederer, 142.

[10] Olga Schnitzler, *Spiegelbild der Freundschaft* (Salzburg: Residenz Verlag), 1962, S. 17.

[11] Bergel (ed.), 75.

[12] He is now director of the *Theater in der Josefstadt* in Vienna and one of the best-known *Regisseurs* of Europe.

[13] Otto P. Schinnerer, "Schnitzler and the Military Censorship: Unpublished Correspondence," *Germanic Review*, V (1930), 243.

[14] Bergel (ed.), 135.

[15] Arthur Schnitzler, I, 110.

NOTES ON THE BIBLIOGRAPHY
AND ABBREVIATIONS USED

General Arrangement: The bibliography is divided into sixteen parts, each designated by a capital letter. Parts A through S are works by Arthur Schnitzler, English and French translations, and criticism (including reviews); parts X through Z consist of general criticism (including reviews of more than one work), dissertations, and research in progress. In each part the arrangement of entries is first chronological by year of publication, then alphabetical for multiple entries in the same year, and finally, in the case of works by Schnitzler, the following typical order: German editions (beginning with the "Erstdruck"), English translations ("e"), French translations ("f"), and criticism ("x") – – all in chronological-alphabetical fashion. Thus item number "B7f.1" indicates a narrative work (B), the seventh in chronological-alphabetical order (7), a French translation (f), and the first in this classification (.1). Entries in parts X and Y are numbered in a strictly consecutive manner; those in part Z by type of research.

Chronology: The date of publication is used to order the individual items chronologically. Works with later printings or editions are ordered by the first of these; books by Schnitzler are ordered in the same manner with later printings or editions (Auflagen) recorded in the same entry.

Alphabetization: In the case of title, the first word (excluding articles) is used; in the case of authors, the surname (disregarding "von" for German authors) is used. Anonymous entries are placed before all others of the same year. The indices of Schnitzler titles and of personal names should be noted.

Periodicals: The periodical title is given in brief form; following is given the volume number or *Jahrgang* or *année* in Arabic numbers, the issue or *Heft* number in small Roman numerals; then the date (except when obvious) and the pagination. Abbreviations in the appropriate language are used in each instance. The index of periodicals with full titles and places of publication should be noted.

Books: Following the title, the author or editor, if any and not obvious, is given in parentheses. Then the imprint: place of publication, publisher, date (except when obvious), and pagination. If the books appears as part of a series, the series title follows in parentheses.

9

Abbreviations in the appropriate language are used in each instance. *Analytics*: The collected works, anthologies, and school editions are analyzed by their individual works. In such cases a brief title of the larger work, followed by the number of the work in the bibliography, date, and pages, is given. Thus "*Erzählende Schriften* [#J5.], 1928, Bd. I, S. 9-117" indicates that full bibliographical information will be found in item #J5.

ABBREVIATIONS USED

anon.	anonymous	no.	number, nombre
AS	Arthur Schnitzler	Nr.	Nummer
Aufl.	Auflage, Auflagen	o. J.	ohne Jahr
Bd., Bde.	Band, Bände	p.	page, pages
col.	column, columns	repr.	reprinted, reprint
diss.	dissertation	rev., revs.	review, reviews
ed., eds.	editor, editors	S.	Seite, Seiten
ff.	and following	sér.	série
fr.	from	Sp.	Spalte, Spalten
H.	Heft, Hefte	t.	tome
introd.	introduction	tr., trs.	translator, translators
Jg.	Jahrgang	tsd.	tausend
n. d.	no date	vol.	volume

FREQUENTLY CITED SOURCES

JIASRA – Journal of the International Arthur Schnitzler Research Association
PMLA – Publications of the Modern Language Association of America
SiAS – Studies in Arthur Schnitzler:
    Centennial Commemorative Volume. (Herbert W. Reichert & Herman Salinger, eds.) Chapel Hill: University of North Carolina Press, 1963, vi, 116 p. (University of North Carolina. Studies in the Germanic Languages and Literatures, No. 42).

Information of additional or corrected items would be appreciated by the author for inclusion in a possible later supplement.

OUTLINE OF THE BIBLIOGRAPHY

13

PART A: POEMS

1880

A1.   "Liebeslied der Balledrine." *Der Freie Landesbote*, 13. Nov. [Signed "Arth. Schn."]

1886

A2.1   "Wie wir so still an einem Tische sassen." *An der schönen blauen Donau*, 1, xx, 1. Nov., S. 600. [In "Briefkasten."]

A2.2   – – *Die deutsche Lyrik des 19. Jahrhunderts: Eine poetische Revue.* (Theodor von Sosnosky, ed.) Stuttgart: J. G. Cotta, 1901, S. 396.

A2.3   – – *Deutsche Lyrik aus Österreich seit Grillparzer.* (Camill Hoffmann, ed.) Berlin: Meyer & Jessen, 1912, S. 157. [Title: "Wie wir so still . . ."]

1889

A3.1   "Am Flügel." *An der schönen blauen Donau*, 4, i, S. 12. [Signed "Anatol."]

A3.2   – – *Wiener Zeitschrift für Musik*, 1908, Nr. 1.

A3.3   – – *Deutsche Lyrik aus Österreich seit Grillparzer.* (Camill Hoffmann, ed.) Berlin: Meyer & Jessen, 1912, S. 159-160.

A4.   "Der Blasierte." *An der schönen blauen Donau*, 4, xix, S. 449. [Signed "Anatol."]

A5.   "Liebesgeständnis." *An der schönen blauen Donau*, 4, xvi, S. 374. [Signed "Anatol."]

A6.   "Lieder eines Nervösen. I. Landpartie. II. Apathie. III. Beim Souper. IV. Moderne Erfahrung und Philosophie." *An der schönen blauen Donau*, 4, xiii, S. 297. [Signed "Anatol."]

1890

A7.   "An die Alten." *An der schönen blauen Donau*, 5, vi, S. 132. [Signed "Anatol."]

A8.   "An gar Manche." *An der schönen blauen Donau*, 5, xxii, S. 520. [Signed "Anatol."]

A9.   "Der And're." *An der schönen blauen Donau*, 5, xiii, S. 302. [Signed "Anatol."]

A10.   "Intermezzo." *An der schönen blauen Donau*, 5, xvi, S. 373. [Signed "Anatol."]

A11.   "Wildenstein." *An der schönen blauen Donau*, 5, x, S. 232. [Signed "Anatol."]

1891

A12.1   "Morgenandacht." *Die Gesellschaft*, 7-1, ii, Feb., S. 189-190.

A12.2   – – *Der Merker*, 3, ix, 1. Mai-H., 1912, S. 322-323.

A13.1   "Tagebuchblatt." *Moderne Rundschau*, 3, ii, 15. Apr., S. 58.

A13.2   – – *Der Merker*, 3, ix, 1. Mai-H., 1912, S. 321-322.

14

A14.1   "Anfang vom Ende." *Deutsche Dichtung,* 12, viii, 15. Juli, S. 192.

A14.2   – – *Theateralmanach für das Münchner Schauspielhaus: Saison 1900.* (Paul Busse, ed.) S. 88.

A14.3   – – *Die deutsche Lyrik des 19. Jahrhunderts: Eine poetische Revue.* (Theodor von Sosnosky, ed.) Stuttgart: J. G. Cotta, 1901, S. 396-397.

A14.4   – – *Moderne Deutsche Lyrik.* (Hans Benzmann, ed.) Leipzig: Philipp Reclam jun., 1903, S. 484. [2. Aufl., 1907, S. 511; 3. Aufl., 1913, S. 445; not in the 4. Aufl., 1924.]

A14.5   – – *Neue Deutsche Gedichte.* (Hermann Beutenmüller, ed.) Leipzig: Xenien, 1908, S. 165.

A14.6   – – *Dichtergrüsse: Neue deutsche Lyrik.* (Elise Polko, ed.) Leipzig: C. F. Amelang, 1909, S. 97.

A14.7   – – *Die Quelle,* 4, ix/x, 1. Juni 1911, S. 13.

A14.8   – – *Deutsche Lyrik aus Österreich seit Grillparzer.* (Camill Hoffmann, ed.) Berlin: Meyer & Jessen, 1912, S. 157-158.

A14.9   – – *Der Merker,* 3, ix, 1. Mai-H., 1912, S. 1-4 (special paging). [With music by Richard Mandl.]

1893

A15.   "Der gute Irrtum." *Die Gesellschaft,* 9-4, xi, Nov., S. 1416.

A16.1   "Ohnmacht." *Die Gesellschaft,* 9-3, ix, Sept., S. 1118.

A16.2   – – *Die deutsche Lyrik des 19. Jahrhunderts: Eine poetische Revue.* (Theodor von Sosnosky, ed.) Stuttgart: J. G. Cotta, 1901, S. 395-396.

A16.3   – – *Moderne Deutsche Lyrik.* (Hans Benzmann, ed.) Leipzig: Philipp Reclam jun., 1903, S. 483-484. [2. Aufl., 1907, S. 510-511; 3. Aufl., 1913, S. 444; 4. Aufl., 1924, S. 339.]

A16.4   – – *Neue Deutsche Gedichte.* (Hermann Beutenmüller, ed.) Leipzig: Xenien, 1908, S. 164.

A16.5   – – *Deutsche Lyrik aus Österreich seit Grillparzer.* (Camill Hoffmann, ed.) Berlin: Meyer & Jessen, 1912, S. 156-157.

1898

A17.   "Käme ein Grosser uns wieder." *Prager Tagblatt,* 25. Dez.

1899

A18.1   "Zum Abschied." *Illustriertes Wiener Extrablatt,* 21. Mai.

A18.2   – – *Deutsche Lyrik aus Österreich seit Grillparzer.* (Camill Hoffmann, ed.) Berlin: Meyer & Jessen, 1912, S. 158-159. [Title "Abschied."]

1902

A19.   "An ein Mädchen." *Schwarz auf Weiss: Humor und Satyre beliebter Autoren und Künstler.* Leipzig: Heinrich Blömer, S. 119.

1912

A20.   "Lebewohl." *Der Merker,* 3, ix, 1. Mai-H., S. 323.

A21.1   "Wandernde Musikanten." *Der Tag* (Wien), 9. Mai, S. 22.

A21.2   – – *Prager Tagblatt*, 9. Mai.

A22.   "Orchester des Lebens." *Österreichische Dichtergabe: Ungedrucktes von Hugo von Hofmannsthal, Max Mell, Arthur Schnitzler, Karl Schönherr, Anton Wildgans.* Wien: Wiener Bibliophilen-Gesellschaft, S. 38. [Fr. "Ungedruckte Gedichte aus vergangener Zeit, 1880-1884."]

A23.   "Rendez-vous." *Österreichische Dichtergabe* [as in #A22.], S. 37.

A24.   "Therese." *Österreichische Dichtergabe* [as in #A22.], S. 39.

A25.   "Ein Ton." *University of Kentucky Notes from the Schnitzler Archive*, 1, Apr., 1961, p. 2.

A26.   "Beträchtlich stört mein junges Liebesglück." *Anatol* [#C4.22], S. 145. [Unpublished poem from "Anatol."]

PART B: NARRATIVE WORKS

1886

BI. ER WARTET AUF DEN VAZIERENDEN GOTT: SKIZZE
BI.1   – – *Deutsche Wochenschrift*, 4, H. 50, 12. Dez. 1886, S. 644. [Signed "Arth. Sch."]
BI.2   – – *Kleine Komödie* [#J7.], 1932, S. 13-18.
BI.3   – – *Erzählende Schriften* [#J10.], 1961, Bd. I, S. 11-14.

1889

B2. AMERIKA: SKIZZE
B2.1   – – *An der schönen blauen Donau*, 4, ix, 1889, S. 197.
B2.2   – – *Kleine Komödie* [#J7.], 1932, S. 9-12.
B2.3   – – *Erzählende Schriften* [#J10.], 1961, Bd. I, S. 15-17.

ENGLISH TRANSLATION

B2e.1   "America." *Decision*, 3, i/ii, Jan./Feb., 1942, p. 35-36. [Franzi Ascher, tr.]

B3. DER ANDERE: AUS DEM TAGEBUCH EINES
HINTERBLIEBENEN
B3.1   – – *An der schönen blauen Donau*, 4, xxi, 1889, S. 490-492.
B3.2   – – *Kleine Komödie* [#J7.], 1932, S. 34-43.
B3.3   – – *Erzählende Schriften* [#J10.], 1961, Bd. I, S. 40-46.
B3.4   – – *Erzählungen* [#K16.], 1965, S. 7-15.

B4. MEIN FREUND YPSILON: AUS DEN PAPIEREN EINES
ARZTES
B4.1   – – *An der schönen blauen Donau*, 4, ii, 1889, S. 25-28.
B4.2   – – *Illustrierter österreichischer Volks-Kalender für das Jahr 1906.* (Wien), 62,
1906, S. 23-30.
B4.3   – – *Illustriertes Wiener Extrablatt*, 25. Dez. 1912.
B4.4   – – *Kleine Komödie* [#J7.], 1932, S. 134-150.
B4.5   – – *Erzählende Schriften* [#J10.], 1961, Bd. I, S. 28-39.

1891

B5. REICHTUM
B5.1   – – *Moderne Rundschau*, 3, xi, 1. Sept. 1891, S. 385-391; 3, xii, 15. Sept. 1891,
S. 417-423. [Also repr. separately.]
B5.2   – – *Kleine Komödie* [#J7.], 1932, S. 202-248.
B5.3   – – *Erzählende Schriften* [#J10.], 1961, Bd. I, S. 47-78.

B6.   DER SOHN: AUS DEN PAPIEREN EINES ARZTES
B6.1   — — *Freie Bühne für den Entwicklungskampf der Zeit*, 3, i, Jan. 1892, S. 89-94.
B6.2   — — *Kleine Komödie* [#J7.], 1932, S. 172-183.
B6.2a   — — *Der goldene Schnitt: Grosse Erzähler der Neuen Rundschau 1890-1960*. (Christoph Schwerin, ed.) Frankfurt a.M.: S. Fischer, 1959, S. 153-159.
B6.3   — — *Erzählende Schriften* [#J10.], 1961, Bd. I, S. 90-97.
B6.4   — — *Literatur für den Deutschunterricht: Zweite Stufe*. (Bernard Rechtschaffen, Conrad P. Homberger & Victor Bobetsky, eds.) New York: American Book, 1964, p. 18-32. [School edition.]
B6.5   *Spiel im Morgengrauen* [#K17.], 1965, S. 15-33.

FRENCH TRANSLATION

B6f.1   — — "Le fils." *Gringoire*, 2 juin 1933. [Suzanne Clauser, tr.]

B7.   BLUMEN
B7.1   — — *Neue Revue*, 5, xxxiii, 1. Aug. 1894, S. 151-157.
B7.2   — — *Frau des Weisen* [#K1.], 1898, S. 113-133.
B7.3   — — *Erzählende Schriften* [#J1.], 1912, Bd. I, S. 118-129.
B7.4   — — *Erzählende Schriften* [#J3.], 1922, Bd. I, S. 118-129.
B7.5   — — *Erzählende Schriften* [#J5.], 1928, Bd. I, S. 118-129.
B7.6   — — *Stories and Plays* [#S3.], 1930, p. 87-98.
B7.7   — — *Ausgewählte Erzählungen* [#J8.], 1950, S. 81-88.
B7.8   — — *Erzählende Schriften* [#J10.], 1961, Bd. I, S. 220-228.
B7.9   — — *Novellen aus Wien*. (Richard H. Lawson, ed.) New York: Charles Scribner, 1964, p. 5-15. (The Scribner German Series). [School edition.]

ENGLISH TRANSLATIONS

B7e.1   "Flowers." *Viennese Idylls* [#L3.], 1913, p. 1-18. [Frederick Eisemann, tr.]
B7e.2   "Crumbled Blossoms." *The Dial*, 68, vi, June, 1920, p. 711-718. [Pierre Loving, tr.]
B7e.3   "Flowers." *Beatrice* [#L8.], 1926, p. 121-136. [Elsie M. Lang, tr.]
B7e.4   "Flowers." *Great Stories of All Nations: One Hundred Sixty Complete Short Stories from the Literatures of All Periods and Countries*. (Maxim Lieber & Blanche Colton Williams, eds.) New York: Brentano's, 1927, p. 505-511.

FRENCH TRANSLATIONS

B7f.1   "Fleurs." *Pénombre des âmes* [#M2.], 1929, p. 35-48. [Suzanne Clauser, tr.]
B7f.2   "Fleurs." *Mademoiselle Else* [#M4.], 1932, p. 124-136. [Suzanne Clauser, tr.]

B8.   DIE DREI ELIXIERE
B8.1   — — *Moderner Musen-Almanach auf das Jahr 1894: Ein Jahrbuch deutscher Kunst*, 2, 1894, S. 44-49.
B8.2   — — *Kleine Komödie* [#J7.], 1932, S. 151-157.
B8.3   — — *Erzählende Schriften* [#J10.], 1961, Bd. I, S. 79-83.

B9.   STERBEN: NOVELLE
B9.1   — — *Neue Deutsche Rundschau*, 5, x, Okt. 1894, S. 969-988; 5, xi, Nov. 1894, S. 1073-1101; 5, xii, Dez. 1894, S. 1179-1191.

B9.2	– –	Berlin: S. Fischer, 1895, 138 S. [Auflagen:
	1.	1895
	2.	1898
	3.	1901
	4.	1904
	5.	1906
	6.	1909
	7.-8.	1911
	11.-12.	1923 (Text of #J1., Bd. I, S. 9-117.)]

B9.3   – – *Erzählende Schriften* [#J1.], 1912, Bd. I, S. 9-117.
B9.4   – – *Erzählende Schriften* [#J3.], 1922, Bd. I, S. 9-117.
B9.5   – – *Erzählende Schriften* [#J5.], 1928, Bd. I, S. 9-117.
B9.6   – – *Ausgewählte Erzählungen* [#J8.], 1950, S. 7-80.
B9.7   – – *Erzählende Schriften* [#J10.], 1961, Bd. I, S. 98-175.
B9.8   – – *Erzählungen* [#K16.], 1965, S. 16-114.

FRENCH TRANSLATIONS

B9f.1   "Mourir." *Semaine littéraire*, lxix-lxxiv, 27 avril – 1. juin, 1895, p. 197-201; 210-215; 220-225; 237-239; 243-246; 255-257. [Gaspard Valette, tr.]
B9f.2   *Mourir*. Paris: Perrin, 1896, 269 p. [Gaspard Valette, tr.]
B9f.3   *Mourir*. Paris: F. Rieder, 1925, 189 p. (Les prosateurs étrangers modernes). [Alzir Hella & O. Bournac, trs. Introd. by Maurice Scheyer.]

CRITICISM

B9x.1   Sosnosky, Theodor von. *Deutsche Revue*, 20 (Bd. 3), i, Juli 1895, S. 123-124
B9x.2   Weitbrecht, Richard. *Blätter für litterarische Unterhaltung*, 11. Apr. 1895, S. 237
B9x.3   Werner, Richard Maria. "Tod und Sterben." *Monatsschrift für neue Litteratur* 1, v, Feb. 1897, S. 355-364. [Repr. in slightly revised form in *Vollendete und Ringende: Dichter und Dichtungen der Neuzeit*. Minden in Westf.: J. C. C. Bruns, 1900, S. 270-279. – – Comparison with work by Ignaz Dombrowski.]

B10.   DER WITWER
B10.1   – – *Wiener Allgemeine Zeitung*, 25. Dez. 1894.
B10.2   – – *Kleine Komödie* [#J7.], 1932, S. 19-33.
B10.3   – – *Aus unserer Zeit: Dichter des zwanzigsten Jahrhunderts*. (Ian C. Loram & Leland R. Phelps, eds.) New York: W. W. Norton, 1956, p. 169-183. [School edition; 2nd. edition, 1965, p. 235-251.]
B10.4   – – *Erzählende Schriften* [#J10.], 1961, Bd. I, S. 229-238.
B10.5   – – *Spiel im Morgengrauen* [#K17.], 1965, S. 35-55.

1895

B11.   DIE KLEINE KOMÖDIE
B11.1   – – *Neue Deutsche Rundschau*, 6, viii, Aug. 1895, S. 779-798.
B11.2   – – *Kleine Komödie* [#J7.], 1932, S. 276-321.
B11.3   – – *Erzählende Schriften* [#J10.], 1961, Bd. I, S. 176-207.

1896

B12.   EIN ABSCHIED
B12.1   – – *Neue Deutsche Rundschau*, 7, ii, Feb. 1896, S. 115-124.
B12.2   – – *Meisterwerke der zeitgenössischen Novellistik*. (Lothar Schmidt, ed.) Breslau,

Leipzig, Wien: L. Frankenstein, 1897, S. 7-26. ["1. Jg., 1. Bd."]
B12.3 – – *Frau des Weisen* [#K1.], 1898, S. 37-71.
B12.4 – – *Erzählende Schriften* [#J1.], 1912, Bd. I, S. 130-151.
B12.5 – – *Erzählende Schriften* [#J3.], 1922, Bd. I, S. 130-151.
B12.6 – – *Erzählende Schriften* [#J5.], 1928, Bd. I, S. 130-151.
B12.7 – – *Ausgewählte Erzählungen* [#J8.], 1950, S. 89-103.
B12.8 – – *Erzählende Schriften* [#J10.], 1961, Bd. I, S. 239-254.

ENGLISH TRANSLATIONS

B12e.1 "A Farewell." *English Review*, 12, Aug., 1912, p. 49-64. [Beatrice Marshall, tr.]
B12e.2 "The Farewell." *Viennese Idylls* [#L3.], 1913, p. 121-152. [Frederick Eisemann, tr.]
B12e.3 "A Farewell." *Beatrice* [#L8.], 1926, p. 137-162. [Elsie M. Lang, tr.]
B12e.4 "A Farewell." *Great German Short Novels and Stories.* (Victor Lange, ed.) New York: Modern Library, 1952, p. 363-379. (The Modern Library of the World's Best Books). [Beatrice Marshall, tr.]

FRENCH TRANSLATION

B12f.1 "L'adieu." *Gringoire*, 12 sept. 1930. [Suzanne Clauser, tr.]

1897

B13. DER EHRENTAG
B13.1 – – *Die Romanwelt*, 5-1, xvi, 1897, S. 507-516.
B13.2 – – *Frau des Weisen* [#K1.], 1898, S. 73-112.
B13.3 – – *Erzählende Schriften* [#J1.], 1912, Bd. I, S. 173-196.
B13.4 – – *Der Strom*, 3, xii, März 1914, S. 359-372.
B13.5 – – *Die Weltliteratur: Die besten Romane und Novellen aller Zeiten und Völker.* München: Walther C. F. Hirth, 1917. (Nr. 19).
B13.6 – – *Erzählende Schriften* [#J3.], 1922, Bd. I, S. 173-196.
B13.7 – – *Erzählende Schriften* [#J5.], 1928, Bd. I, S. 173-196.
B13.8 – – *Stories and Plays* [#S3.], 1930, p. 34-57.
B13.9 – – *Grosse Szene* [#K14.], 1959, S. 37-60.
B13.10 – – *Erzählende Schriften* [#J10.], 1961, Bd. I, S. 278-295.
B13.11 – – *Spiel im Morgengrauen* [#K17.], 1965, S. 57-93.

ENGLISH TRANSLATIONS

B13e.1 "The Hour of Fame." *Beatrice* [#L8.], 1926, p. 189-220. [Elsie M. Lang, tr.]
B13e.2 "The Jest." *Rejections of 1927.* (Charles H. Baker, ed.) Garden City, N. Y.: Doubleday, Doran, 1928, p. 171-194. [Agnes Jacques, tr.]

FRENCH TRANSLATIONS

B13f.1 "L'apothése." *Gringoire*, 8 sept. 1929. [Suzanne Clauser, tr.]
B13f.2 "L'apothése." *Pénombre des âmes* [#M2.], 1929, p. 169-197. [Suzanne Clauser, tr.]
B13f.3 "L'apothése." *Mademoiselle Else* [#M4.], 1932, p. 200-226. [Suzanne Clauser, tr.]

B14. DIE FRAU DES WEISEN
B14.1 – – *Die Zeit*, 10, cxviii, 2. Jan. 1897, S. 15-16; 10, cxix, 9. Jan. 1897, S. 31-32;

10, cxx, 16. Jan. 1897, S. 47-48.
B14.2   – – *Frau des Weisen* [‡K1.], 1898, S. 1-36.
B14.3   – – *Erzählende Schriften* [‡J1.], 1912, Bd. I, S. 152-172.
B14.4   – – *Erzählende Schriften* [‡J3.], 1922, Bd. I, S. 152-172.
B14.5   – – *Dreifache Warnung* [‡K10.], 1924, S. 3-26.
B14.6   – – *Erzählende Schriften* [‡J5.], 1928, Bd. I, S. 152-172.
B14.7   – – *Ausgewählte Erzählungen* [‡J8.], 1950, S. 105-119.
B14.8   – – *Erzählende Schriften* [‡J10.], 1961, Bd. I, S. 262-277.
B14.9   – – *Novellen aus Wien.* (Richard H. Lawson, ed.) New York: Charles Scribners, 1964, p. 17-35. (The Scribner German Series). [School edition.]

ENGLISH TRANSLATIONS

B14e.1   "The Sage's Wife." *Viennese Idylls* [‡L3.], 1913, p. 19-52. [Frederick Eisemann tr.]
B14e.2   "She Never Knew." *Fortnightly Review*, 101, dlxv, Jan. 1, 1914, p. 165-177. [Beatrice Marshall, tr.]
B14e.3   "She Never Knew." *Vanity Fair*, 27, iv, Dec., 1926, p. 81 ff.
B14e.4   "The Wife of the Wise Man." *Beatrice* [‡L8.], 1926, p. 163-188. [Elsie M. Lang, tr.]
B14e.5   "She Never Knew." *Short Stories from Vanity Fair 1926-1927*. New York: Horace Liveright, 1928, p. 353-375.

FRENCH TRANSLATIONS

B14f.1   "La femme d'un sage." *Gringoire*, 15 nov. 1929. [Suzanne Clauser, tr.]
B14f.2   "La femme d'un sage." *Pénombre des âmes* [‡M2.], 1929, p. 199-224. [Suzanne Clauser, tr.]

B15.   DIE TOTEN SCHWEIGEN
B15.1   – – *Cosmopolis*, 8, xxii, Oct., 1897, p. 193-211.
B15.2   – – *Frau des Weisen* [‡K1.], 1898, S. 135-170.
B15.3   – – *Erzählende Schriften* [‡J1.], 1912, Bd. I, S. 197-219.
B15.4   – – *Griechische Tänzerin* [‡K8.], 1914, S. 53-84.
B15.5   – – *Erzählende Schriften* [‡J3.], 1922, Bd. I, S. 197-219.
B15.6   – – *Erzählende Schriften* [‡J5.], 1928, Bd. I, S. 197-219.
B15.7   – – *Ausgewählte Erzählungen* [‡J8.], 1950, S. 121-136.
B15.8   – – *Die schönsten Erzählungen aus Österreich: Hausbuch unvergänglicher Prosa.* Wien: Kurt Desch, 1958, S. 215-228.
B15.9   – – *Erzählende Schriften* [‡J10.], 1961, Bd. I, S. 296-312.
B15.10   – – *Deutschland Erzählt: Sechsundvierzig Erzählungen.* (Benno von Wiese, ed.) Frankfurt a.M.: Fischer Bücherei, 1962, S. 19-33. (Fischer Bücherei, Nr. 500).
B15.11   – – *Spiel im Morgengrauen* [‡K17.], 1965, S. 95-129.

ENGLISH TRANSLATIONS

B15e.1   "The Dead Are Silent." *Short Story Classics: Foreign.* (William Patten, ed.) New York: P. F. Collier, 1907, Vol. III, p. 953-977. [Courtland H. Young, tr.]
B15e.2   "The Dead Are Silent." *Smart Set*, 40, iii, July, 1913, p. 59-65.
B15e.3   "The Dead Are Silent." *Viennese Idylls* [‡L3.], 1913, p. 153-182. [Frederick Eisemann, tr.]
B15e.4   "Dead Men Tell No Tales." *Fortnightly Review*, 101, dlxx, June 1, 1914, p. 1109-1122. [Beatrice Marshall, tr.]
B15e.5   "The Dead Are Silent." *The Greatest Short Stories.* New York: P. F. Collier, Vol. VII, p. 101-127. [Courtland H. Young, tr.]

BI5e.6 "Dead Men Tell No Tales." *Metropolitan*, 44, ii, July, 1916, p. 26-27; 47; 50-52.
BI5e.7 "The Dead Are Silent." *Beatrice* [‡L8.], 1926, p. 221-248. [Elsie M. Lang, tr.]
BI5e.8 "Dead Men Tell No Tales." *Vanity Fair*, 29, ii, Oct., 1927, p. 54ff.
BI5e.9 "Dead Men Tell No Tales." *Short Stories from Vanity Fair 1926-1927*. New York: Horace Liveright, 1928, p. 376-401.
BI5e.10 "The Dead Are Silent." *The Smart Set Anthology*. (Burton Rascoe & Groff Conklin, eds.) New York: Reynal & Hitchcock, 1934, p. 702-714.
BI5e.11 "The Dead Are Silent." *Bachelor's Companion: A Smart Set Collection*. (Burton Rascoe & Groff Conklin, eds.) New York: Grayson, 1944, p. 702-714.
BI5e.12 "The Dead Are Silent." *A World of Great Stories*. (Hiram C. Haydn & John Cournos, eds.) New York: Crown, 1947, p. 447-457. [Frederick Eiseman, tr.]

FRENCH TRANSLATIONS

BI5f.1 "Les morts se taisent." *Pénombre des âmes* [‡M2.], 1929, p. 225-250. [Suzanne Clauser, tr.]
BI5f.2 "Les morts se taisent." *Mademoiselle Else* [‡M4.], 1932, p. 227-251. [Suzanne Clauser, tr.]

CRITICISM

BI5x.1 Wiese, Benno von. "Die Toten schweigen." *Die deutsche Novelle von Goethe bis Kafka: Interpretationen*. Düsseldorf: August Bagel, 1962, Bd. II, S. 261-279.

1899

BI6. UM EINE STUNDE
BI6.1 – – *Neue Freie Presse*, Nr. 12695, 24. Dez. 1899, (Weihnachts-Beilage), S. 29.
BI6.2 – – *Wiener Bilder*, 12, i, 2. Jan. 1907.
BI6.3 – – *Kleine Komödie* [‡J7.], 1932, S. 89-97.
BI6.4 – – *Erzählende Schriften* [‡J10.], 1961, Bd. I, S. 313-318.

1900

BI7. DER BLINDE GERONIMO UND SEIN BRUDER
BI7.1 "Der blinde Hieronymo und sein Bruder." *Die Zeit*, 25, cccxxv, 22. Dez. 1900, S. 190-191; 25, cccxxvi, 29. Dez. 1900, S. 207-208; 26, cccxxvii, 5. Jan. 1901, S. 15-16; 26, cccxxviii, 12. Jan. 1901, S. 31-32.
BI7.2 – – *Griechische Tänzerin* [‡K4.], 1905.
BI7.3 – – *Erzählende Schriften* [‡J1.], 1912, Bd. I, S. 229-260.
BI7.4 – – *Griechische Tänzerin* [‡K8.], 1914, S. 7-52.
BI7.5 – – Erzählung. Mit einer Originalradierung von Ferdinand Schmutzer. Berlin: S. Fischer, 1915, 72 S. ["Herausgegeben 1915 zu Gunsten der im Felde Erblindeten. Druck der Spamerschen Buchdruckerei in Leipzig." In the 1. Aufl.: "200 Exemplare sind numeriert und von Arthur Schnitzler und Ferdinand Schmutzer eigenhändig signiert." 1.-5. Aufl.]
BI7.6 – – *Die Weltliteratur: Die besten Romane und Novellen aller Zeiten und Völker*. München: Walther C. F. Hirth, 1917. (Nr. 19.)
BI7.7 – – *Erzählende Schriften* [‡J3.], 1922, Bd. I, S. 229-260.
BI7.8 – – *Dreifache Warnung* [‡K10.], 1924, S. 34-69.
BI7.9 – – *Österreichische Erzähler*. Leipzig: Philipp Reclam jun., 1924.
BI7.10 – – *Die Welt in Novellen: Eine Auswahl für die Jugend (Deutsche, Nordländer, Angelsachsen)*. Wien, Leipzig: Herz, 1925, S. 21-60.

B17.11   – – Novelle. Mit einer Einleitung von Dr. Robert Reinhard. Wiesbaden: Volksbildungsverein, 1928, 44 S. (Wiesbadener Volksbücher, Nr. 214).

B17.12   – – *Erzählende Schriften* [#J5.], 1928, Bd. I, S. 229-260.

B17.13   – – Edited with Notes and Vocabulary by Lawrence M. Price. Chicago: University of Chicago Press, 1929, xiii, 57 p. (The University of Chicago Junior College Series: German). [School edition. – Also: Boston: D. C. Heath, ix, 57 p. (The Heath-Chicago German Series). – – Boston: D. C. Heath, 1959, xii, 67 p. (Revised edition, illustrated by Richard Floethe.)]

B17.14   – – *Zwei Tiroler Novellen* [#S2.], 1929.

B17.15   – – *Stories and Plays* [#S3.], 1930, p. 3-33.

B17.16   – – *Traum und Schicksal* [#K11.], 1931, S. 327-360.

B17.17   – – *Modern German Prose: Short Stories by Ten Representative Authors.* (E. P. Appelt & Erich Funke, eds.) Boston: D. C. Heath, 1936, p. 71-100. [School edition.]

B17.18   – – *Ausgewählte Erzählungen* [#J8.], 1950, S. 167-188.

B17.19   – – *Two Modern German Stories: Das Wunderkind by Thomas Mann and Der blinde Geronimo und sein Bruder by Arthur Schnitzler.* (Hans & Marian Pollack, eds.) Crawley: University of Western Australia Text Books Board, 1946, p. 17-43. [Revised edition, 1952, 1955. – – School edition.]

B17.20   – – *Der blinde Geronimo* [#S4.], 1956, S. 3-33.

B17.21   – – *Deutsche Erzähler des 20. Jahrhunderts.* (Kurt Böttcher & Paul Günther Krohn, eds.) Berlin: Neues Leben, 1957, Bd. I, S. 84-109.

B17.22   – – *Erzählende Schriften* [#J10.], 1961, Bd. I, S. 367-389.

B17.23   – – *German Stories: Deutsche Novellen.* Stories in the Original German. (Harry Steinhauer, ed.) New York: Bantam Books, 1961, p. 188-238. (A Bantam Dual-Language Book). [School edition.]

B17.24   – – *Erzählungen* [#K16.], 1965, S. 115-144.

ENGLISH TRANSLATIONS

B17e.1   "The Blind Man's Brother." *Canadian Magazine*, 41, v, Sept., 1913, p. 452-466. [Bernard Muddiman, tr.]

B17e.2   "Blind Geronimo and His Brother." *Viennese Idylls* [#L3.], 1913, p. 53-106. [Frederick Eisemann, tr.]

B17e.3   "The Blind Geronimo and His Brother." *Shepherd's Pipe* [#L7.], 1922, p. 15-80. [O. F. Theis, tr.]

B17e.4   "Blind Geronimo and His Brother." *Little Novels* [#L9.], 1929, p. 121-164. [Eric Sutton, tr.]

B17e.5   "Blind Geronimo and His Brother." *Pictorial Review*, 31, iii, Dec., 1929, p. 25-28; 33. [Fortunino Matonia, illus.]

B17e.6   "The Blind Geronimo and His Brother." *The Story Survey.* (Harold Blodgett, ed.) Chicago, Philadelphia, New York: J. B. Lippincott, 1939, p. 657-676. [Dorothy Blodgett, tr.]

B17e.7   "The Blind Geronimo and His Brother." *German Stories: Deutsche Novellen.* (Harry Steinhauer, ed.) New York: Bantam Books, 1961, p. 189-239. (A Bantam Dual-Language Book). [Harry Steinhauer, tr.]

FRENCH TRANSLATIONS

B17f.1   "Géronimo l'aveugle et son frère." *Pénombre des âmes* [#M2.], 1929, p. 49-87. [Suzanne Clauser, tr.]

B17f.2   "Géronimo l'aveugle et son frère." *Mademoiselle Else* [#M4.], 1932, p. 137-172. [Suzanne Clauser, tr.]

B17x.1 Newton, Lester C. *Modern Language* Journal, 15, i, Oct., 1930, p. 81-82. [Rev. of #B17.13.]
B17x.2 Kaufmann, Friedrich W. "Arthur Schnitzler: Der blinde Geronimo und sein Bruder." *Monatshefte für deutschen Unterricht,* 26, vi, Oct., 1934, p. 190-196. [Psychological, textual interpretation.]
B17x.3 Anon. *Monatshefte für deutsche Unterricht,* 52, v, Oct., 1960, p. 264-265. [Rev. of #B17.13, 1959.]
See Also: x282.

B18. LEUTNANT GUSTL: NOVELLE
B18.1 "Lieutenant Gustl." *Neue Freie Presse,* Nr. 13053, 25. Dez. 1900 (Weihnachts-beilage), S. 35-41.
B18.2 *Lieutenant Gustl: Novelle.* Illustriert von M. Coschell. Berlin: S. Fischer, 1901, 80 S. [Auflagen:
   1. – 8. 1901
   9. – 12. 1904-1906 (64 S.)
   14. – 15. 1910 (72 S.)
   16. – 18. 1914
   19. – 21. 1919]
B18.3 – – *Erzählende Schriften* [#J1.], 1912, Bd. I, S. 261-302.
B18.4 – – *Erzählende Schriften* [#J3.], 1922, Bd. I, S. 261-302.
B18.5 – – Berlin: S. Fischer, 1926, 78 S. (Fischers Illustrierte Bücher). ["Buch-druckerei A. Wohlfeld Magdeburg." 1. – 5. Aufl. of the illustrated edition; 22. – 26. Aufl. of #B18.2. "Mit 17 Illustrationen von M. Coschell."]
B18.6 – – *Deutsches Geistesleben der Gegenwart: An Introduction to Contemporary German Literature.* (Otto Koischwitz, ed.) New York: Alfred A. Knopf, 1928, p. 101-105. [Selection. School edition.]
B18.7 – – *Erzählende Schriften* [#J5.], 1928, Bd. I, S. 261-302.
B18.8 – – *Stories and Plays* [#S3.], 1930, p. 99-125.
B18.9 – – Komödie nach Motiven der gleichnamigen Novelle von Arthur Schnitzler. (Ernst Lothar). Frankfurt a.M.: S. Fischer, 1949, 140 S. [Mimeographed stage-edition.]
B18.10 – – *Ausgewählte Erzählungen* [#J8.], 1950, S. 189-216.
B18.11 – – *Schnitzler. Kafka. Mann.* (Henry Hatfield & Jack M. Stein, eds.) Boston: Houghton, Mifflin, 1953, p. 7-48. [School edition.]
B18.12 – – *Unsere Zeit: Die schönsten Erzählungen des zwanzigsten Jahrhunderts.* (Hermann Kesten, ed.) Köln, Berlin: Kiepenheuer & Witsch, 1956, S. 24-50.
B18.13 – – *Erzählende Schriften* [#J10.], 1961, Bd. I, S. 337-366.
B18.14 – – Nachwort und Anmerkungen von Heinz Politzer. Frankfurt a.M.: S. Fischer, 1962, 54 S. (S. Fischer Schulausgaben Texte moderner Autoren). [School edition.]
B18.15 – – *Spiel im Morgengrauen* [#K17.], 1965, S. 131-193.

ENGLISH TRANSLATIONS

B18e.1 "Lieutenant Gustl." *The Dial,* 79, ii, Aug., 1925, p. 89-117. [Kenneth Burke, tr.]
B18e.2 *None But the Brave.* New York: Simon & Schuster, 1926, 74 p. [Richard L. Simon, tr.]
B18e.3 "None But the Brave." *Viennese Novelettes* [#L10.], 1931, p. 393-433. [Richard L. Simon, tr.]

FRENCH TRANSLATION

B18f.1 "Le Lieutenant Gustel." *L'appel des ténèbres* [#M3.], 1932. [Suzanne Clauser, tr.]

B18x.1   Anon. *Die Wage*, 4, xxvii, 1901.
B18x.2   Düsel, Friedrich. *Westermanns Monatshefte*, 46 (Bd. 91), dxli, Okt. 1901, S. 157-158.
B18x.3   Fred, W. "Der Dichter vor dem Ehrengericht." *Die Nation*, 18, xxxix, 29. Juni, 1901, S. 616-617. [Argues against AS's demotion from the reserves for writing the Novelle.]
B18x.4   Klaar, Alfred. *Das Literarische Echo*, 3, xx, Juli 1901, Sp. 1416.
B18x.5   Weitbrecht, Richard. *Schöne Literatur*, 3, i, 4. Jan. 1902, Sp. 3.
B18x.6   Anon. *Saturday Review of Literature*, 3, xix, Dec. 4, 1926, p. 399.
B18x.7   Anon. "Schnitzler's Surgery." *New York Times Book Review*, Oct. 24, 1926, p. 29; 31.
B18x.8   Littell, Robert. *New Republic*, 48, dcxviii, Oct. 6, 1926, p. 201.
B18x.9   Sapin, Ruth. *Literary Digest International Book Review*, 4, xii, Nov., 1926, p.776.
B18x.10 Anon. *The Dial*, 82, ii, Feb., 1927, p. 164.
B18x.11 Lawson, Richard H. "A Reinterpretation of Schnitzler's 'Leutnant Gustl'." *JIASRA*, 1, ii, Spring, 1962, p. 4-19. [Freudian interpretation, raising interesting questions.]
B18x.12 Politzer, Heinz. "Nachwort." *Leutnant Gustl* [#B18.14], 1962, S. 40-50. [Work as literary-scientific experiment.]
B18x.13 Romberg, Bertil. *Studies in the Narrative Technique of the First-Person Novel.* Stockholm, Göteberg, Uppsala: Almqvist & Wiksell, 1962, p. 128-131. [Fr. "The Narrator and His Narrative."]
B18x.14 Jäger, Manfred. "Schnitzlers 'Leutnant Gustl.'" *Wirkendes Wort*, 15, Sept./Okt., 1965, S. 308-316.
See Also: X13,. X14., X15., X207., Y28.

1901

B19.   FRAU BERTHA GARLAN: NOVELLE
B19.1   -- *Neue Deutsche Rundschau*, 12, i, Jan. 1901, S. 41-64; 12, ii, Feb. 1901, S. 181-206; 12, iii, März 1901, S. 237-272.
B19.2   -- Berlin: S. Fischer, 1901, 256 S. [Auflagen:
        1.-2.   1901
        4.   1904
        5.   1906
        6.-7.   1908]
B19.3   -- *New Yorker Staats-Zeitung*, Mai 1901.
B19.4   -- Berlin: S. Fischer, 1912, 181 S. (Fischers Bibliothek zeitgenössischer Romane, 4. Reihe, 9. Bd.) [Later Auflagen:
        70.-77.   1921 (no series title)
        78.-80.   1925 (no series title)]
B19.5   -- *Erzählende Schriften* [#J1.], 1912, Bd. II, S. 9-181.
B19.6   -- *Erzählende Schriften* [#J3.], 1922, Bd. II, S. 9-181.
B19.7   -- *Erzählende Schriften* [#J5.], 1928, Bd. II, S. 9-181.
B19.8   -- *Erzählende Schriften* [#J10.], 1961, Bd. I, S. 390-513.

ENGLISH TRANSLATIONS

B19e.1 *Bertha Garlan*. Boston: Badger, 1913. (Vienna Edition).
B19e.2 *B... G...* A Novel. London: Goschen, 1913, 272 p.
B19e.3 *Bertha Garlan*. A Novel. London: Max Goschen, 1914, 267 p. [J. H. Wisdom & Marr Murray, trs.]

B19e.4   *Bertha Garlan.* New York: Boni & Liveright, 1918, 246 p. (The Modern Library of the World's Best Books, No. 39). [Agnes Jacques, tr. – – Also: New York: The Modern Library, n. d.]

FRENCH TRANSLATION

B19f.1   "Bertha Garlan." *Revue hebdomadaire.* [Suzanne Clauser, tr.]

CRITICISM

B19x.1   Eloesser, Arthur. *Neue Deutsche Rundschau,* 12, vii, Juli 1901, S. 656-657.
B19x.2   Gold, Alfred. *Die Zeit,* 27, cccxliv, 4. Mai 1901, S. 78.
B19x.3   Kempff, Max. *Die Gegenwart,* 30 (Bd. 60), xxvii, 6. Juli 1901, S. 10-11.
See Also: X13., X14., X15.

1902

B20.   ANDREAS THAMEYERS LETZTER BRIEF
B20.1   – – *Die Zeit,* 32, cdviii, 26. Juli 1902.
B20.2   – – *Griechische Tänzerin* [#K4.], 1905.
B20.3   – – *Dämmerseelen* [#K6.], 1907, S. 121-132.
B20.4   – – *Die Quelle,* 4, ix/x, 1. Juni 1911, S. 9-13.
B20.5   – – *Erzählende Schriften* [#J1.], 1912, Bd. I, S. 220-228.
B20.6   – – *Erzählende Schriften* [#J3.], 1922, Bd. I, S. 220-228.
B20.7   – – *Erzählende Schriften* [#J5.], 1928, Bd. I, S. 220-228.
B20.8   – – *Ausgewählte Erzählungen* [#J8.], 1950, S. 161-166.
B20.9   – – *Erzählende Schriften* [#J10.], 1961, Bd. I, S. 514-520.

ENGLISH TRANSLATIONS

B20e.1   "Andreas Thameyer's Last Letter." *Viennese Idylls* [#L3.], 1913, p. 107-120. [Frederick Eisemann, tr.]
B20e.2   "Andreas Thameyer's Last Letter." *Little Novels* [#L9.], 1929, p. 167-178. [Eric Sutton, tr.]

B21.   EXZENTRIK
B21.1   "Excentric." *Jugend,* 2, xxx, 1902, S. 492-493; 495-496.
B21.2   – – *Griechische Tänzerin* [#K4.], 1905.
B21.3   – – *In Lustige Lande: Der Heiteren Geschichten.* (Hermann Beutenmüller, ed.) Leipzig & Berlin: Franz Möser, 1910, Bd. II, S. 305-327.
B21.4   – – *Bunte Skizzen.* München: G. Hirth, 1917, S. 87-100. (Bücherei der Münchner Jugend, Bd. II).
B21.5   – – *Mitropa Zeitung* (Sonderausgabe Berlin), 10. – 16. Nov. 1924.
B21.6   – – *Kleine Komödie* [#J7.], 1932, S. 120-133.
B21.7   – – *Erzählende Schriften* [#J10.], 1961, Bd. I, S. 560-568.

B22.   DIE FREMDE
B22.1   "Dammerseele." *Neue Freie Presse,* Nr. 13553, 18. Mai 1902, (Pfingst-Beilage), S. 31-33.
B22.2   – – *Dämmerseelen* [#K6.], 1907, S. 105-120.
B22.3   – – *Erzählende Schriften* [#J1.], 1912, Bd. II, S. 207-218.
B22.4   – – *Erzählende Schriften* [#J3.], 1922, Bd. II, S. 207-218.
B22.5   – – *Erzählende Schriften* [#J5.], 1928, Bd. II, S. 207-218.
B22.6   – – *Traum und Schicksal* [#K11.], 1931, S. 407-420.
B22.7   – – *Ausgewählte Erzählungen* [#J8.], 1950, S. 245-252.

26

B22.8   – –   *Grosse Szene* [#K14.], 1959, S. 23-35.
B22.9   – –   *Drei Szenen* [#85.], 1960, p. 49-59.
B22.10   – –   *Erzählende Schriften* [#J10.], 1961, Bd. I, S. 551-559.
B22.11   – –   *Die gute neue Zeit*. (E. Pablé & H. Weigel, eds.) Salzburg: Residenz Verlag, 1962, S. 11-21.
B22.12   – –   *Spiel im Morgengrauen* [#K17.], 1965, S. 195-215.

ENGLISH TRANSLATION

B22e.1   "The Stranger." *Little Novels* [#L9.], 1929, p. 39-54. [Eric Sutton, tr.]

FRENCH TRANSLATION

B22f.1   "L'étrangère." *Gringoire*, 2 mai 1930. [Suzanne Clauser, tr.]

CRITICISM

B22x.1   Benn, Joachim. *Das Literarische Echo*, 16, x, 15. Feb. 1914, Sp. 666-667.

B23.   DIE GRIECHISCHE TÄNZERIN
B23.1   – –   *Die Zeit*, 28. Sept. 1902 (Beilage zu Nr. 2)   .
B23.2   – –   *Griechische Tänzerin* [#K4.], 1905.
B23.3   – –   *Erzählende Schriften* [#J1.], 1912, Bd. I, S. 303-317.
B23.4   – –   *Griechische Tänzerin* [#K8.], 1914, S. 157-177.
B23.5   – –   *Erzählende Schriften* [#J3.], 1922, Bd. I, S. 303-317.
B23.6   – –   *Erzählende Schriften* [#J5.], 1928, Bd. I, S. 303-317.
B23.7   – –   *Ausgewählte Erzählungen* [#J8.], 1950, S. 217-226.
B23.8   – –   *Erzählende Schriften* [#J10.], 1961, Bd. I, S. 569-579.

ENGLISH TRANSLATIONS

B23e.1   "The Greek Dancer." *The Dial*, 71, iii, Sept., 1921, p. 253-264. [Pierre Loving, tr.]
B23e.2   "The Greek Dancer." *Stories from the Dial*. New York: Lincoln Macveagh, 1924, p. 167-189. [Pierre Loving, tr.]
B23e.3   "The Greek Dancing-Girl." *Little Novels* [#L9.], 1929, p. 57-76.

FRENCH TRANSLATION

B23f.1   "La danseuse grecque." *Gringoire*, 21 fév. 1930. [Suzanne Clauser, tr.]

1903

B24.   DIE GRÜNE KRAWATTE
B24.1   – –   *Neues Wiener Journal*, 25. Okt. 1903.
B24.2   – –   *Kleine Komödie* [#J7.], 1932, S. 117-119.
B24.3   – –   *Erzählende Schriften* [#J10.], 1961, Bd. I, S. 549-550.

1904

B25.   DAS SCHICKSAL DES FREIHERRN VON LEISENBOHG: NOVELLETTE
B25.1   – –   *Neue Rundschau*, 15, vii, Juli 1904, S. 829-842.
B25.2   – –   *Dämmerseelen* [#K6.], 1907, S. 9-40.

B25.3   – – *Erzählende Schriften* [#J1.], 1912, Bd. II, S. 182-206.
B25.4   – – *Erzählende Schriften* [#J3.], 1922, Bd. II, S. 182-206.
B25.5   – – *Erzählende Schriften* [#J5.], 1928, Bd. II, S. 182-206.
B25.6   – – *Traum und Schicksal* [#K11.], 1931, S. 421-447.
B25.7   – – *Ausgewählte Erzählungen* [#J8.], 1950, S. 227-243.
B25.8   – – *Erzählende Schriften* [#J10.], 1961, Bd. I, S. 580-597.

ENGLISH TRANSLATIONS

B25e.1 "The Fate of the Baron von Leisenbohg." *The Dial*, 75, vi, Dec., 1923, p. 565-582. [Kenneth Burke, tr.]

B25e.2 "The Fate of the Baron von Leisenbohg." *The Best Continental Short Stories of 1923-1924 and the Yearbook of the Continental Short Story.* (Richard Eaton, ed.) Boston: Small, Maynard, 1924, p. 3-21. [Kenneth Burke, tr.]

B25e.3 "The Fate of the Baron." *Little Novels* [#L9.], 1929, p. 3-36. [Eric Sutton, tr.]

B25e.4 "The Fate of the Baron." *Great German Short Novels and Stories.* (Bennett A. Cerf, ed.) New York: Modern Library, 1933, p. 241-261. (The Modern Library of the World's Best Books). [Eric Sutton, tr.]

B25e.5 "The Fate of the Baron." *Tellers of Tales: 100 Short Stories from the United States, England, France, Russia and Germany.* (William S. Maugham, ed.) New York: Doubleday, Doran, 1939, p. 407-420. [Eric Sutton, tr.]

B25e.6 "The Fate of the Baron." *Bachelor's Quarters: Stories from Two Worlds.* (Norman Lockridge, ed.) New York: Biltmore, 1944, p. 74-86.

B25e.7 "Fate of the Baron." *Crimes of Passion.* (Herbert J. Salomon, ed.) Garden City, N. Y.: Garden City Books, 1947.

FRENCH TRANSLATIONS

B25f.1 "Le destin du baron de Leisenbohg." *Gringoire*, 26 mai 1929. [Suzanne Clauser, tr.]

B25f.2 "Le destin du baron de Leisenbohg." *Pénombre des âmes* [#M2.], 1929, p. 7-23. [Suzanne Clauser, tr.]

B25f.3 "Le destin du baron de Leisenbohg." *Mademoiselle Else* [#M4.], 1932, p. 99-123. [Suzanne Clauser, tr.]

1905

B26.   DAS NEUE LIED: ERZÄHLUNG
B26.1   – – *Neue Freie Presse*, Nr. 14608, 23. Apr. 1905 (Oster-Beilage), S. 31-34.
B26.2   – – *Dämmerseelen* [#K6.], 1907, S. 79-104.
B26.3   – – *Erzählende Schriften* [#J1.], 1912, Bd. II, S. 249-269.
B26.4   – – *Griechische Tänzerin* [#K8.], 1914, S. 128-156.
B26.5   – – *Erzählende Schriften* [#J3.], 1922, Bd. II, S. 249-269.
B26.6   – – *Erzählende Schriften* [#J5.], 1928, Bd. II, S. 249-269.
B26.7   – – *Erzählende Schriften* [#J10.], 1961, Bd. I, S. 620-634.

ENGLISH TRANSLATION

B26e.1 "The New Song." *The Dial*, 79, v, Nov., 1925, p. 355-369. [Kenneth Burke, tr.]

FRENCH TRANSLATION

B26f.1 "La nouvelle chanson." *Gringoire*, 25 juil. 1930. [Suzanne Clauser, tr.]

28

B27.	DIE WEISSAGUNG
B27.1	– – *Neue Freie Presse*, Nr. 14850, 24. Dez. 1905 (Weihnachtsbeilage), S. 31-38.
B27.2	– – *Dämmerseelen* [#K6.], 1907, S. 41-77.
B27.3	– – *Schatzkammer: Eine Auslese bester Erzählungen und grösserer Bruchstücke aus berühmten Romanen und epischen Gedichten der Weltliteratur.* (Norbert Falk, ed.) Berlin & Wien: Ullstein, 1909, S. 497-514.
B27.4	– – *Erzählende Schriften* [#J1.], 1912, Bd. II, S. 219-248.
B27.5	– – *Griechische Tänzerin* [#K8.], 1914, S. 85-127.
B27.6	– – *Der Wiener Bote: Illustrierte Kalender für Stadt- und Landleute auf das Jahr 1921*, 52, 1921, S. 45-57.
B27.7	– – *Erzählende Schriften* [#J3.], 1922, Bd. II, S. 219-248.
B27.8	– – *Erzählende Schriften* [#J5.], 1928, Bd. II, S. 219-248.
B27.9	– – *Zwei Tiroler Novellen* [#S2.], 1929.
B27.10	– – *Stories and Plays* [#S3.], 1930, p. 58-86.
B27.11	– – *Erzählende Schriften* [#J10.], 1961, Bd. I, S. 598-619.

ENGLISH TRANSLATIONS

B27e.1	"The Prophecy." *Selected Austrian Short Stories*. (Marie Busch, ed.) Oxford University Press & London: Humphrey Milford, 1928, p. 246-279. (World's Classics, No. 337). [Marie Busch, tr.]
B27e.2	"The Prophecy." *Little Novels* [#L9.], 1929, p. 79-118. [Eric Sutton, tr.]

FRENCH TRANSLATION

B27f.1	"La prédiction." *Gringoire* 30 jan. 1931. [Suzanne Clauser, tr.]

CRITICISM

B27x.1	Lawson, Richard H. "An Interpretation of 'Die Weissagung'." *SiAS*, 1963, p. 71-78.

1907

B28.	DIE GESCHICHTE EINES GENIES
B28.1	– – *Arena*, 2, xii, März 1907, S. 1290-1292.
B28.2	– – *Kleine Komödie* [#J7.], 1932, S. 75-78.
B28.3	– – *Erzählende Schriften* [#J10.], 1961, Bd. I, S. 959-961.

B29.	DER TOTE GABRIEL: NOVELLE
B29.1	– – *Neue Freie Presse*, Nr. 15352, 19. Mai 1907 (Pfingstbeilage), S. 31-35.
B29.2	– – *Erzählende Schriften* [#J1.], 1912, Bd. II, S. 285-301.
B29.3	– – *Masken und Wunder* [#K7.], 1912, S. 137-163.
B29.4	– – *Rigasche Zeitung*, 19. Sept. 1912.
B29.5	– – *Erzählende Schriften* [#J3.], 1922, Bd. II, S. 285-301.
B29.6	– – *Erzählende Schriften* [#J5.], 1928, Bd. II, S. 285-301.
B29.7	– – *Erzählende Schriften* [#J10.], 1961, Bd. I, S. 973-984.

ENGLISH TRANSLATION

B29e.1	"Dead Gabriel." *Little Novels* [#L9.], 1929, p. 195-217. [Eric Sutton, tr.]

FRENCH TRANSLATION

B29f.1	"L'ombre de Gabriel." *Pénombre des âmes* [#M2.], 1929, p. 149-168. [Suzanne Clauser, tr.]

B30. DER TOD DES JUNGGESELLEN: NOVELLE
B30.1 – – *Österreichische Rundschau*, 15, i, 1. Apr. 1908, S. 19-26. [Also repr. separately.]
B30.2 – – *Erzählende Schriften* [#J1.], 1912, Bd. II, S. 270-284.
B30.3 – – *Masken und Wunder* [#K7.], 1912, S. 73-96.
B30.4 – – *Erzählende Schriften* [#J3.], 1922, Bd. II, S. 270-284.
B30.5 – – *Erzählende Schriften* [#J5.], 1928, Bd. II, S. 270-284.
B30.6 – – *Ausgewählte Erzählungen* [#J8.], 1950, S. 253-263.
B30.7 – – *Erzählende Schriften* [#J10.], 1961, Bd. I, S. 962-972.

ENGLISH TRANSLATIONS

B30e.1 "The Death of a Bachelor." *Little Novels* [#L9.], 1929, p. 259-279. [Eric Sutton, tr.]
B30e.2 "The Death of a Bachelor." *Yisröel: The First Jewish Omnibus.* (Joseph Leftwich, ed.) London: John Heritage, 1933, p. 360-371. [Eric Sutton, tr. – Also: New York: Beechhurst, 1952, p. 289-297; New York & London: Thomas Yoseloff, 1963, p. 267-275.]
B30e.3 "The Death of a Bachelor." *A Treasury of Doctor Stories by the World's Great Authors.* (Noah D. Fabricant & Heinz Werner, eds.) New York: Grosset & Dunlap, 1946, p. 239-250. [Eric Sutton, tr.]
B30e.4 "The Bachelor's Death." *German Stories and Tales.* (Robert Pick, ed.) New York: Alfred A. Knopf, 1954, p. 151-162. (The Borzoi Series of Stories and Tales). [Richard & Clara Winston, trs.]

FRENCH TRANSLATION

B30f.1 "La mort du vieux garçon." *Pénombre des âmes* [#M2.], 1929, p. 101-119. [Suzanne Clauser, tr.]

B31. DER WEG INS FREIE: ROMAN
B31.1 – – *Neue Rundschau*, 19, i-vi, Jan. – Juni 1908, S. 31-71; 183-221; 327-361; 471-517; 643-693; 801-857.
B31.2 – – Berlin: S. Fischer, 1908, 491 S. [Auflagen:
    1. – 20. 1908
    21. – 22. 1911
    23. – 25. 1913 (460 S.)
    26. – 28. 1916
    34. – 38. 1920
    39. 1922
    43. – 45. 1924
    83. – 86. 1928
    87. – 136. 1929 (#B31.8)]
B31.3 "Paralipomena zum Weg ins Freie." *Jüdischer Almanach*, Nr. 5670, 1910, S. 24-26.
B31.4 – – *Erzählende Schriften* [#J1.], 1912, Bd. III, 460 S.
B31.5 – – *Erzählende Schriften* [#J3.], 1922, Bd. III, 460 S.
B31.6 "Heinrich Bermanns Familie." *Menorah*, 2, viii/ix, Aug./Sept. 1924, S. 11. [An unpublished chapter.]
B31.7 – – *Erzählende Schriften* [#J5.], 1928, Bd. III 460 S.
B31.8 – – Berlin: Sieben Stäbe, 1929, 445 S. (Bücher der Epoche, Serie A: Deutsche Autoren, Bd. 6). [Introd. by Lyonel Dunin; "Vorwort zur neuen Ausgabe: Werk und Widerhall (Aus dem Buch der Sprüche und Bedenken) von Arthur Schnitzler." 1. – 50. Tsd.; 87. – 136. Tsd. of #B31.2.]
B31.9 – – *Erzählende Werke* [#J10.], 1961, Bd. I, S. 635-958.

B31e.1   *The Road to the Open.* New York: Alfred A. Knopf, 1923, 412 p. [Horace Samuel, tr. 1 – 2 printing, 1923. – – Also: London: George Allen & Unwin.]

CRITICISM

B31x.1   Anon. *Heimgarten,* Dez. 1908.
B31x.2   Anon. *Der Kunstwart,* 22, i, 1. Okt.-H., 1908, S. 41-43. [Signed "W. R."]
B31x.3   Bergmann, Hugo. *Ost und West,* 8, viii/ix, Aug./Sept. 1908, Sp. 491-496. [AS incisive in his treatment of the Jewish question.]
B31x.4   Blech, Thekla. *Dr. Blochs Wochenschrift,* Nr. 42, 17. Okt. 1908, S. 737 ff.
B31x.5   Busse, Carl. *Velhagen & Klasings Monatshefte,* 23, ii, Okt. 1908, S. 317-319.
B31x.6   Geiger, Ludwig. *Allgemeine Zeitung des Judentums,* 72, xxxv, 1908, S. 415-418.
B31x.7   Handl, Willi. *Neue Rundschau,* 19, xii, Dez. 1908, S. 1851-1852.
B31x.8   Hofmiller, Josef. *Süddeutsche Monatshefte,* 5-2, ix, Sept. 1908, S. 342-345.
B31x.9   Kienzl, Hermann. *Das Literarische Echo,* 11, i, 1. Okt. 1908, Sp. 28-30.
B31x.10 Pollatschek, Stefan. *Die Gegenwart,* Nr. 34, 1908, S. 125 ff.
B31x.11 Servaes, Franz. *Das Blaubuch,* 3, xxxvii, 1908, S. 1111-1115.
B31x.12 Spiero, H. *Die Grenzboten,* Nr. 50, 1908, S. 548-549.
B31x.13 Anon. *Österreichische Rundschau,* 18, 1909, S. 79-80.
B31x.14 Anon. *Der Türmer,* Apr. 1909, S. 92.
B31x.15 Anders, Immanuel Ernst. "Aus Arthur Schnitzlers Buch 'Der Weg ins Frei'." *Der Kunstwart,* 22, xx, 2. Juli-H., 1909, S. 75-77 [Preface and excerpt.]
B31x.16 Goldbeck, Eduard. *Die Zukunft,* 66, Nr. 24, 13. März 1909, S. 417-418.
B31x.17 Hauschner, August. *Die Hilfe,* 17, iii, 1909, S. 59.
B31x.18 Schmidt, Erich. *Deutsche Rundschau,* 35 (Bd. 138), v, Feb. 1909, S. 313-314. [Fr. "Literarische Rundschau." – – AS avoids every possibility for tragedy.]
B31x.19 Stössl, Otto. *Österreichische Rundschau,* 18, i, 1. Jan. 1909, S. 79-80.
B31x.20 Tonnelat, Ernest. "Un roman viennois." *Revue de Paris,* 4, xiv, 15 juil. 1909, p. 367-382. [Discussion of principal characters with excerpts in French; work possessed of "une grandeur tragique."]
B31x.21 Anon. *Literary Digest International Book Review,* 1, iv, Mar., 1923, p. 52.
B31x.22 Boynton, H. W. *The Bookman,* 57, ii, Apr., 1923, p. 208-209. [Fr. "Best Quality, Imported."]
See Also: x233.

1911

B32.   DIE DREIFACHE WARNUNG
B32.1   – – *Die Zeit,* Nr. 3122, 4. Juni 1911 (Die Pfingst-Zeit).
B32.2   – – *S. F. V.: Das XXV. Jahr.* Berlin: S. Fischer, 1911, S. 328-333.
B32.3   – – *Erzählende Schriften* [#J1.], 1912, Bd. II, S. 338-343.
B32.4   – – *Masken und Wunder* [#K7.], 1912, S. 181-190.
B32.5   – – *Legenden und Märchen unserer Zeit.* (Emil Kläger, ed.) Wien & Leipzig: Artur Wolf, 1917, S. 69-72.
B32.6   – – *Erzählende Schriften* [#J3.], 1922, Bd. II, S. 338-343.
B32.7   – – *Dreifache Warnung* [#K10.], 1924, S. 27-33.
B32.8   – – *Erzählende Schriften* [#J5.], 1928, Bd. II, S. 338-343.
B32.9   – – *Modern German Stories.* (Allen W. Porterfield, ed.) Boston: D. C. Heath, 1928, p. 111-116. [School edition.]
B32.10 – – *Programm des Theaters in der Josefstadt: Spielzeit 1931-1932.* Heft 5, 1932.
B32.11 – – *Ausgewählte Erzählungen* [#J8.], 1950, S. 291-294.
B32.12 – – *Weit ist das Land: Erzählkunst aus Österreich.* Wien: Amandus, 1959, Bd. II: Blüte des Übergangs, S. 439-442.

B32.13 — — *Drei Szenen* [#85.], 1960, p. 60-64.
B32.14 — — *Erzählende Schriften* [#J10.], 1961, Bd. II, S. 7-10.

ENGLISH TRANSLATION

B32e.1 "The Triple Warning." *Great Short Stories of the World: A Collection of Complete Short Stories Chosen from the Literatures of All Periods and Countries.* (Barrett H. Clark & Maxim Lieber, eds.) New York: Robert M. McBride, 1925, p. 284-285. [Barrett H. Clark, tr.]

B33. DIE HIRTENFLÖTE: NOVELLE
B33.1 — — *Neue Rundschau,* 22, ix, Sept. 1911, S. 1249-1273.
B33.2 — — Mit 9 Radierungen von Ferdinand Schmutzer. Wien: Deutsch-Österreichischer Verlag, 1912, 104 S. ["Dieses Buch wurde im Auftrage des Deutsch-Österreichischen Verlags in Wien in einer einmaligen Auflage von vierhundert in der Presse numerierten Exemplaren in der Druckerei Christoph Reisser's Söhne in Wien hergestellt, die Einbände wurden nach einem Entwurf von Prof. Josef Hoffmann in der Wiener Werkstätte angefertigt."]
B33.3 — — *Erzählende Schriften* [#J1.], 1912, Bd. II, S. 344-386.
B33.4 — — *Masken und Wunder* [#K7.], 1912, S. 9-72.
B33.5 — — *Erzählende Schriften* [#J3.], 1922, Bd. II, S. 344-386.
B33.6 — — *Erzählende Schriften* [#J5.], 1928, Bd. II, S. 344-386.
B33.7 — — *Traum und Schicksal* [#K11.], 1931, S. 361-405.
B33.8 — — *Ausgewählte Erzählungen* [#J8.], 1950, S. 295-323.
B33.9 — — *Der blinde Geronimo* [#84.], 1956, S. 35-76.
B33.10 — — *Erzählende Schriften* [#J10.], 1961, Bd. II, S. 11-41.

ENGLISH TRANSLATION

B33e.1 "The Shepherd's Pipe." *Shepherd's Pipe* [#L7.], 1922, p. 15-80. [O. F. Theis, tr.]

FRENCH TRANSLATION

B33f.1 "La flûte du pâtre." *L'appel des ténèbres* [#M3.], 1932. [Suzanne Clauser, tr.]
See Also: B41x.18.

B34. DER MÖRDER: NOVELLE
B34.1 — — *Neue Freie Presse,* Nr. 16804, 4. Juni 1911 (Pfingstbeilage), S. 31-38.
B34.2 — — *Reuch* (Petersburg), 1. Juni 1911.
B34.3 — — *Erzählende Schriften* [#J1.], 1912, Bd. II, S. 312-337.
B34.4 — — *Masken und Wunder* [#K7.], 1912, S. 97-136.
B34.5 — — Mit 8 Holzschnitten von Ernst Huber. Wien: Paul Knepler, 1922, 83 S. ["Dieses Buch wurde über Auftrag des Verlages Paul Knepler in der Offizin F. Rollinger gedruckt und in der Kunstwerkstätte dieser Anstalt in handgearbeitetes Kleisterpapier gebunden. Hundert Exemplare wurden als Luxusausgabe auf feinstem Papier abgezogen und in der Kunstwerkstätte für Buchbinderei A. Günther in Edelleder handgebunden."]
B34.6 — — *Erzählende Schriften* [#J3.], 1922, Bd. II, S. 312-337.
B34.7 — — *Erzählende Schriften* [#J5.], 1928, Bd. II, S. 312-337.
B34.8 — — *Ausgewählte Erzählungen* [#J8.], 1950, S. 273-290.
B34.9 — — *Erzählende Schriften* [#J10.], 1961, Bd. I, S. 992-1010.

ENGLISH TRANSLATIONS

B34e.1 "The Murderer." *Shepherd's Pipe* [#L7.], 1922, p. 81-120. [O. F. Theis, tr.]
B34e.2 "The Murderer." *Little Novels* [#L9.], 1929, p. 221-255. [Eric Sutton, tr.]

B34f.1 "L'assassin." *Pénombre des âmes* [#M2.], 1929, p. 121-148. [Suzanne Clauser, tr.]
B34f.2 "L'assassin." *Mademoiselle Else* [#M4.], 1932, p. 173-199. [Suzanne Clauser, tr.]

B35. DAS TAGEBUCH DER REDEGONDA: NOVELLETTE
B35.1 – – *Süddeutsche Monatshefte*, 9-1, i, Okt. 1911, S. 1-7.
B35.2 – – *Erzählende Schriften* [#J1.], 1912, Bd. II, S. 302-311.
B35.3 – – *Masken und Wunder* [#K7.], 1912, S. 165-180.
B35.4 – – *S. F. V.: Das 26. Jahr.* Berlin: S. Fischer, 1912, S. 221-231.
B35.5 – – *Erzählende Schriften* [#J3.], 1922, Bd. II, S. 302-311.
B35.6 – – *Erzählende Schriften* [#J5.], 1928, Bd. II, S. 302-311.
B35.7 – – *Die deutsche Novelle: 1880-1933.* (H. Steinhauer, ed.) New York: W. W. Norton, 1936, p. 33-44. (Gateway Books). [School edition. – – "Expanded edition," *1880-1950*, 1958, p. 53-61.]
B35.8 – – *Ausgewälte Erzählungen* [#J8.], 1950, S. 265-271.
B35.9 – – *Erzählende Schriften* [#J10.], 1961, Bd. I, S. 985-991.
B35.10 – – *Spiel im Morgengrauen* [#K17.], 1965, S. 217-231.

B35e.1 "Redegonda's Diary." *Little Novels* [#L9.], 1929, p. 181-192. [Eric Sutton, tr.]
B35e.2 "Redegonda's Diary." *Love Throughout the Ages: Love Stories of All Nations.* (Robert Lynd, ed.) New York: Coward-McCann, 1932, p. 609-614. [Eric Sutton, tr.]

B35f.1 "Le journal de Radegonde." *Pénombre des âmes* [#M2.], 1929, p. 89-99. [Suzanne Clauser, tr.]

B35x.1 Ikeda, Yûzô. "Das Tagebuch der Redegonda: Eine Bemerkung über Schnitzlers Novellistik." *Doitsu Bungaku*, 18, Mai 1957, S. 66-71. [On the combining of dream and reality in the work.]
B35x.2 Lawson, Richard H. "Schnitzler's 'Das Tagebuch der Redegonda'." *Germanic Review*, 35, iii, Oct., 1960, p. 202-213. [Freudian interpretation.]
B35x.3 Reik, Theodor. *The Need to Be Loved.* New York: Farrar, Strauss, 1963. [Discussion from psychiatric point of view.]

1913

B36. FRAU BEATE UND IHR SOHN: NOVELLE
B36.1 – – *Neue Rundschau*, 24, ii, Feb. 1913, S. 302-322; 24, iii, März 1913, S. 502-516; 24, iii, Apr. 1913, S. 603-628.
B36.2 – – Berlin: S. Fischer, 1913, 155 S. ["Druck der Spamerschen Buchdruckerei zu Leipzig." Auflagen:
    1. – 12. 1913
    13. 1917
    14. – 15. 1919
    16. – 18. 1922 (Text of #J3., Bd. IV, S. 7-106.)]
B36.3 – – *Erzählende Schriften* [#J3.], 1922, Bd. IV, S. 7-106.
B36.4 – – *Erzählende Schriften* [#J5.], 1928, Bd. IV, S. 7-106.
B36.5 – – *Traum und Schicksal* [#K11.], 1931, S. 227-326.
B36.6 – – *Erzählende Schriften* [#J10.], 1961, Bd. II, S. 42-112.

B36e.1   *Beatrice: A Novel.* New York: Simon & Schuster, 1926, iv, 173 p. [Agnes Jacques, tr. 1-3 printings, 1926; 4, 1928.]

B36e.2   "Beatrice." *Beatrice* [♯L8.], 1926, p. 1-120. [Agnes Jacques, tr.]

B36e.3   "Beatrice." *Viennese Novelettes* [♯L10.], 1931, p. 297-392. [Agnes Jacques, tr.]

FRENCH TRANSLATION

B36f.1   *Madame Béate et son fils: Roman.* Paris: Victor Attinger, 1929, 186 p. [A. Hella & O. Bournac, trs.]

CRITICISM

B36x.1   Anon. *Velhagen & Klasings Monatshefte*, 28, Okt. 1913, S. 309-310.

B36x.2   Anon. *Westermanns Monatshefte*, 115-1, dclxxxv, Sept. 1913, S. 156-157. ["H.L."]

B36x.3   Heilborn, Ernst. *Das Literarische Echo*, 15, xix, 1. Juli 1913, Sp. 1371-1372.

B36x.4   Pinthus, Karl. *Zeitschrift für Bücherfreunde*, 5-1, iv, Juli 1913 (Beiblatt), S. 162.

B36x.5   Schumann, Wolfgang. *Der Kunstwart*, 27, iv, 2. Nov.-H., 1913, S. 305-306.

B36x.6   Bertaux, F. *La nouvelle revue française*, 6, lxii, 1. fév. 1914, p. 359-360.

B36x.7   Ratislav, J. *Xenien*, 7, Apr.-H., 1914, S. 250; 253.

B36x.8   Reik, Theodor. *Imago*, 3, vi, Dez. 1914, S. 537-539.

B36x.9   Littell, Philip. *New Republic*, 2, xx, Mar. 20, 1915, p. 186. [Repr. as "A Schnitzler Story." *Books and Things.* New York: Harcourt, Brace & Howe, 1919, p. 141-147.]

B36x.10   Anon. *The Independent*, 116, No. 3965, May 29, 1926, p. 645.

B36x.11   Anon. *New Republic*, 46, dxcviii, May 19, 1926, p. 414. [Signed "M.H."]

B36x.12   Anon. *New Yorker*, 2, xii, May 8, 1926, p. 60. [Signed "P.C."]

B36x.13   Crawford, John W. "Schnitzler Portrays the Indian Summer of a Woman's Life." *New York Times Book Review*, June 6, 1926, p. 9.

B36x.14   Egloff, Max A. "Trick or Truth?" *Saturday Review of Literature*, 2, xlii, May 15, 1926, p. 785.

B36x.15   Leonard, Baird. *Life*, 87, No. 2271, May 13, 1926, p. 40.

B36x.16   Sapin, Ruth. *Literary Digest International Book Review*, 4, ix, Aug., 1926, p. 584-585.

B36x.17   Loiseau, H. *Revue de l'enseignement des langues vivantes*, 46, xi, nov. 1929, p. 407-408.

1917

B37.   DOKTOR GRÄSLER, BADEARZT: ERZÄHLUNG

B37.1   – – *Berliner Tageblatt*, 46, lxxiv-cxli, 10. Feb. – 18 März 1917. [In 31 installments.]

B37.2   – – Berlin: S. Fischer, 1917, 222 S. ["Druck der Spamerschen Buchdruckerei in Leipzig." Auflagen:
       1. – 26.   1917
       27. – 29.   1922 (Text of ♯J3., Bd. IV, S. 107-238.)
       30. – 32.   1951 (♯B37.6)]

B37.3   – – *Erzählende Schriften* [♯J3.], 1922, Bd. IV, S. 107-238.

B37.4   – – *Erzählende Schriften* [♯J5.], 1928, Bd. IV, S. 107-238.

B37.5   – – *Die Roman-Rundschau*, Nr. 9, 1930, S. 7-91.

B37.6   ■ – Frankfurt a.M.: S. Fischer, 1951, 184 S. [Constitutes the 30. – 32. Aufl. of ♯B37.2. Also: Lizenzausgabe, Wien: Österreichische Buchgemeinschaft, 1951, 187 S. (Ausgabe für die Österreichische Buchgemeinschaft, Bd. 51).]

B37.7   – – *Erzählende Schriften* [♯J10.], 1961, Bd. II, S. 113-205.

B37e.1   "Doctor Graesler." *The Dial*, 73, i, July, 1922, p. 1-22; 73, ii, Aug., 1922, p. 162-180; 73, iii, Sept., 1922, p. 246-270; 73, iv, Oct., 1922, p. 411-424; 73, v, Nov., 1922, p. 509-524. [Paul Zeisler, tr.]

B37e.2   *Dr. Graesler*. New York: Thomas Seltzer, 1923, 180 p. [E. C. Slade, tr. – Also: New York: Simon & Schuster, 1930, 176 p.; London: Chapman & Hall, 1924, 180 p.]

CRITICISM

B37x.1   Anon. *Donauland*, 1917 (Bd. II), S. 872.
B37x.2   Anon. *Zeitschrift für Bücherfreunde*, 10, (1. Beilage), 1917, S. 79.
B37x.3   Heilborn, Ernst. *Das Literarische Echo*, 20, ii, 15. Okt. 1917, Sp. 116-117.
B37x.4   Wantoch, Hans. *Die Schaubühne*, 13, xxxviii, 20. Sept. 1917, S. 273-275.
B37x.5   Edschmid, Kasimir. *Das Literarische Echo*, 20, viii, 15. Jan. 1918, Sp. 474-475. [Repr. fr. the *Frankfurter Zeitung*.]
B37x.6   Anon. *Times Literary Supplement*, 23, No. 1191, Nov. 13, 1924, p. 728.
B37x.7   Muir, Edwin. "Irony and Pity." *The Freeman*, 8, ccvii, Feb. 27, 1924, p. 596.
B37x.8   Muir, Edwin. *Nation and the Athenaeum*, 36, No. 4935, Nov. 29, 1924, p. 334; 336.
B37x.9   Wright, Cuthbert. "De senectute." *The Dial*, 79, i, July, 1925, p. 68-71.
B37x.10   Anon. *American Mercury*, 29, lxxix, July, 1930, p. xxvi; xxviii.
B37x.11   Purdy, Theodore, Jr. "Diagnosis of a Physician." *Saturday Review of Literature*, 6, xlix, June 28, 1930, p. 1156.
B37x.12   Robbins, F. L. *Outlook and Independent*, 154, xvii, Apr. 23, 1930, p. 666-667.

1918

B38.   CASANOVAS HEIMFAHRT: NOVELLE
B38.1   – – *Neue Rundschau*, 29, vii, Juli 1918, S. 884-912; 29, viii, Aug. 1918, S. 1022-1046; 29, ix, Sept. 1918, S. 1147-1176.
B38.2   – – Berlin: S. Fischer, 1918, 182 S. ["Druck der Spamerschen Buchdruckerei in Leipzig." Auflagen:
     1. – 15.   1918
     16. – 40.   1919
     41. – 44.   1921 (#B38.3)
     45. – 49.   1929]
B38.3   – – Mit fünf Zeichnungen von Hans Meid. Berlin: S. Fischer, 1921, 170 S. [1. – 4. Aufl.; 41. – 44. Aufl. of #B38.2.]
B38.4   – – *Erzählende Schriften* [#J3.], 1922, Bd. IV, S. 239-371.
B38.5   – – *Erzählende Schriften* [#J5.], 1928, Bd. IV, S. 239-371.
B38.6   – – *Ausgewählte Erzählungen* [#J8.], 1950, S. 447-534.
B38.7   – – Frankfurt a.M.: S. Fischer, 1952, 175 S. (Fischer Bücherei, Bd. 14).
B38.8   – – *Erzählende Schriften* [#J10.], 1961, Bd. II, S. 231-323.

ENGLISH TRANSLATIONS

B38e.1   *Casanova's Homecoming*. New York: Private Printing for Subscribers Only, 1921, 201 p. [Eden & Cedar Paul, trs. 1250 copies printed.]

B38e.2   *Casanova's Homecoming*. New York: Thomas Seltzer, 1922, 201 p. (Eden & Cedar Paul, trs. 1-2 printing, 1922; 3, 1923.]

B38e.3   *Casanova's Homecoming*. London: Brentano's, 1923, 175 p. [Eden & Cedar Paul, trs.]

B38e.4   *Casanova's Homecoming.* New York: Simon & Schuster, 1930, 187 p. (The Inner Sanctum Novels). [Introd. by Otto P. Schinnerer, p. vii-xii. Eden & Cedar Paul, trs. – Also: Toronto: Musson, 199 p.]
B38e.5   *Casanova's Homecoming.* Drawings by Rockwell Kent. New York: Private Printing for the Sylvan Press, 1947, 153 p. ["This large paper edition, designed by Lewis F. White, is limited to 1499 numbered copies for the United States and the same number for the British Empire. Ten unnumbered copies have been struck off for reviewers." – Also: Toronto: Ambassador; Citadel Press, 1949.]
B38e.6   *Casanova's Homecoming.* New York: Avon, 1948, 126 p. (New Avon Library, No. 160). [Eden & Cedar Paul, trs. – N. Y. court decision, p. 123-126.]
B38e.7   *Casanova's Homecoming.* With Illustrations by Robin Jacques. Introduction by Ilsa Barea. London: Weidenfeld & Nicolson, 1954, ix, 130 p. [Maurice Eden Paul and Cedar Paul, trs. – Also: London: World Distributors, 1959, 128 p.]

FRENCH TRANSLATION

B38f.1   *Le retour de Casanova.* Paris & Neuchâtel: Victor Attinger, 1930, 187 p. [Maurice Rémon, tr.]

CRITICISM

B38x.1   Albert, Henri. *Mercure de France,* 132, cdxcviii, 16 mars 1919, p. 338.
B38x.2   Düsel, Friedrich. *Westermanns Monatshefte,* 63 (Bd. 126-2), dccli, März 1919, S. 95-96.
B38x.3   Eloesser, Arthur. *Deutsche Rundschau,* 45 (Bd. 180), x, Juli 1919, S. 152.
B38x.4   Heilborn, Ernst. *Das Literarische Echo,* 21, viii, 15. Jan. 1919, Sp. 503-504.
B38x.5   Weiglin, Paul. *Velhagen & Klasings Monatshefte,* 33, vii, März 1919, S. 104-105.
B38x.6   Burke, Kenneth. "Modifying the 18th Century." *The Dial,* 71, vi, Dec., 1921, p. 707-710. [Thought-provoking criticism; the work displays the triumph and reduction to absurdity of AS's method.]
B38x.7   Hergesheimer, Joseph. "Casanova Passes." *The Nation,* 113, No. 2945, Dec. 14, 1912, p. 705-706.
B38x.8   Tree, Ronald. *The Forum,* 68, vi, Dec., 1922, p. 1085.
B38x.9   Wright, Cuthbert. "A Defence of Don Juan." *The Freeman,* 6, clii, Feb. 7, 1923, p. 523-524.
B38x.10   Anon. *Publisher's Weekly,* 118, vii, Aug. 16, 1930, p. 595; 118, xiii, Sept. 27, 1930, p. 1532; 118, xiv, Oct. 4, 1930, p. 1615; 118, xviii, Nov. 1, 1930, p. 2083. [Reports on the New York trial and the vindication of charges of obscenity against the work.]
B38x.11   Anon. *Saturday Review of Literature,* 7, xviii, Nov. 22, 1930, p. 372. [Letter to the editor.]
B38x.12   Séqur, N. *Revue mondiale,* 201, 1936, p. 80.

1924

B39.   FRÄULEIN ELSE: NOVELLE
B39.1   – – *Neue Rundschau,* 35, x, Okt. 1924, S. 993-1051.
B39.2   – – Berlin, Wien, Leipzig: Paul Zsolnay, 1924, 136 S. ["Von diesem Buche wurden 100 Exemplare numeriert und vom Autor signiert. Druck der Gesellschaft für graphische Industrie, Wien, VI. Einbandentwurf Rudolf Geyer." Auflagen:
          1. – 25. Tsd.   1924
          26. – 35. Tsd.   1925
          36. – 45. Tsd.   1926
          46. – 60. Tsd.   1928

61. – 70. Tsd.   1929 (Special edition honoring Elisabeth Bergner.)]
B39.3   – –   *Erzählende Schriften* [#J5.], 1928, Bd. VI, S. 9-95.
B39.4   – –   Eingeleitet von Gustav Keyhl. Wien: Globus, 1946, 83 S. (Tagblatt Bibliothek, Nr. 1258). ["Umschlagentwurf von Kóra."]
B39.5   – –   *Ausgewählte Erzählungen* [#J8.], 1950, S. 535-588.
B39.6   – –   *Erzählende Schriften* [#J10.], 1961, Bd. II, S. 324-381.
B39.7   – –   *Erzählungen* [#K16.], 1965, S. 145-219.

ENGLISH TRANSLATIONS

B39e.1   *Fräulein Else: A Novel.* New York: Simon & Schuster, 1925, iii, 145 p. [Robert A. Simon, tr. 1-4 printing, 1925; 5-7, 1926; 8-9, 1927; 10, 1931.]
B39e.2   *Fräulein Else.* London: A. M. Philpot, 1925, 149 p. [F. H. Lyon, tr.]
B39e.3   *Fräulein Else.* Illustrated by Donia Nachshen. London: Constable, 1929, vi, 159 p. [F. H. Lyon, tr. – Also: 1939, 157 p.]
B39e.4   "Fräulein Else." *Viennese Novelettes* [#L10.], 1931, p. 119-200. [Robert A. Simon, tr.]
B39e.5   "Fräulein Else." *The Silver Treasury: Prose and Verse for Every Mood.* (Jane Manner, ed.) New York & London: Samuel French, 1934, p. 234-253. [Robert A. Simon, tr.]

FRENCH TRANSLATIONS

B39f.1   *Mademoiselle Else.* Paris: Stock, Delamain & Boutelleau, 1926, 173 p. (Le cabinet cosmopolite, no. 9). [Clara K. Pollaczek, tr. – Also: 1929, 169 p.]
B39f.2   "Mademoiselle Else." *Mademoiselle Else* [#M4.], 1932, p. 7-96. [Clara K. Pollaczek, tr.]

CRITICISM

B39X.1   Anon. *Der Kreis*, 2, iii, März 1925, S. 49-50. [Signed "W.P."]
B39X.2   Anon. *Times Literary Supplement*, 24, No. 1244, Nov. 19, 1925, p. 773.
B39X.3   Brandenburg, Hans. *Schöne Literatur*, 26, xii, Dez. 1925, S. 543.
B39X.4   Kennedy, P. C. *New Statesman*, 26, dclvi, Nov. 21, 1925, p. 178.
B39X.5   Krell, Max. *Die Literatur*, 27, vii, Apr. 1925, S. 428-429.
B39X.6   Lee, Rose. *New York Times Book Review*, Sept. 6, 1925, p. 12.
B39X.7   Lesser, Jonas. *Wissen und Leben*, 18, xi/xii, 10. Juli 1925, S. 763-765.
B39X.8   Littell, Robert. *New Republic*, 44, dlxxi, Nov. 11, 1925, p. 312-313.
B39X.9   Loveman, Amy. *Saturday Review of Literature*, 2, xviii, Nov. 28, 1925, p. 335.
B39X.10   Muir, Edwin. *Nation and the Athenaeum*, 38, xii, Dec. 19, 1925, p. 440.
B39X.11   Schacht, Roland. *Das Blaue Heft*, 6, xiii, 1. Apr., 1925, S. 360-364.
B39X.12   Shultz, Sidney. *Literary Digest International Book Review*, 4, i, Dec., 1925, p. 66.
B39X.13   Sternberg, Julian. *Moderne Welt*, 6, xv, 1925, S. 21.
B39X.14   Strecker, K. *Velhagen & Klasings Monatshefte*, 39, 1925, S. 470.
B39X.15   Salinger, Herman. *Nassau Literary Magazine*, 81, vii, Mar., 1926, p. 334-337.
B39X.16   Anon. *Jüdische Rundschau*, 30, 1928, S. 380.
B39X.17   Anon. "Graphologie im Film." *Die Literatur*, 31, viii, Mai 1929, S. 437-438. [Film version. Signed "L.W."]
B39X.18   Roberts, R. E. *New Statesman*, 34, dcclxvii, 1930, p. ix.
B39X.19   Anon. *Illustrated London News*, 181, No. 4885, Dec. 3, 1932, p. 910; 912. [Stage version.]
B39X.20   Anon. "Violation." *New Statesman*, 4, xciii, Dec. 3, 1932, p. 691. [Stage version]
B39X.21   Oswald, Victor A., Jr., & Veronica Pinter Mindess. "Schnitzler's 'Fräulein Else' and the Psychoanalytic Theory of Neuroses." *Germanic Review*, 26, iv, Dec., 1951, p. 279-288. [Freud's contribution: analysis. AS's: synthesis. Else narcissistic.]

B39x.22 Hoppe, Klaus D. "Psychoanalytic Remarks on Schnitzler's 'Fräulein Else'."
JIASRA, 3, i, Spring, 1964, p. 4-8.
See Also: Y28.

1925

B40.   DIE FRAU DES RICHTERS: NOVELLE
B40.1   – – *Vossische Zeitung*, 7. – 15. Aug. 1925.
B40.2   – – Berlin: Propyläen, 1925, 135 S. (Das kleine Propyläen-Buch). [1. – 10. Tsd.]
B40.3   – – *Erzählende Schriften* [#J5.], 1928, Bd. VI, S. 99-175.
B40.4   – – *Ausgewählte Erzählungen* [#J8.], 1950, S. 325-373.
B40.5   – – *Erzählende Schriften* [#J10.], Bd. II, S. 382-433.

CRITICISM

B40x.1   Fürst, Ludwig. *Die Literatur*, 28, iv, Jan. 1926, S. 239.

B41.   TRAUMNOVELLE
B41.1   – – *Die Dame*, 53, vi-xii, 1. Dez.-H., 1925 – 1. März-H., 1926.
B41.2   "Ein Maskenball." *Prager Tagblatt*, 25. Dez. 1926. [Selection.]
B41.3   "Die Maskenleihanstalt." *Das vierzigste Jahr: 1886-1926*. Berlin: S. Fischer, 1926, S. 252-260. [Selection.]
B41.4   – – Berlin: S. Fischer, 1926, 136 S. ["Titelbild von Hans Meid. In Holz geschnitten von Oskar Bangemann. Druck der Spamerschen Buchdruckerei in Leipzig." Auflagen:
         1. – 25.   1926
         26. – 30.   1927]
B41.5   – – *Erzählende Schriften* [#J5.], 1928, Bd. IV, S. 179-282.
B41.6   – – *Traum und Schicksal* [#K11.], 1931, S. 5-110.
B41.7   – – *Flucht in die Finsternis* [#K12.], 1939, S. 119-224.
B41.8   – – *Traumnovelle*. [#K13.], 1948, S. 5-105.
B41.9   – – *Erzählende Schriften* [#J10.], 1961, Bd. II, S. 434-504.

ENGLISH TRANSLATIONS

B41e.1   "Fridolin and Albertine." *Vanity Fair*, 27, ii, Oct., 1926, p. 50-52 ff.; 27, iii, Nov., 1926, p. 53 ff. [Erich Posselt, tr.]
B41e.2   *Rhapsody: A Dream Novel*. New York: Simon & Schuster, 1927, 167 p. [Otto P. Schinnerer, tr. 1-2 printing, 1927; 4, 1929.]
B41e.3   *Rhapsody: A Dream Novel*. Illustrated by Donia Nachshen. London: Constable, 1928, 192 p. [Otto P. Schinnerer, tr. – Limited edition, 1000 copies.]
B41e.4   "Rhapsody." *Viennese Novelettes* [#L10.], 1931, p. 201-296. [Otto P. Schinnerer, tr.]
B41e.5   "Pierrette." *Heart of Europe: An Anthology of Creative Writing in Europe 1920-1940*. (Klaus Mann & Hermann Kesten, eds.) New York: L. B. Fischer, 1943, p. 583-588. [Mary P. Bittner, tr. Selection.]
B41e.6   "Pierrette." *The Best of Modern European Literature: Heart of Europe*. (Klaus Mann & Hermann Kesten, eds.) Philadelphia: Blakiston, 1945, p. 583-588. [Mary P. Bittner, tr. Selection.]

FRENCH TRANSLATION

B41f.1   "Rapsode." *Les dernières cartes* [#M5.], 1953. [Dominique Auclères, tr.]

B41X.1   Düsel, Friedrich. *Westermanns Monatshefte*, 140-2, dcccxxxix, Juli 1926, S. 577-578.
B41X.2   Leontion. *Freie Welt*, 7, cxliv, 1926, S. 26.
B41X.3   Reuter, Gabriele. *New York Times Book Review*, July 4, 1926, p. 18.
B41X.4   Stolz, Friedrich. *Der Kunstwart*, 40, iii, Dez. 1926, S. 189-190.
B41X.5   Strecker, K. *Velhagen & Klasings Monatshefte*, 41-1, 1926, S. 230.
B41X.6   Wiegler, Paul. *Neue Rundschau*, 37, ix, Sept. 1926, S. 335-336.
B41X.7   Anon. *New Republic*, 50, dcxliv, Apr. 6, 1927, p. 203-204. [Signed "P. L."]
B41X.8   Anon. *The Dial*, 83, i, July, 1927, p. 76.
B41X.9   Anon. *Living Age*, 332, No. 4304, Apr. 15, 1927, p. 747-748.
B41X.10   Anon. *The Outlook*, 145, vxii, Apr. 27, 1927, p. 537-538.
B41X.11   Anon. "Schnitzler Merges Dream and Reality." *New York Times Book Review*, Mar. 27, 1927, p. 5.
B41X.12   Bates, Ernest Sutherland. "A Blithe Tragedy." *Saturday Review of Literature*, 3, xxxix, Apr. 23, 1927, p. 752.
B41X.13   Keulers Dr. *Der Gral*, 21, v. Feb. 1927, S. 317-318.
B41X.14   Rostosky, Fritz. *Schöne Literature,* 28, i, Jan. 1927, S. 15.
B41X.15   Salinger, Herman. *Nassau Literary Magazine*, 82, viii, Apr., 1927, p. 297-298.
B41X.16   Sapin, Ruth. "Dream and Reality." *The Nation*, 124, No. 3224, Apr. 20, 1927, p. 456-457.
B41X.17   Rey, William H. "Das Wagnis des Guten in Schnitzlers Traumnovelle." *German Quarterly*, 35, iii, May, 1962, p. 254-264. [Detailed analysis; AS's successful development of the husband-wife relationship.]
B41X.18   Schrimpf, Hans Joachim. "Arthur Schnitzlers 'Traumnovelle'" *Zeitschrift für deutsche Philologie*, 82, ii, 1963, S. 172-192. [Structural interpretation through contrast with "Die Hirtenflöte."]

1926

B42.   SPIEL IM MORGENGRAUEN: NOVELLE
B42.1   – – *Berliner Illustrierte Zeitung*, 35, xlix-lii; 36, i-ii, 5. Dez. 1926 – 9. Jan. 1927.
B42.2   – – Berlin: S. Fischer, 1927, 159 S. ["Druck von C. G. Röder G.m.b.H., Leipzig. Einbandentwurf von Hans Meid." 1. – 25. Aufl.]
B42.3   "Die Spieler." *Almanach 1928.* Berlin: S. Fischer, 1927, S. 145-151.
B42.4   – – *Traum und Schicksal* [♯K11.], 1931, S. 111-226.
B42.5   – – *Flucht in die Finsternis* [♯K12.], 1939, S. 5-118.
B42.6   – – *Ausgewählte Erzählungen* [♯J8.], 1950, S. 375-446.
B42.7   – – *Erzählende Schriften* [♯J10.], 1961, Bd. II, S. 505-581.
B42.8   – – *Die Grossen Meister: Deutsche Erzähler des 20. Jahrhunderts*. Bertelsmann, 1964.
B42.9   – – *Spiel im Morgengrauen* [♯K17.], 1965, S. 233-391.

ENGLISH TRANSLATIONS

B42e.1   *Daybreak*. New York: Simon & Schuster, 1927, 204 p. [William A. Drake, tr. 1-2 printing, 1927; 3, 1928]
B42e.2   "Daybreak." *Viennese Novelettes* [♯L10.], 1931, p. 1-118. [William A. Drake, tr.]

FRENCH TRANSLATION

B42f.1   "Les dernières cartes." *Les dernières cartes* [♯M5.], 1953. [Dominique Auclères, tr.]

B42x.1   Anon. *Living Age*, 333, Nr. 4319, Dec. 1, 1927, p. 1028. [Repr. fr. *Times Literary Supplement*.]
B42x.2   Anon. *Westermanns Monatshefte*, 142-2, dcccli, Juli 1927, S. 573.
B42x.3   Anon. *Zwiebelfisch*, 20, 1927, S. 204.
B42x.4   Bates, Ernest Sutherland. "Character and Destiny." *Saturday Review of Literature*, 4, xix, Dec. 3, 1927, p. 371-372.
B42x.5   Joseph, Michael. *The Bookman*, 65, vi, Aug., 1927, p. 724-725.
B42x.6   Lee, Rose. "Schnitzler's Tragedy Has a Light Tough." *New York Times Book Review*, Nov. 27, 1927, p. 5.
B42x.7   Schwabach, Erik-Ernst. *Zeitschrift für Bücherfreunde*, 19, iv, Juli/Aug. 1927 (Beiblatt), Sp. 164-165.
B42x.8   Wiegler, Paul. *Die Literatur*, 30, iii, Dez. 1927, S. 177.
B42x.9   Wittmer, Felix. *Neue Zeit*, 9, xviii, 1. Okt. 1927, S. 11-12.
B42x.10   Anon. *Books Abroad*, 2, i, Jan., 1928, p. 80-81. [Signed "W. A. W."]
B42x.11   Anon. *New Yorker*, 3, xlviii, Jan. 14, 1928, p. 72-73. [Signed "N. H."]
B42x.12   Hansen, Harry. *Harper's Magazine*, 156, ii, Jan., 1928, p. vi.
B42x.13   Lütkemeyer, M. *Neue Bücher*, 5, iii/iv, 1928, S. 8.

1928

B43.   THERESE: CHRONIK EINES FRAUENLEBENS
B43.1   ‑‑ Berlin: S. Fischer, 1928, 392 S. (Arthur Schnitzler: Gesammelte Werke). ["Druck vom Bibliographischen Institut in Leipzig." Auflagen:
       1. – 30.   1928
       31. – 35.   1929
       43. Tsd.   1949 (#B43.4)]
B43.2   "Der Sohn." *Almanach 1929*. Berlin: S. Fischer, 1928, S. 151-157. [Selection.]
B43.3   ‑‑ *Erzählende Schriften* [#J5.], 1928, Bd. V, 392 S.
B43.4   ‑‑ Wien: Bermann-Fischer, 1949, 392 S. (Gesammelte Werke in Einzelbänden). ["Gedruckt und gebunden bei R. Kiesel zu Salzburg." Constitutes 43. Tsd. of #B43.1.]
B43.5   ‑‑ *Weit ist das Land: Erzählkunst aus Österreich*. Wien: Amandus, 1959, Bd. II: Blüte des Überganges, S. 421-438. [Selection.]
B43.6   ‑‑ *Erzählende Schriften* [#J10.], 1961, Bd. II, S. 625-881.
B43.7   ‑‑ Frankfurt a.M. & Hamburg: Fischer Bücherei, 1962, 312 S. (Fischer Bücherei, Nr. 433). ["Umschlagentwurf: Horst Riehl; Gesamtherstellung: Hanseatische Druckanstalt."]

ENGLISH TRANSLATION

B43e.1   *Theresa: The Chronicle of a Woman's Life*. New York: Simon & Schuster, 1928, 460 p. [William A. Drake, tr. 1-4 printing, 1928. – Also: London: Constable, 1929.]

FRENCH TRANSLATION

B43f.1   *Thérèse: Chronique d'une vie de femme*. Roman. Préface de Louis Gillet. Paris: Albin Michel, 1931, 313 p. (Collection des maîtres de la littérature étrangère). [Suzanne Clauser, tr.]

CRITICISM

B43x.1   Anon. *New Yorker*, Oct. 6, 1928.
B43x.2   Anon. *Time*, 12, xv, Oct. 8, 1928, p. 45-46.

B43X.3   Anon. *American Mercury*, 15, lx, Dec., 1928, p. lxxx.
B43X.4   Chase, Cleveland B. "Schnitzler Abandons His Spontaneity in a Grim Study."
         New York Times Book Review, Nov. 25, 1928, p. 2.
B43X.5   Eaton, G. D. *Plain Talk*, 3, vi, Dec., 1928, p. 756-757.
B43X.6   Galantière, Lewis. *The Bookman*, 68, iv, Dec., 1928, p. 481.
B43X.7   Krutch, Joseph Wood. "The Nonentity as Hero." *The Nation*, 127, No. 3306,
         Nov. 14, 1928, p. 523-524.
B43X.8   Luschnat, D. *Literarische Welt*, 5, xxiv, 1928, S. 5.
B43X.9   Matthews, T. S. *New Republic*, 56, dccxxvi, Oct. 31, 1928, p. 308.
B43X.10 Michel, Hermann. *Das Deutsche Buch*, 8, xi/xii, Nov./Dez. 1928, S. 348.
B43X.11 Purdy, Theodore, Jr. "Chronicle of a Woman's Life." *Saturday Review of
         Literature*, 5, xvi, Nov. 10, 1928, p. 336.
B43X.12 Randall, A. W. G. "A New Schnitzler." *Saturday Review of Literature* 4, lii,
         July 21, 1928, p. 1053.
B43X.13 Reuter, Gabriele. *New York Times Book Review*, July 22, 1928, p. 8.
B43X.14 Rose, Donald F. *Forum*, 80, vi, Dec., 1928, p. xx.
B43X.15 Silber, Boris. *Literarische Welt*, 15. Juni 1928.
B43X.16 Spenlé, Jean-Edouard. *Mercure de France*, 208, dccxxxi, 1 dec. 1928, p. 462-463.
B43X.17 Strecker, K. *Velhagen & Klasings Monatshefte*, 43-1, 1928, S. 115.
B43X.18 Zuckerkandl, Viktor. *Neue Rundschau*, 39, ix, Sept. 1928, S. 334-335.
B43X.19 Ben-Gavriël. *Jüdische Rundschau*, 34, 1929, S. 25.
B43X.20 Gillet, Louis. "Thérèse ou les amours viennoises." *Revue des deux mondes*, 9
         (t. 2), 15 juil. 1929, p. 452-453.
B43X.21 Raunick, S. Metzenthin. *Books Abroad*, 3, i, Jan., 1929, p. 76.
B43X.22 Rubin, H. *Zeitschrift für Sexualwissenschaft*, 15, 1929, S. 499.
B43X.23 Seltzer, Edith G. "A Caseworker Looks at Schnitzler." *The Survey*, 61, vii,
         Jan. 1, 1929, p. 451-452.
B43X.24 Wiegler, Paul. *Die Literatur*, 32, xii, Sept. 1930, S. 721-722.

1931

B44.   FLUCHT IN DIE FINSTERNIS: NOVELLE
B44.1   – – *Vossische Zeitung*, 13. – 30. Mai 1931.
B44.2   – – *Neues Wiener Tagblatt*, 19. Juli – 19. Aug. 1931.
B44.3   – – Berlin: S. Fischer, 1931, 172 S. ["Einband und Schutzumschlag: Hans
         Meid. Druck der Spamerschen Buchdruckerei in Leipzig." 1. – 15. Aufl.]
B44.4   – – *Almanach 1932*. Berlin: S. Fischer, 1931, S. 111-115. [Selection.]
B44.5   – – *Flucht in die Finsternis* [#K12.], 1939, S. 225-349.
B44.6   – – *Traumnovelle* [#K13.], 1948, S. 107-226.
B44.7   – – *Erzählende Schriften* [#J10.], 1961, Bd. II, S. 902-985.

ENGLISH TRANSLATION

B44e.1   *Flight into Darkness*. New York: Simon & Schuster, 1931, 152 p. [William
         A. Drake, tr.]

FRENCH TRANSLATIONS

B44f.1   "L'appel des ténèbres." *Le Revue de France*, 15 juil. 1932. [Suzanne Clauser, tr.]
B44f.2   "L'appel des ténèbres." *L'Appel des ténèbres* [#M3.], 1932. [Suzanne Clauser, tr.]

CRITICISM

B44X.1   Anon. "Schnitzler's Last." *New York Times Book Review*, Nov. 15, 1931, p. 7.
B44X.2   Heilborn, Ernst. *Die Literatur*, 34, iii, Dez. 1931, S. 165-166.

B44x.3   Porterfield, Allen W. *Outlook and Independent*, 159, xi, Nov. 11, 1931, p. 344-345.
B44x.4   Ruppel, K. H. *Neue Rundschau*, 42, xii, Dez. 1931, S. 842-843.
B44x.5   Slochower, Harry. *New Republic*, 69, dccclxxxv, Nov. 18, 1931, p. 22-23.
B44x.6   Borttscheller, H. *Münchener Medizinische Wochenschrift*, 79, 1932, S. 443.
B44x.7   Dangerfield, George. "Malade imaginaire." *Saturday Review of Literature*, 8, xxvii, Jan. 23, 1932, p. 473.
B44x.8   Fränkl. *Goetheanum*, 11, 1932, S. 251.
B44x.9   Muret, Maurice. "A propos d'une oeuvre posthume." *Journal des débats*, 39-1, No. 1999, 17 juin 1932, p. 963-965.
B44x.10   Weiss, Robert O. "A Study of the Psychiatric Elements in Schnitzler's 'Flucht in die Finsternis'." *Germanic Review*, 33, iv. Dec., 1958, p. 251-275. [A psychiatric case-study; Robert suffering from a paranoid type of schizophrenia.]
See Also: X258, Y32.

B45.   WOHLTATEN, STILL UND REIN GEGEBEN
B45.1   – – *Neues Wiener Tagblatt*, 25. Dez. 1931 (Weihnachtsbeilage), S. 27-28. ["Aus dem Nachlass."]
B45.2   – – *Kleine Komödie* [#J7.], 1932, S. 98-107.
B45.3   – – *Erzählende Schriften* [#J10.], 1961, Bd. I, S. 521-527.

ENGLISH TRANSLATION

B45e.1   "Charity's Reward." *Living Age*, 342, No. 4386, Mar., 1932, p. 48-52.

FRENCH TRANSLATION

B45f.1   "Un bienfait n'est jamais perdu." *Gringoire*, 6 mai 1932.

1932

B46.   DIE BRAUT: STUDIE
B46.1   – – *Kleine Komödie* [#J7.], 1932, S. 108-116.
B46.2   – – *Erzählende Schriften* [#J10.], 1961, Bd. I, S. 84-89.

B47.   DER EMPFINDSAME
B47.1   – – *Neue Rundschau*, 43, v, Mai 1932, S. 663-669. [Fr. "Drei Geschichten aus dem Nachlass." "Geschrieben im Jahre 1895."]
B47.2   – – *Kleine Komödie* [#J7.], 1932, S. 50-59.
B47.3   – – *Erzählende Schriften* [#J10.], 1961, Bd. I, S. 255-261.

FRENCH TRANSLATION

B47f.1   "Le sensitif." *Candide*, 10, 16 nov. 1933. [Suzanne Clauser, tr.]

B48.   ERBSCHAFT
B48.1   – – *Kleine Komödie* [#J7.], 1932, S. 165-171.
B48.2   – – *Erzählende Schriften* [#J10.], 1961, Bd. I, S. 18-22.

B49.   EIN ERFOLG
B49.1   – – *Neue Rundschau*, 43, v, Mai 1932, S. 669-678. [Fr. "Drei Geschichten aus dem Nachlass." "Geschrieben im Jahre 1900."]
B49.2   – – *Kleine Komödie* [#J7.], 1932, S. 60-74.
B49.3   – – *Erzählende Schriften* [#J10.], 1961, Bd. I, S. 528-537.

B50.   FRÜHLINGSNACHT IM SEZIERSAAL: PHANTASIE
B50.1   – – *Jahrbuch Deutscher Bibliophilen und Literaturfreunde*, 18/19, 1932/1933, S. 86-91. ["Aus dem Nachlass."]
B50.2   – – *Almanach. Das sechsundsiebzigste Jahr*. Frankfurt a.M.: S. Fischer, 1962, S. 12-17. [Prefatory note by Heinz Politzer.]
See Also: x313.

B51.   DER FÜRST IST IM HAUSE
B51.1   – – *Arbeiter-Zeitung* (Wien), Nr. 135, 15. Mai 1932.
B51.2   – – *Kleine Komödie* [#J7.], 1932, S. 158-164.
B51.3   – – *Erzählende Schriften* [#J10.], 1961, Bd. I, S. 23-27.

B52.   DIE KOMÖDIANTIN
B52.1   – – *Berliner Tageblatt*, Nr. 299, 15. Mai 1932, S. 2-3.

B53.   KOMÖDIANTINNEN: HELENE, FRITZI
B53.1   – – *Kleine Komödie* [#J7.], 1932, S. 184-201.
B53.2   – – *Erzählende Schriften* [#J10.], 1961, Bd. I, S. 208-219.

B54.   LEGENDE (FRAGMENT)
B54.1   – – *Kleine Komödie* [#J7.], 1932, S. 79-88.
B54.2   – – *Erzählende Schriften* [#J10.], 1961, Bd. I, S. 538-544.

B55.   DER LETZTE BRIEF EINES LITERATEN: NOVELLE
B55.1   – – *Neue Rundschau*, 43, i, Jan. 1932, S. 14-37.
B55.2   – – *Ausgewählte Erzählungen* [#J8.], 1950, S. 137-159.
B55.3   – – *Erzählende Schriften* [#J10.], 1961, Bd. II, S. 206-230.

B56.   DIE NÄCHSTE
B56.1   – – *Neue Freie Presse*, Nr. 24259, 27. März 1932 (Osterbeilage), S. 33-39.
B56.2   – – *Kleine Komödie* [#J7.], 1932, S. 249-275.
B56.3   – – *Erzählende Schriften* [#J10.], 1961, Bd. I, S. 319-336.

B57.   DER SEKUNDANT
B57.1   – – *Vossische Zeitung*, 1. – 4. Jan. 1932.
B57.2   – – *Erzählende Schriften* [#J10.], 1961, Bd. II, S. 882-901.
B57.3   – – *Spiel im Morgengrauen* [#K17.], 1965, S. 393-435.

B58.   WELCH EINE MELODIE
B58.1   – – *Neue Rundschau*, 43, v, Mai 1932, S. 659-663. [Fr. "Drei Geschichten aus dem Nachlass." "Geschrieben im Jahre 1885."]
B58.2   – – *Kleine Komödie* [#J7.], 1932, S. 44-49.
B58.3   – – *Erzählende Schriften* [#J10.], 1961, Bd. I, S. 7-10.

                                    1937

B59.   ABENTEURERNOVELLE
B59.1   – – Mit 16 Zeichnungen von W. Müller Hofmann. Wien: Bermann-Fischer, 1937, 95 S. ["Gesamtausstattung von Professor Müller Hofmann. Druck des Textes von Jahoda & Siegel, Wien III."]
B59.2   – – *Erzählende Schriften* [#J10.], 1961, Bd. II, S. 582-624.

                               CRITICISM

B59x.1   Eloesser, Arthur. *Jüdische Rundschau*, 42, lxii, 1937, S. 8.

                                     43

B60.   BOXERAUFSTAND: ENTWURF ZU EINER NOVELLE
B60.1   – – *Neue Rundschau*, 68, i, 1957, S. 84-87.
B60.2   – – *Erzählende Schriften* [#J10.], 1961, Bd. I, S. 545-548.

B61.   PARABELN
B61.1   – – *Almanach: Das neunundsiebzigste Jahr*. Frankfurt a.M.: S. Fischer, 1965,
        S. 148-150. ["Aus dem Nachlass."]
See Also: F21.

PART C: DRAMAS

1888

C1.   DAS ABENTEUER SEINES LEBENS: LUSTSPIEL IN EINEM AUFZUGE
C1.1   − − Wien: Dr. O. F. Eirich, 1888. [Stage manuscript.]
C1.2   − − *Anatol* [#C4.22], 1964, S. 118-140.

1890

C2.   ALKANDIS LIED: DRAMATISCHES GEDICHT IN EINEM AUFZUG
C2.1   − − *An der schönen blauen Donau*, 5, xvii/xviii, 1890, S. 398-400; 424-426.
C2.2   − − *Dramatische Werke* [#J11], 1962, Bd. I, S. 7-25.

1891

C3.   DAS MÄRCHEN: SCHAUSPIEL IN DREI AUFZÜGEN
C3.1   − − 1891. [Stage manuscript.]
C3.2   − − Dresden & Leipzig: E. Pierson, 1894, 111 S. [Constitutes 1. Aufl. of #C3.3.]
C3.3   − − Berlin: S. Fischer, 1902, 200 S. ["Buchdruckerei Roitzsch vorm. Otto Roack & Co." Auflagen:
     1. 1894 (#C3.2)
     2. 1902
     3. 1910
     4. 1923 [(Text of #J4., Bd. I, S. 107-204.)]
C3.4   − − *Theaterstücke* [#J2.], 1912, Bd. I, S. 109-204.
C3.5   − − *Theaterstücke* [#J4.], 1922, Bd. I, S. 109-204.
C3.6   − − *Theaterstücke* [#J6.], 1928, Bd. I, S. 109-204.
C3.7   − − *Dramatische Werke* [#J11.], 1962, Bd. I, S. 125-200.

CRITICISM

C3x.1   Marholm, Laura. *Die Zukunft*, 8, 25. Aug. 1894, S. 368-371.
C3x.2   Kummer, Friedrich. *Blätter für literarische Unterhaltung*, Nr. 2, 10. Jan. 1895, S. 27-28.
C3x.3   Anon. *Academy and Literature*, 82, Nr. 2074, Feb. 3, 1912, p. 146-147.
C3x.4   Palmer, John. *Saturday Review*, 113, No. 2936, Feb. 3, 1912, p. 139.
C3x.5   Teweles, Heinrich. "Das Märchen.". *Der Merker*, 3, ix, Mai 1912, S. 347-348. [Teweles, theater director in Prague.]
See Also: F8.

1893

C4.   ANATOL. [The cycle as follows: Einleitung von Loris (Hugo von Hofmannsthal). Die Frage an das Schicksal. Weihnachtseinkäufe. Episode. Denksteine. Abschiedssouper. Agonie. Anatols Hochzeitsmorgen.]

C4.1	"Episode." *An der schönen blauen Donau*, 4, xviii, 1889, S. 424-426.
C4.2	"Anatols Hochzeitsmorgen." *Moderne Dichtung*, 2, i, 1. Juli 1890, S. 431-442.
C4.3	"Die Frage an das Schicksal." *Budapester Tagblatt*, 13. Mai 1890.
C4.4	"Die Frage an das Schicksal. "*Moderne Dichtung*, 1, v, 1. Mai 1890, S. 299-306.
C4.5	"Denksteine." *Moderne Rundschau*, 3, iv, 15. Mai 1891, S. 151-154.
C4.6	"Weihnachts-Einkäufe." *Frankfurter Zeitung*, Nr. 358, 24. Dez. 1891, S. 1-2. [Two speakers are "Er" and "Sie."]
C4.7	"Weihnachtseinkäufe. "*Das Rendezvous*, Nr. 8-10, Weihnachten, 1892, S. 15-18.
C4.8	– – Mit einer Einleitung von Loris. Berlin: Bibliographisches Bureau, 1893, iii, 138 S. ["Druck von G. Pätz in Naumburg a. S." Constitutes the 1. Aufl. of #C4.9.]
C4.9	– – Berlin: S. Fischer, 1895, 138 S. ["Umschlag von Th. Th. Heine." Auflagen:
	1. 1893 (#C4.8)
	2. 1895
	3. 1899
	7. – 8. 1905 (146 S.)
	10. 1908
	11. – 15. 1911
	16. – 18. 1914
	23. – 26. 1920
	27. – 29. 1923
	30. – 32. 1927]
C4.10	– – Illustriert von M. Coschell. Berlin: S. Fischer, 1901, 206 S. ["Gedruckt bei A. Seydel & Cie., Berlin SW. 13." 1. – 3. Aufl.]
C4.11	– – *Theaterstücke* [#J2.], 1912, Bd. I, S. 9-107.
C4.12	– – *Theaterstücke* [#J4.], 1922, Bd. I, S. 9-107.
C4.13	– – *Theaterstücke* [#J6.], 1928, Bd. I, S. 9-107.
C4.14	"Aus 'Anatols Hochzeitsmorgen'." *Deutsche Dichtung unserer Zeit: Von der Sinnenkunst zur Seelenkunst (1880-1930).* (Ernst Rose, ed.) New York: Prentice-Hall, 1930, p. 109-115. [School edition.]
C4.15	"Aus Anatol." *Moderne Einakter.* (Hans Jaeger, ed.) New York: F. S. Crofts, 1938, p. 1-26. [Contains "Weihnachtseinkäufe" and "Abschiedssouper." School edition.]
C4.16	"Die Frage an das Schicksal." *Four German One-Act Plays.* (Gilbert J. Jordan, ed.) New York: Henry Holt, 1951, p. 1-18. [Expurgated school edition.]
C4.17	– – *Meisterdramen* [#S5.], 1955, S. 7-84.
C4.18	*Drei Szenen aus Anatol* [#S5.], 1960, p. 1-48. [School edition containing "Die Frage an das Schicksal," "Episode," "Abschiedssouper."]
C4.18a	"Weihnachtseinkäufe." *Lebendige Literatur: Deutsches Lesebuch für Anfänger.* (Frank G. Ryder & E. Allen McCormick, eds.) Boston: Houghton Mifflin, 1960, p. 228-247. [School edition.]
C4.19	– – *Österreichisches Theater des XX. Jahrhunderts: Schnitzler, Hofmannsthal, Mell, Csokor, Billinger, Lernet-Holenia, Horvàth.* (Joachim Schondorff, ed.) München: Albert Langen, Georg Müller, 1961, S. 37-109. [Note on AS by Oskar Maurus Fontana, S. 19-21.]
C4.20	– – *Dramatische Werke* [#J11.], 1962, Bd. I, S. 27-104.
C4.21	"Süsses Mädel: Eine bisher unveröffentlichte Anatol-Szene." *Forum* (Wien), 9, ci, Mai 1962, S. 220-222.
C4.22	*Anatol: Anatol-Zyklus. Anatols Grössenwahn. Das Abenteuer seines Lebens.* (Ernst L. Offermanns, ed.) Berlin: Walter de Gruyter, 1964, 202 S. (Komedia: Deutsche Lustspiele vom Barock bis zur Gegenwart, Nr. 6). [Also contains: "Ursprünglicher Schluss zu Anatols Hochzeitsmorgen," S. 140-145, and "Beträchtlich stört mein junges Liebesglück" (unpublished poem from "Anatol"), S. 145. First AS-critical edition: "Editionsbericht," "Zur Entstehungsgeschichte," "Gattungsgeschichtliche Einordnung," "Zur Analyse der Stücke," "Zur Wirkungsgeschichte," "Literatur."]

C4e.1 "Questioning the Irrevocable." *The Drama: Its History, Literature and Influence on Civilization.* (Alfred Bates, ed.) London & New York: Athenian Society (Smart & Stanley), 1903, Vol. XII: German Drama, p. 329-344. ["Die Frage an das Schicksal." W. H. H. Chambers, tr.]

C4e.2 *Anatol: A Sequence of Dialogues.* Paraphrased for the English Stage by Granville Barker. London: Sidgwick & Jackson, 1911, 125 p. [Also: New York: M. Kennerley, 1911; Boston: Little, Brown, 1916. English titles: "Ask No Questions and You'll Hear No Stories." "A Christmas Present." "An Episode." "Keepsakes." "A Farewell Supper." "Dying Pangs." "The Wedding Morning." – 1st & 2nd impressions, 1911; 3rd impression, 1913.]

C4e.3 "A Christmas Present." *International*, 4, i, June, 1911, p. 6-7. ["Weihnachtseinkäufe." Granville Barker, tr.]

C4e.4 "An Episode." *International*, 4, ii, July, 1911, p. 23-24. [Granville Barker, tr.]

C4e.5 "Anatol." *Green Book Magazine*, 8, v, Nov., 1912, p. 818-824. [Excerpts. Granville Barker, tr.]

C4e.6 "Anatol." *Anatol* [#L5.], 1917, p. 1-97. [Grace Isabel Colbron, tr.]

C4e.7 "A Christmas Present." *The Warner Library: The World's Best Literature.* New York: Warner Library, 1917, Vol. XXI, p. 12922d-12922k. ["Weihnachtseinkäufe." Granville Barker, tr.]

C4e.8 "The Affairs of Anatol." *Motion Picture Classic*, 12, iv, June, 1921, p. 37-41. ["Fictionized by permission from the Cecil B. de Mille production of the scenario by Jeanie Macpherson, adapted from the play by Arthur Schnitzler, by Gladys Hall."]

C4e.9 "Christmas Purchases." *The Columbia Course in Literature.* New York: Columbia University Press, 1928, Vol. IX, p. 561-568. ["Weihnachtseinkäufe." Bayard Quincy Morgan, tr.]

C4e.10 "Dissolution: A Viennese Comedy of Love." *Golden Book Magazine*, 16, xcii, Aug., 1932, p. 175-180. ["Agonie." Grace Isabel Colbron, tr.]

C4e.11 *The Affairs of Anatol: A Cycle of One-Act Plays.* Version by Harley Granville-Barker. New York: Samuel French, 1933.

C4e.12 "The Affairs of Anatol." *Reigen* [#L11.], 1933, p. 73-169. [Grace Isabel Colbron, tr.]

C4e.13 "Episode." *Golden Book Magazine*, 17, xcvii, Jan., 1933, p. 70-77. [Grace Isabel Colbron, tr.]

C4e.14 "A Farewell Supper: A Comedy." *Fifty One-Act Plays.* (Constance M. Martin, ed.) London: Victor Gollancz, 1934, p. 961-976. ["Abschiedssouper." H. Granville-Barker, tr.]

C4e.15 "Anatol." *Sixteen Famous European Plays.* (Bennett A. Cerf & Van H. Cartmell, eds.) New York: Modern Library, 1943, p. 667-730. (The Modern Library of the World's Best Books). [Grace Isabel Colbron, tr.]

C4e.16 "A Farewell Supper." *Reading Drama: A Method of Analysis with Selections for Study.* (Fred B. Millett, ed.) New York: Harper, 1950, p. 47-62. ["Abschiedssouper." H. Granville-Barker, tr.]

C4e.17 "Anatol." *From the Modern Repertoire: Series Three.* (Eric Bentley, ed.) Bloomington: Indiana University Press, 1956, p. 175-240. [Harley Granville-Barker, tr.]

C4f.1 "Un souvenir! Scène dramatique tirée d'Anatole." *Revue d'art dramatique*, 1, vi, avril, 1897, p. 416-423. ["Denksteine." August Monnier & Georges Montignac, trs.]

C4f.2 *Souper d'adieu: comédie en un acte.* Adaptée par Maurice Vaucaire. Paris: Société d'Editions Littéraires et Artistiques, 1905, 33 p. ["Abschiedssouper."]

C4f.3 "Anatole." *Anatole* [#M1.], 1913, p. 1-234. [Maurice Rémon & Maurice Vaucaire, trs.]

C4x.1   Anon. *Die Gegenwart*, Nr. 5, 4. Feb. 1893.
C4x.2   Anon. *Das Magazin*, Nr. 18, 6. Mai 1893.
C4x.3   Kraus, Karl. *Die Gesellschaft*, 9-1, i, Jan. 1893, S. 109-110.
C4x.4   Kerr, Alfred. *Die Nation*, 16, xxvi, 25. März 1899, S. 377.
C4x.5   Hatvany, Ludwig. *Pan*, 1, iv. 16. Dez. 1910, S. 132-133.
C4x.6   Kienzel, Hermann. *Bühne und Welt*, 13-1, Dez. 1910, S. 257.
C4x.7   Anon. *Academy and Literature*, 80, No. 2026, Mar. 4, 1911, p. 268.
C4x.8   Anon. *The Athenaeum*, No. 4351, Mar. 18, 1911, p. 314-316. [Two reviews.]
C4x.9   Anon. *The Bookman*, 34, ii, Oct., 1911, p. 205-206.
C4x.10   Anon. "Dialogues for Adults." *New York Times Book Review*, Aug. 13, 1911, p. 496.
C4x.11   Anon. *Illustrated London News*, 138, No. 3752, Mar. 18, 1911, p. 370.
C4x.12   Anon. *Velhagen & Klasings Monatshefte*, 25. Feb. 1911, S. 230.
C4x.13   Frenzel, Karl. *Deutsche Rundschau*, 37 (Bd. 147), ix, Juni 1911, S. 468.
C4x.14   Anon. *American Playwright*, 1, xi, Nov. 15, 1912, p. 367-368.
C4x.15   Anon. *New York Dramatic Mirror*, 68, No. 1765, Oct. 16, 1912, p. 6-7.
C4x.16   Anon. *New York Dramatic News*, 56, Oct. 19, 1912, p. 19.
C4x.17   Anon. *The Theatre*, 16, cxli, Nov., 1912, p. ix-x.
C4x.18   Metcalfe. *Life*, 60, No. 1565, Oct. 24, 1912, p. 2051.
C4x.19   Ruhl, Arthur. *Collier's* 50, vii, Nov. 2, 1912, p. 18; 34.
C4x.20   vom Baur, E. E. "Schnitzler's 'Anatol' a New Form of Play." *The Theatre*, 16, cxl, Oct., 1912, p. 106; 108; 110.
C4x.21. White, Matthew, Jr. "A Delightful Philanderer." *Munsey's* Magazine, 48, iii, Dec., 1912, p. 527.
C4x.22   Anon. *Bluebook*, 16, Jan., 1913, p. 458-462.
C4x.23   DeFoë, Louis. *Red Book Magazine*, 20, May, 1913, p. 497-500.
C4x.24   Hamilton, Clayton. *Everybody's Magazine*, 28, i, Jan., 1913, p. 111.
C4x.25   Pollock, Channing. *Green Book Magazine*, 9, i, Jan., 1913, p. 67-78.
C4x.26   Anon. "The Affairs of Anatol: Rakishness in the Guise of Reform." *The Dramatist*, 12, iv, Oct., 1921, p. 1083-1085.
C4x.27   Polgar, Alfred. *Die Weltbühne*, 21, xii, 24. März 1925, S. 444.
C4x.28   Anon. *Theatre Magazine*, 53, iii, Mar., 1931, p. 25.
C4x.29   Chatfield-Taylor, Otis. *Outlook and Independent*, 157, v, Feb. 4, 1931, p. 190.
C4x.30   Leonard, Baird. *Life*, 97, No. 2518, Feb. 6, 1931, p. 18.
C4x.31   Skinner, Richard Dana. *The Commonweal*, 13, xiv, Feb. 4, 1931, p. 385.
C4x.32   van Doren, Mark. *The Nation*, 132, No. 3422, Feb. 4, 1931, p. 134-135.
C4x.33   Van Rensselaer Wyatt, Euphemia. *Catholic World*, 132, dccxcii, Mar., 1931, p. 720-721.
C4x.34   LoCicero, Vincent. *JIASRA*, 4, i, Spring, 1965, p. 27. [Rev. of #C4.22.]
See Also: x9, x39, x131, x324.

1896

C5.   LIEBELEI: SCHAUSPIEL IN DREI AKTEN

C5.1   ── Berlin: S. Fischer, 1896, 142 S. ["Druck von Max Schmersow vorm. Zahn & Baendel, Kirchhain N.-L." Auflagen:
         1. 1896
         3. 1899

4. 1901
6. 1905
7. 1907
9. 1909
10. – 11. 1911
12. 1914
20. – 21. 1922 (Text of #J4., Bd. II, S. 201-267.)
23. 1925
24. – 25. 1928 (67 S.)
26. – 27. 1933]

C5.2   "Liebelei, Erstes Bild." *Widmungen zur Feier des siebzigsten Geburtstages Ferdinand von Saars.* (Richard Specht, ed.) Wien: Wiener Verlag, 1903, S. 175-196. [Fr. the original version; Fritz and Theodor meet in a Viennese dancing-school.]

C5.3   – – Oper in drei Akten. Von Franz Neumann. Text nach dem gleichnamigen Schauspiel von Arthur Schnitzler. Berlin: S. Fischer; Mainz: B. Schott, 1910, 77 S. ["Buchdruckerei Roitzsch, Albert Schulze, Roitzsch." Text changed and shortened.]

C5.4   "Das arme Mädel." *Der Merker*, 3, ix, 1. Mai-H., 1912, (facsimile page). [First sketch of the work.]

C5.5   – – *Theaterstücke* [#J2.], 1912, Bd. I. S. 205-267.
C5.6   – – *Theaterstücke* [#J4.], 1922, Bd. I, S. 205-267.
C5.7   – – *Theaterstücke* [#J6.], 1928, Bd. I, S. 205-267.
C5.8   – – *Great Dramas Retold.* (Erich Hofacker, ed.) New York: Oxford University Press, 1931, p. 106-115. (Oxford Library of German Texts). [Retold in prose. School edition.]

C5.9   "Liebelei. Erstes Bild der unbekannten Urfassung des Schauspiels." *Wiener Tag*, 25. Dez. 1931. [Reprint of #C5.2.]

C5.10 – – *Meisterdramen* [#J9.], 1955, S. 85-134.
C5.11 – – *Liebelei* [#K15.], 1960, S. 5-68.
C5.12 – – *Dramatische Werke* [#J11.], 1962, Bd. I, S. 215-264.

ENGLISH TRANSLATIONS

C5e.1 "Light-O'-Love: A Drama in Three Acts." *The Drama*, No. 7, Aug., 1912, p. 14-77. [Bayard Quincy Morgan, tr. Also as separate reprint: Chicago: Dramatic Publishing Co., 1912, 77 p.]

C5e.2 *Playing with Love (Liebelei).* Chicago: A. C. McClurg, 1914, ix, 101 p. [P. Morton Shand, tr. Prologue by Hofmannsthal, tr. by Trevor Blakemore. Foreward by P. Morton Shand. – Also: London: Gay & Hancock, 1914.]

C5e.3 "From 'Light O' Love'." *The Columbia University Course in Literature.* New York: Columbia University Press, 1928, Vol. IX, p. 568-573. [Bayard Quincy Morgan, tr. Selection.]

C5e.4 "Light-O'-Love." *Modern Continental Plays.* (Samuel Marion Tucker, ed.) New York & London: Harper, 1929, p. 669-695. [Bayard Quincy Morgan, tr.]

C5e.5 "Light-O'-Love." *Twenty-Five Modern Plays.* (Samuel M. Tucker, ed.) New York & London: Harper, 1931, p. 565-591. [Bayard Quincy Morgan, tr. – Also: 1948 edition revised by Alan S. Downer, p. 97-123.]

C5e.6 "Light-O'-Love." *Contemporary Drama: European Plays.* (Ernest B. Watson & Benfield Pressey, eds.) New York: Charles Scribner, 1931, Vol. I, p. 391-458. [Bayard Quincy Morgan, tr.]

C5e.7 "Light-O'-Love." *Continental Plays.* (Thomas H. Dickinson, ed.) Boston: Houghton Mifflin, 1935, Vol. I, p. 215-265. [Bayard Quincy Morgan, tr.]

C5e.8 "Light-O'-Love." *Contemporary Drama: European; English and Irish; American Plays.* (Ernest B. Watson & Benfield Pressey, eds.) New York: Charles Scribner, 1941, p. 96-118. [Bayard Quincy Morgan, tr.]

C5f.1   *Amourette. Pièce en trois actes.* Adaptée de Arthur Schnitzler par Jean Thorel. Paris: Société des Auteurs Dramatiques, 1897. [Stage manuscript.]

C5f.2   "Liebelei (amourette): pièce en trois actes." *La petite illustration,* no. 648, 4 nov., 1933, p. 1-20. [Suzanne Clauser, tr. – Also as separate reprint: Paris: L'Illustration, 1933, 20 p.]

CRITICISM

C5x.1   Anon. *Die Zukunft,* 14, 14. März 1896, S. 528.

C5x.2   Bie, Oskar. *Der Kunstwart,* 9, xi, 1. Märzheft, 1896, S. 168-169.

C5x.3   Schlenther, Paul. *Preussische Jahrbücher,* 85, iii, Sept. 1896, S. 493-495.

C5x.4   Sittenberger, Hans. *Das Literarische Echo,* 1, viii, 15. Jan. 1899, Sp. 474-475.

C5x.5   Anon. *Illustrated London News,* 134, No. 3657, May 22, 1909, p. 740.

C5x.6   Anon. *New York Dramatic Mirror,* 68, No. 1772, Dec. 4, 1912, p. 7.

C5x.7   Clark, Barrett Harper. "Schnitzler." *The Continental Drama of Today: Outlines for Its Study.* New York: Henry Holt, 1914, p. 119-124. [Notes on "Liebelei."]

C5x.8   Ritscher, Wolf. "Schnitzlers Dramatik und der [sic] Kino." *Phöbus,* 1, i, Apr. 1914, S. 47-48. [Film version.]

C5x.9   Clark, Barrett Harper. "Arthur Schnitzler." *A Study of the Modern Drama: A Handbook for the Study and Appreciation of the Best Plays, European, English and American, of the Last Century.* New York & London: D. Appleton, 1925, p. 100-104. [Study-guide.]

C5x.10   Porché, François. *Revue de Paris,* 40 (t. 5), xx, 15 oct., 1933, p. 938-939.

See Also: x2, x39, x288.

c6.   DIE ÜBERSPANNTE PERSON

c6.1   – – *Simplicissimus,* 1, iii, 18. Apr. 1896, S. 3; 6.

c6.2   – – Berlin: S. Fischer, 1932, 7 S. [Stage manuscript.]

c6.3   – – *Kaffeehaus: Literarische Spezialitäten und amouröse Gusto-Stückln aus Wien.* (Ludwig Plakolb, ed.) München: R. Piper, 1959, S. 12-19.

c6.4   – – *Dramatische Werke* [#J11.], 1962, Bd. I, S. 201-205.

See Also: x238.

1897

c7.   HALBZWEI: EIN AKT

c7.1   – – *Die Gesellschaft,* 13-2, iv, Apr. 1897, S. 42-49.

c7.2   – – Berlin: S. Fischer, 1932, 11 S. [Stage manuscript.]

c7.3   – – *Dramatische Werke* [#J11.], 1962, Bd. I, S. 207-213.

See Also: x238.

1898

c8.   FREIWILD: SCHAUSPIEL IN DREI AKTEN

c8.1   – – Berlin: S. Fischer, 1898, 158 S. ["Druck der Freyhoffschen Buchdruckerei in Nauen." Auflagen:
       1.   1898
       2.   1902 ("veränderte Auflage," 163 S.)
       3.   1908 (158 S.)
       20. – 21. 1922 (Text of #J4., Bd. I, S. 271-346.)]

c8.2   "Die Duellforderung." *Die Meisterwerke der deutschen Literatur (von Klopstock bis zur Gegenwart): In Auszügen.* (G. Burghard, ed.) Paris: Edouard Cornély, 1907, p. 492-501. [Selection. School edition.]

c8.3	– – *Theaterstücke* [‡J2.], 1912, Bd. I, S. 269-346.
c8.4	– – *Theaterstücke* [‡J4.], 1922, Bd. I, S. 269-346.
c8.5	– – *Theaterstücke* [‡J6.], 1928, Bd. I, S. 269-346.
c8.6	– – *Dramatische Werke* [‡J11.], 1962, Bd. 1, S. 265-326.

ENGLISH TRANSLATION

c8e.1   *Free Game.* Boston: Badger, 1913. [Paul H. Grummann, tr.]

CRITICISM

c8x.1   Anon. *Die Gegenwart*, 50, xlvi, 14. Nov. 1896, S. 318.
c8x.2   Anon. *Velhagen & Klasings Monatshefte*, 11-1, 1896, S. 572 ff.
c8x.3   Bie, Oskar. *Der Kunstwart*, 10, iv, 2. Nov.-H., 1896, S. 58-59.
c8x.4   Heilborn, Ernst. *Die Nation*, 14, vi, 7. Nov. 1896, S. 94-95.
c8x.5   Kerr, Alfred. "Das neue Ritterdrama. "*Neue Deutsche Rundschau*, 7, xii, Dez. 1896, S. 1228-1232.
c8x.6   Neumann-Hofer, Otto. "Drei." *Magazin für Litteratur des In- und Auslandes*, 65, xlvi, 14. Nov. 1896, Sp. 1407-1411.
c8x.7   Osborn, Max. "Stücke zum Thema 'Ehre". "*Monatsschrift für neue Litteratur und Kunst*, 1, iii, Dez. 1896, S. 223-228. [Comparison with other works.]
c8x.8   Neumann-Hofer, Otto. *Cosmopolis*, 5, xiii, Jan. 1897, p. 290-292.
c8x.9   Gold, Alfred. *Die Zeit*, 14, clxxvi, 12. Feb. 1898, S. 106.
c8x.10   Rena, E. *Internationales Litteraturblatt*, 5, 1898, S. 259-261.
c8x.11   Schik, F. *Wiener Rundschau*, 3, 1898, S. 277-278.
c8x.12   Anon. *Kritik*, Nr. 1, 1905.
c8x.13   Anon. *The Bookman*, 25, i, Mar., 1907, p. 8-9.
See *Also*: x2, x9, x33.

c9.   PARACELSUS: SCHAUSPIEL IN EINEM AKT

c9.1	– – *Cosmopolis*, 12, xxxv, Nov. 1898, p. 489-527.
c9.2	– – *Der grüne Kakadu* [‡K2.], 1899, S. 1-57.
c9.3	– – *Theaterstücke* [‡J2.] 1912, Bd. II, S. 9-57.
c9.4	– – *Theaterstücke* [‡J4.], 1922, Bd. II, S. 9-57.
c9.5	– – *Theaterstücke* [‡J6.], 1928, Bd. II, S. 9-57.
c9.6	– – *Dramatische Werke* [‡J11.], 1962, Bd. I, S. 465-498.

ENGLISH TRANSLATION

c9e.1   "Paracelsus: A Play in Verse in One Act." *Green Cockatoo* [‡LI.], 1913, p. 85-124. [Horace B. Samuel, tr.]

CRITICISM

c9x.1   Stockum, Theodorus Cornelis van. "Schnitzlers 'Paracelsus' als 'Homo ludens'." *Neophilologus*, 40, iii, 1956, S. 201-206. [Repr. in *Von Friedrich Nicolai bis Thomas Mann: Aufsätze zur deutschen und vergleichenden Literaturgeschichte*. Groningen: J. B. Wolters, 1962, S. 274-279. – Historical deviations; Paracelsus, not Cyprian, the real hero.]

1899

C10.   DIE GEFÄHRTIN: SCHAUSPIEL IN EINEM AKT

C10.1	– – *Der grüne Kakadu* [‡K2.], 1899, S. 59-94.
C10.2	– – *Theaterstücke* [‡J2.], 1912, Bd. II, S. 59-79.

c10.3   — — *Theaterstücke* [#J4.], 1922, Bd. II, S. 59-79.
c10.4   — — *Theaterstücke* [#J6.], 1928, Bd. II, S. 59-79.
c10.5   — — *Dramatische Werke* [#J11.], 1962, Bd. I, S. 499-514.

ENGLISH TRANSLATIONS

c10e.1   "The Wife: A Play." *Current Literature*, 39, v. Nov., 1905, p. 553-556. [Abridged.]
c10e.2   "The Mate." *Green Cockatoo* [#L1.], 1913, p. 59-84. [Horace B. Samuel, tr.]
c10e.3   "His Helpmeet." *International*, 9, vii, July, 1915, p. 207-211. [Pierre Loving, tr.]
c10e.4   "His Helpmate." *Comedies of Words* [#L6.], 1917, p. 160-182. [Pierre Loving, tr.]

FRENCH TRANSLATION

c10f.1   "La Compagne." *Anatole* [#M1.], 1913, p. 235-275. [Maurice Rémon & Maurice Vaucaire, trs.]

CRITICISM

c10x.1   Kienzel, Hermann. *Bühne und Welt*, 12-1, i, Okt. 1909, S. 50-51.

c11.   DER GRÜNE KAKADU: GROTESKE IN EINEM AKT
c11.1   — — *Neue Deutsche Rundschau*, 10, iii, März 1899, S. 282-308.
c11.2   — — *Der grüne Kakadu* [#K2.], 1899, S. 95-178.
c11.3   — — *Theaterstücke* [#J2.], 1912, Bd. II, S. 81-127.
c11.4   — — *Theaterstücke* [#J4.], 1922, Bd. II, S. 81-127.
c11.5   — — *Der grüne Kakadu* [#S1.], 1928, p. 1-51.
c11.6   — — *Theaterstücke* [#J6.], 1928, Bd. II, S. 81-127.
c11.7   — — *Meisterdramen* [#J9.], 1955, S. 135-171.
c11.8   — — Oper in einem Akt. Von Richard Mohaupt. Text nach dem Schauspiel von Arthur Schnitzler. Wien, Zürich, London: Universal Edition, 1958, 71 S. ["Druck: Typographische Anstalt, Wien." Adaptation, ten scenes.]
c11.9   — — *German Literature Since Goethe*. (Ernst Feise & Harry Steinhauer, eds.) Boston: Houghton Mifflin, 1959, Vol. II: An Age of Crisis, 1870-1950, p. 108-128. [School edition.]
c11.10   — — *Spiele in einem Akt: 35 exemplarische Stücke*. (Walter Höllerer, ed.) Frankfurt a.M.: Suhrkamp, 1961, S. 89-118.
c11.11   — — *Dramatische Werke* [#J11.], 1962, Bd. I, S. 515-552.

ENGLISH TRANSLATIONS

c11e.1   "The Duke and the Actress: A Play in One Act." *Poet Lore*, 21, iv, July/Aug., 1910, p. 257-284. [Hans Weysz, tr. Also as separate reprint in the series "Poet Lore Plays," Boston: R. G. Badger, 1910.]
c11e.2   "The Green Cockatoo: A Grotesque in One Act." *Green Cockatoo* [#L1.], 1913, p. 1-58. [Horace B. Samuel, tr.]
c11e.3   "The Green Cockatoo: A Grotesque in One Act." *The German Classics: Masterpieces of German Literature Translated into English*. (Kuno Francke, ed.) New York: German Publication Society, 1914, Vol. XX, p. 289-331. [Horace B. Samuel, tr.]
c11e.4   "The Green Cockatoo: Grotesquery in One Act." *Anatol* [#L5.], 1917, p. 183-226. [Grace Isabel Colbron, tr.]
c11e.5   "The Green Cockatoo: Grotesquery in One Act." *Golden Book Magazine*, 4, xxiii, Nov., 1926, p. 637-653. [Grace Isabel Colbron, tr.]
c11e.6   "The Green Cockatoo." *Plays for the College Theater*. (Garrett H. Leverton, ed.) New York & London: Samuel French, 1932, p. 245-261. [Ethel van der Veer, tr.]

CI1e.7 "The Green Cockatoo: Grotesquery in One Act." *Reigen* [#LII.], 1933, p. 257-301. [Grace Isabel Colbron, tr.]
CI1e.8 "The Green Cockatoo: A Grotesque in One Act." *Thirty Famous One Act Plays.* (Bennett Cerf & Van H. Cartmell, eds.) Garden City, N. Y.: Garden City, 1943, p. 131-163. [Ethel van der Veer, tr. – Also: New York: Modern Library, 1949. (The Modern Library of the World's Best Books).]

CRITICISM

CI1x.1 Lublinski, S. *Das Literarische Echo,* 2, iv, 15. Nov. 1899, Sp. 227. [Fr. "Wiener Romantik."]
CI1x.2 Anon. *Magazin für Litteratur,* 70, xxi, 25. Mai 1901, Sp. 508-509. [Signed "J. G.]
CI1x.3 Duquesnel, Félix. *Le Théâtre,* 6, cxviii, 2 nov. 1903, p. 2.
CI1x.4 Anon. *Kritik,* Nr. 10, 1905.
CI1x.5 Anon. *New York Dramatic Mirror,* 63, No. 1635, Apr. 23, 1910, p. 7.
CI1x.6 Anon. *Theatre Magazine,* 11, cxi, May, 1910, p. xxix.
CI1x.7 Hamilton, Clayton. *The Bookman,* 31, iv, June, 1910, p. 418.
CI1x.8 Bab. Julius. *Der Merker,* 3, ix, Mai 1912, S. 331-334. [This AS's best work.]
CI1x.9 Anon. *Academy and Literature,* 85, No. 2165, Nov. 1, 1913, p. 565-566.
CI1x.10 Barretto, Larry. *The Bookman,* 63, i, Mar., 1926, p. 82-83.
CI1x.11 Schinnerer, Otto P. "The Suppression of Schnitzler's 'Der grüne Kakadu' by the Burgtheater: Unpublished Correspondence." *Germanic Review,* 6, ii, Apr. 1931, p. 183-192. [Difficulties with the authorities of the Burgtheater because of the disfavor of high court officials.]
CI1x.12 Nelson, Robert James. "Schnitzler: The Play as Clinic." *Play Within a Play: The Dramatist's Conception of His Art: Shakespeare to Anouilh.* New Haven: Yale University Press, 1958, p. 115-122. [Double frame; reality-illusion problems.]
See Also: x17, x33, x393.

CI2. DAS VERMÄCHTNIS: SCHAUSPIEL IN DREI AKTEN
CI2.1 – – Berlin: S. Fischer, 1899, 191 S. ["Freyhoffs Buchdruckerei in Nauen." Auflagen:
1. 1899
2. 1901
3. 1912 (152 S.)
4. 1922
1923 (Text of #J4., Bd. I, S. 349-438.)]
CI2.2 – – *Theaterstücke* [#J2.], 1912, Bd. I, S. 347-439.
CI2.3 – – *Theaterstücke* [#J4.], 1922, Bd. I, S. 347-439.
CI2.4 – – *Theaterstücke* [#J6.], 1928, Bd. I, S. 347-439.
CI2.5 – – *Dramatische Werke* [#J11.], 1962, Bd. I, S. 391-464.

ENGLISH TRANSLATION

CI2e.1 "The Legacy: Drama in Three Acts." *Poet Lore,* 22, iv, July/Aug., 1911, p. 241-308. [Mary L. Stephenson, tr.]

CRITICISM

CI2x.1 Anon. *Preussische Jahrbücher,* 94, ii, Nov. 1898, S. 358-361.
CI2x.2 Berg, Leo. *Umschau,* 2, xlviii, 26. Nov. 1898, S. 809-810.
CI2x.3 Burckhard, Max. *Die Zeit,* 17, 1898, S. 154-155.
CI2x.4 Busse, C. *Deutsches Wochenblatt,* 4, 1898, S. 512-514.
CI2x.5 Harden, Maximilian. *Die Zukunft,* 25, 15. Okt. 1898, S. 133-136.

CI2x.6   Heilborn, Ernst. *Die Nation*, 16, iii, 15. Okt. 1898, S. 41-42.
CI2x.7   Kerr, Alfred. *Neue Deutsche Rundschau*, 9, xii, Dez. 1898, S. 1319.
CI2x.8   Lothar, Rudolf. *Die Wage*, 1, 1898, S. 814-815.
CI2x.9   Schlaikjer, Erich. *Der Kunstwart*, 12, iii, 1. Nov.-H., 1898, S. 103-104.
CI2x.10   Schmidt, Lothar. *Das Literarische Echo*, 1, iii, 1. Nov. 1898, Sp. 195.
CI2x.11   Steiner, Rudolf. *Das Magazin für Litteratur*, 67, xli, 15. Okt. 1898, Sp. 977-978.
CI2x.12   Zoozmann, Richard. *Bühne und Welt*, 1-1, iii, Okt. 1898, S. 142.
CI2x.13   Jellinek, Arthur L. *Das Literarische Echo*, 1, vii, 1. Jan. 1899, S. 466.
CI2x.14   Vallette, Gaspard. *Semaine littéraire*, 7, cclxxii, 18 mars, 1899, p. 120-124.
CI2x.15   Weber, C. Hanns von. *Die Gesellschaft*, 15-1, vi, 1899, S. 440-441.
See Also: x39.

1900

CI3.   REIGEN: ZEHN DIALOGE. GESCHRIEBEN WINTER 1896/97
CI3.1   – – 1900. [Private printing limited to 200 copies.]
CI3.2   – – Buchschmuck von Berthold Löffler. Wien & Leipzig: Wiener Verlag,
          1903, 250 S. [Auflagen:
          1. – 27. Tsd.   1903   ("Von diesem Buche wurden 25 numerierte Exemplare
                                 auf Büttenpapier abgezogen und vom Autor signiert.")
          36. – 40. Tsd. 1903   ("Von diesem Buche wurden 100 Exemplare auf echt
                                 Büttenpapier abgezogen, in Leder gebunden, hand-
                                 schriftlich numeriert und vom Autor persönlich
                                 signiert.")
          41. – 43. Tsd. n.d.
          44. – 46. Tsd. n.d.]
CI3.3   – – Berlin & Wien: Benjamin Harz, 1914, 254 S. [59. – 99. Tsd. of #CI3.2.]
CI3.4   – – Mit zehn Illustrationen nach Radierungen von Stefan Eggeler. Wien,
          Leipzig, Bern: Frisch, 1921, 161 S. ["Dieses Buch wurde im Jahre 1921 vom
          Frisch & Co. Verlag in Wien herausgegeben und in der eigenen Anstalt des
          Verlages in einer einmaligen Auflage von 3000 numerierten Exemplaren her-
          gestellt. Die ersten 150 Exemplare sind in Halbleder gebunden und vom Autor
          und vom Künstler signiert. Nr. 151 bis 3000 wurden in Ganzleinen ausgegeben.
          Dieses Exemplar trägt die Nummer . . ."]
CI3.5   – – Mit zehn Original-Radierungen von Stefan Eggeler. Wien: Ernst Wil-
          hartitz, 1922, 161 S. ["Dieses Buch wurde im Jahr 1922 vom Verlag Ernst
          Wilhartitz in Wien herausgegeben und in der eigenen Anstalt des Verlags in
          einer einmaligen Auflage von 50 römisch numerierte Exemplaren hergestellt.
          Die Exemplare enthalten Original-Radierungen, sind in Ganzleder gebunden
          und vom Autor und vom Künstler signiert."]
CI3.6   – – Berlin & Wien: Benjamin Harz, 1923, 127 S. ["Als hundertstes Tsd." of
          #13.2. "In Tausend numerierten Exemplaren . . . für den Verlag Benjamin
          Harz in Berlin und Wien unter typographischer Leitung von Lazarus Gold-
          schmiedt im Sommer 1923 in der Offizin von W. Drugulin in Leipzig her-
          gestellt."]
CI3.7   – – Berlin: S. Fischer, 1931, 166 S. ["Gedruckt bei Poeschel & Trepte in
          Leipzig." 101. – 104. Aufl. of #13.2.]
CI3.8   – – Berlin: Onkel Toms Hütte, P. Steegemann, 1951, 82 S. (Die Bank der
          Spötter, Bd. 7), ["Umschlagzeichnung von Emil Orlik; Gesamtherstellung:
          Graphische Gesellschaft Grunewald, G.m.b.H., Berlin-Grunewald." 1. – 3.
          Tsd. 1951; 7. – 9. Tsd. 1952; 13. – 15. Tsd. 1954.]
CI3.9   – – *Meisterdramen* [#J9.], 1955, S. 515-582.
CI3.10   – – *Liebelei* [#K15.], 1960, S. 69-154.
CI3.11   – – *Dramatische Werke* [#J11.], 1962, Bd. I. S. 327-390.

54

C13e.1   *Hands Around: A Cycle of Ten Dialogues.* Completely Rendered into English. Authorized Translation. New York: Privately Printed for Subscribers, 1920, xiii, 233 p. [L. D. Edwards & F. L. Glaser, trs. Introd. by the same. "Of this edition, intended for private circulation only, 1475 copies have been printed after which the type has been distributed. This is copy number ... – English scene titles: "The Girl of the Streets and the Soldier." "The S. and the Parlour Maid." "The P. M. and the Young Man." "The Y. M. and the Young Wife." "The Y. W. and the Husband." "The H. and the Sweet Young Miss." "The S. Y. M. and the Poet." "The P. and the Actress." "The A. and the Count." "The C. and the Girl of the Streets." – Also: Privately Printed for Members of the Schnitzler Society, 1929.]

C13e.2   *Couples.* Ten Dialogues Rendered from the German by Lily Wolfe and E. W. Titus. Including a Translation of the Opinion of the State Court at Berlin in Vindication of the Fitness of the Play for Performance in Public. Ten Engravings by Polia Chentoff. Paris: Edward W. Titus, 1927, 111 p.

C13e.3   *Hands Round: A Roundelay in Ten Dialogues.* Illustrated by Rene Gockings. New York: Julian Press, 1929, 158 p. [Keene Wallis, tr.]

C13e.4   "Reigen (Hands Around): Ten Dialogues." *Reigen* [#L11.], 1933, p. 1-72. [Marya Mannes, tr.]

C13e.5   "Round Dance: Ten Dialogues." *From the Modern Repertoire: Series One.* (Eric Bentley, ed.) Bloomington, Indiana: Indiana University Press, 1949, p. 121-175. [Keene Wallis, tr.]

C13e.6   *Merry-Go-Round (Reigen).* With Illustrations by Philip Gough. Introduction by Ilsa Barea. London: Weidenfeld & Nicholson, 1953, xiii, 90 p. [Frank & Jacqueline Marcus, trs. – English scene titles: "The Prostitute and the Soldier." "The S. and the Chambermaid." "The C. and the Young Gentleman." "The Y. G. and the Young Married Woman." "The Y. M. W. and the Husband." "The H. and the Sweet Girl." "The S. G. and the Poet." "The P. and the Actress." "The A. and the Count." "The Count and the Prostitute." – Also: British Book Centre, 1954.]

C13e.7   "Fragments from La Ronde." *Stories of Scarlet Women.* New York: Avon, 1955. [Eric Bentley, tr.]

C13e.8   "La Ronde: Ten Dialogues." *The Modern Theater.* (Eric Bentley, ed.) Garden City, N. Y.: Doubleday, 1955, Vol. II, p. 145-224. (Doubleday Anchor Books). [Eric Bentley, tr.]

C13e.9   *La Ronde (Reigen).* Illustrated by Philip Gough. London: Harborough, 1959, 124 p. (Ace Books). [Frank & Jacqueline Marcus, trs.]

C13e.10   "La Ronde: Ten Dialogues." *Masters of the Modern Drama.* (Haskell M. Block & Robert G. Shedd, eds.) New York: Random House, 1962, p. 245-269. [Hans Weigert & Patricia Newhall, trs.]

C13e.11   *Dance of Love.* New York: Universal Publishing & Distributing Corporation, 1965, 126 p. (Award Book A 142). [Keene Wallis, tr. Illustrated by Rene Gockings. Introd. by Daniel Seltzer.]

FRENCH TRANSLATIONS

C13f.1   *La ronde: Dix scenes dialoguées.* Paris: P. V. Stock, 1912, 278 p. [Maurice Rémon & Wilhelm Bauer, trs.]

C13f.2   *La ronde: Dix dialogues.* Paris: Librairie Stock, Delamain et Boutelleau, 1931, 188 p. [Maurice Rémon, W. Bauer & Suzanne Clauser, trs.]

CRITICISM

C13x.1   Anon. *Die Gesellschaft,* 3, 1900, S. 251. [Signed "M. G. C."]
C13x.2   Kerr. Alfred. *Neue Deutsche Rundschau,* 11, vi, Juni 1900, S. 666.

C13x.3   Anon. *Die Wage*, 6, 1903, S. 23.

C13x.4   Conrad, M. G. "Der Staatsanwalt und die Kultur." *Freistaat*, 5, 1903, S. 493-494.

C13x.5   Danegger, Adolf. "Arthur Schnitzlers 'Reigen' und die Kritik." *Freistaat*, 5, xxviii, 1903, S. 549-550.

C13x.6   Greiner, Leo. *Das Literarische Echo*, 5, xx, 15. Juli 1903, Sp. 1433.

C13x.7   Kausen, A. "Akademisch-dramatische 'Sauspiele'." *Die Wahrheit*, 9, 1903, S. 331-334.

C13x.8   Salten, F. "Arthur Schnitzler und sein 'Reigen'." *Die Zeit*, 7. Nov. 1903.

C13x.9   Strauss, Rudolf. "Der Pornograph Schnitzler." *Die Wage*, 6-1, xxvii, 27. Juni 1903, S. 812-814.

C13x.10   Törnsee, Fr. *Neue Bahnen*, 3, 1903, S. 245.

C13x.11   von der March, Ottokar. *Neue Bahnen*, 3, 23 Juni 1903, S. 367-369.

C13x.12   Weber, Leopold. *Der Kunstwart*, 16, xx, 2. Juli-H., 1903, S. 380-382.

C13x.13   Aram, Kurt. *Das Literarische Echo*, 6, vii, 1. Jan. 1904, Sp. 512-513.

C13x.14   Anon. *Nouvelle Revue*, sér. 4, 2, 1912, p. 282.

C13x.15   Dimier, L. *Polybiblion*, 125 (2 sér., t. 67), 1912, p. 26.

C13x.16   Anon. "Moabiter 'Reigen'." *Das Blaue Heft*, 3, ix, 26. Nov. 1921, S. 262-264.

C13x.17   Anon. "Das Urteil im Reigen-Prozess." *Deutsche Bühne*, 13, x, 7. März 1921, S. 164-166. [Repr. of court decision.]

C13x.18   Anon. *Komödie*, 2, viii, 19. Feb. 1921.

C13x.19   Eloesser, Arthur. *Freie Deutsche Bühne*, 2, xx, 9. Jan. 1921, S. 443-445.

C13x.20   Harden, Maximilan. *Die Zukunft*, 112, 8. Jan. 1921, S. 51-57.

C13x.21   Klaar, Alfred. "Schnitzlers 'Reigen'." *Deutsche Bühne*, 13, i, 3. Jan. 1921, S. 1-2.

C13x.22   Oberlaender, L. G. *Allgemeine Rundschau*, 18, v, 29. Jan. 1921, S. 58.

C13x.23   Thamerus, W. "Der 'Reigen' einer entarteten Kunst." *Allgemeine Rundschau*, 18, viii, 19. Feb. 1921, S. 92-93.

C13x.24   Tögel, Fritz. *Arthur Schnitzlers "Reigen."* Leipzig: Neulandhaus, Walther Tietz, 1921, S. 3-8. (Flugschrift 2: Sonderdruck aus *Neues Land*, H. 1.)

C13x.25   Weil, Robert. *Das Reigenereignis und andere Ereignisse*. Wien: Halm & Goldmann, 1921, 32 S. [Signed "Homunkulus."]

C13x.26   Westerich, Thomas. "'Reigen' und 'Venuswagen'." *Deutschvölkische Blätter*, 36, iv, 24. Nov. 1921, S. 1.

C13x.27   Bartels, Adolf. "Der Reigen-Prozess." *Deutsches Schrifttum*, 14, i, 1922, S. 1-3.

C13x.28   Dehnow, Fritz. "Der Prozess um den 'Reigen'." *Zeitschrift für Sexualwissenschaft*, 9, ix, Dez. 1922, S. 250-257.

C13x.29   Eckhardt, Johannes. "Schnitzler 'Reigen' und Weismantels 'Totentanz 1921'." *Die Bergstadt*, 10, v. Feb. 1922, S. 440-441.

C13x.30   Heine, Wolfgang. *Der Kampf um den Reigen: Vollständiger Bericht über die sechstägige Verhandlung gegen Direktion und Darsteller des Kleinen Schauspielhauses Berlin*. Berlin: Ernst Rowohlt, 1922, 448 S. [Introd. by Wolfgang Heine, S. 5-16. Fascinating account of the Berlin "Reigen" trial, of more interest to the historian and sociologist than to the literary critic. Praises the acquittal as a victory for freedom of the spirit.]

C13x.31   Kleibömer, Georg. "Zu Schnitzlers 'Reigen'." *Deutsches Volkstum*, 4, v. Mai 1922, S. 156-158.

C13x.32   Stapel, Wilhelm. "Das Geschäft mit Sexualien: Die Reigen Presse." *Deutsches Volkstum*, 4, v, Mai, 1922, S. 145-154.

C13x.33   Stapel, Wilhelm. "Ein Schlusswort zum Reigen Prozess." *Deutsches Volkstum*, 4, ix, Nov. 1922, S. 368-369.

C13x.34   Wrobel, Ignaz. "Brunner im Amt." *Die Weltbühne*, 18, xxxvi, 7. Sept. 1922, S. 266-267.

C13x.35   Dukes, Ashley, "Arthur Schnitzler." *The Youngest Drama: Studies of Fifty Dramatists*. London: Ernest Benn, 1923, p. 42-44. [Also: Chicago: Sergel, 1924.]

C13x.36   Endell, Fritz. "Der 'Reigen' in Amerika." *Deutsches Volkstum*, 5, vii, Juli 1923, S. 284-286. [Problems of censorship.]

CI3x.37 Anon. "When Judges Disagree." *Publisher's Weekly*, 116, xxiv, Dec. 14, 1929, p. 2758-2759.
CI3x.38 Schinnerer, Otto P. "The History of Schnitzler's 'Reigen'." *PMLA*, 46, iii, Sept., 1931, p. 839-859. [Fate of the book and stage-history; play counterpart of "Anatol" and a better work.]
CI3x.39 Austruy, Henri. *La nouvelle revue*, 55 (t. 121), cdlxxxv, 15. oct. 1932, p. 313.
CI3x.40 Porché, François. *Revue de Paris*, 39, xxi, 1. nov. 1932, p. 211-213.
CI3x.41 Bentley, Eric. "Round Dance (1897)." *From the Modern Repertoire: Series One* Bloomington, Indiana: Indiana University Press, 1949, p. 385-387.
CI3x.42 Anon. "Rondo der Liebe." *Die Gegenwart*, 5, 15. Dez. 1950, S. 18-19. [Signed "M. V. B."]
CI3x.43 Anon. "Reigen-Parodie: Gelegenheit macht Liebe." *Der Spiegel*, 7, xx, 13. Mai 1953, S. 31-32.
CI3x.44 Bentley, Eric. *New Republic*, 130, xiv, Apr. 5, 1954, p. 21. [Repr. as "Reigen Comes Full Circle." *The Dramatic Event: An American Chronicle*. New York: Horizon, 1954, p. 209-212.]
CI3x.45 Abel, Paul. "Parodierung von Schnitzlers Reigen." *Archiv für Urheber-, Film-, Funk- und Theaterrecht*. 20, v/vi, 1. Okt. 1955, S. 377-380. [Legal decision on the parody "Reigen 51."]
CI3x.46 Malcolm, Donald. *New Yorker*, 36, xiv, May 21, 1960, p. 117-118.
CI3x.47 Hannum, Hunter. "Killing Time." Aspects of Schnitzler's 'Reigen'." *Germanic Review*, 37, iii, May, 1962, p. 190-206. [AS's paradox of the aesthetic life.]
CI3x.48 Marcuse, Ludwig. "Der 'Reigen'-Prozess: Sex, Politik und Kunst 1920 in Berlin." *Der Monat*, 14, clxviii, Sept. 1962, S. 48-55; 14, clxix, Okt. 1962, S. 34-46. [Repr. as "Berlin 1920: Sex, Politik und Kunst – im Reigen." *Obszön: Geschichte einer Entrüstung*. München: Paul List, 1962, S. 207-263.]

See Also: FI3.

1901

CI4. LEBENDIGE STUNDEN: SCHAUSPIEL IN EINEM AKT
CI4.1 − − *Neue Deutsche Rundschau*, 12, xii, Dez. 1901, S. 1297-1306.
CI4.2 − − *Lebendige Stunden* [#K3.], 1902, S. 7-35.
CI4.3 − − *Theaterstücke* [#J2.], 1912, Bd. II, S. 326-342.
CI4.4 − − *Theaterstücke* [#J4.], 1922, Bd. II, S. 326-342.
CI4.5 − − *Theaterstücke* [#J6.], 1928, Bd. II, S. 326-342.
CI4.6 − − *Das deutsche Drama: 1880-1933*. (H. Steinhauer, ed.) New York: W. W. Norton, 1938, Vol. I: From Naturalism to Expressionism, p. 119-140. (Gateway Books). [School edition.]
CI4.7 − − *Meisterdramen* [#J9.], 1955, S. 173-186.
CI4.8 − − *Dramatische Werke* [#J11.], 1962, Bd. I, S. 690-702.

ENGLISH TRANSLATIONS

CI4e.1 "Living Hours: A Play in One Act." *Poet Lore*, 17, i, Spring, 1906, p. 36-45. [Helen Tracy Porter, tr.]
CI4e.2 "Vital Moments. "*International*, 3, i, Dec., 1910, p. 7-9; 16. [Edward Goodman, tr. Abridged.]
CI4e.3 "Living Hours." *Living Hours* [#L2.], 1913. [Paul H. Grummann, tr.]
CI4e.4 "Living Hours." *Anatol* [#L5.], 1917, p. 101-116. [Grace Isabel Colbron, tr.]
CI4e.5 "Living Hours." *Stratford Journal*, 4, iii, Mar., 1919, p. 155-166. [Colin Clements & Alice Ernst, trs.]
CI4e.6 "Living Hours." *Chief Contemporary Dramatists: Second Series*. (Thomas H. Dickinson, ed.) Boston: Houghton Mifflin, 1921, p. 493-503. [Grace Isabel Colbron, tr.]

c14e.7 "Living Hours." *Ten Minute Plays*. (Pierre Loving, ed.) New York: Brentano's, 1923, p. 37-57. [Porter Davitts, tr.]
c14e.8 "Living Hours." *Reigen* [#LII.], 1933, p. 171-188.

c15. DER SCHLEIER DER BEATRICE: SCHAUSPIEL IN FÜNF AKTEN
c15.1 – – Berlin: S. Fischer, 1901, 215 S. ["Freyhoffs Buchdruckerei in Nauen." Auflagen:
   1. – 2. 1901
   3.   1905
   4.   1910
   5.   1919
   6.   1922 (Text of #J4., Bd. II, S. 127-323.)]
c15.2 "Der Schleier der Beatrice (Zwei Fragmente aus der ersten Fassung)." *Der Merker*, 3, ix, 1. Mai-H., 1912, S. 357-360.
c15.3 – – *Theaterstücke* [#J2.], 1912, Bd. II, S. 129-323.
c15.4 – – *Theaterstücke* [#J4.], 1922, Bd. II, S. 129-323.
c15.5 – – *Theaterstücke* [#J6.], 1928, Bd. II, S. 129-323.
c15.6 – – *Dramatische Werke* [#J11.], 1962, Bd. I, S. 553-679.

CRITICISM

c15x.1 Fred, W. *Die Nation*, 18, xxxiv, 25. Mai 1901, S. 544.
c15x.2 Freund, Erich. *Das Literarische Echo*, 3, vii, Jan. 1901, Sp. 493-495.
c15x.3 Kerr. Alfred. *Neue Deutsche Rundschau*, 12, v, Mai 1901, S. 437-438.
c15x.4 Lorenz. M. *Preussische Jahrbücher*, 105, Juli 1901, S. 165-168.
c15x.5 Anon. *Die Gegenwart*, 32 (Bd. 63), xi, 14. März 1903, S. 174.
c15x.6 Düsel, Friedrich. *Westermanns Monatshefte*, 94, viii, Mai 1903, S. 302-303.
c15x.7 Frenzel, Karl. *Deutsche Rundschau*, 29 (Bd. 115), viii, Mai 1903, S. 296-298.
c15x.8 Harden, Maximilan. "Der Schleier der Beatrice." *Die Zukunft*, 42, xxvi, 28. März 1903, S. 517-530. [In spite of its defects AS's best drama of late; AS here gotten away from romantic philandering for more important things.]
c15x.9 Heilborn, Ernst. *Die Nation*, 20, xxiv, 14. März 1903, S. 380-381.
c15x.10 Lienhard, F. *Deutsche Monatschrift für das gesamte Leben der Gegenwart*, 4, Apr. 1903, S. 143-146.
c15x.11 Poppenberg, Felix. *Der Türmer*, 5, vii, Apr. 1903, S. 71-72.
c15x.12 Schönhoff, L. *Der Kunstwart*, 16, xiii, 1. Apr.-H., 1903, S. 37-38.
c15x.13 Strecker, Karl. *Deutschland*, 2, ii, Mai 1903, S. 259-263.
c15x.14 Stümcke, Heinrich. *Bühne und Welt*, 5, xiii, Apr. 1903, S. 571-572.
c15x.15 Polgar, Alfred. *Die Weltbühne*, 21, xxiv, 16. Juni 1925, S. 893-894.
c15x.16 Schinnerer, Otto P. "Schnitzler's 'Der Schleier der Beatrice'." *Germanic Review*, 7, iii, July, 1932, p. 263-279. [A genetic study based on AS's own observations, followed by the stage history of the play. Numerous bibliographical references, including newspaper reviews.]
See Also: F16., x14., x15., x27., x236., x394.

c16. SYLVESTERNACHT: EIN DIALOG
c16.1 – – *Jugend*, 1, viii, 1901, S. 118-119; 121-122.
c16.2 – – *Zwanglose Hefte für die Besucher des Schiller-Theaters*, (Neue Reihe), 27, 1910.
c16.3 – – *Der bunte Almanach auf das Jahr 1914*. Wien & Leipzig: Deutsch-Österreichischer Verlag, 1914, S. 75-88.
c16.4 *Dramatische Werke* [#J11.], 1962, Bd. I, S. 681-688.

CRITICISM

c16x.1 Arnold, Robert F. *Die Literatur*, 29, vi, März 1927, S. 353-354.

C17.   DIE FRAU MIT DEM DOLCHE: SCHAUSPIEL IN EINEM AKT
C17.1   – – *Lebendige Stunden* [#K3.], 1902, S. 37-70.
C17.2   – – *Theaterstücke* [#J2.], 1912, Bd. II, S. 343-369.
C17.3   – – Nach Arthur Schnitzler. Text und Musik von Wl. Reibikow. Op. 41.
          Moskau, Leipzig: P. Jurgenson, ca. 1915. [German translation of a Russian
          adaptation.]
C17.4   – – *Theaterstücke* [#J4.], 1922, Bd. II, S. 343-369.
C17.5   – – *Theaterstücke* [#J6.], 1928, Bd. II, S. 343-369.
C17.6   – – *Dramatische Werke* [#J11.], 1962, Bd. I, S. 702-718.

ENGLISH TRANSLATIONS

C17e.1   "The Lady with the Dagger: A Drama." *Poet Lore*, 15, ii, Summer, 1904, p.
          1-18. [Helen Tracy Porter, tr. Repr. separately in the series "Poet Lore Plays,"
          Boston: Richard G. Badger, 1904, p. 1-18.]
C17e.2   "The Woman with the Dagger." *Fortnightly Review*, 91, dx, June 1, 1909, p.
          1179-1191. [Horace B. Samuel, tr.]
C17e.3   "The Lady with the Dagger." *International*, 4, 1911, p. 92 ff. [Paul Grumman, tr.]
C17e.4   "The Lady with the Dagger." *Living Hours* [#L2.], 1913, [Paul Grummann, tr.]
C17e.5   "The Lady with the Dagger." *Anatol* [#L5.], 1917, p. 117-135. [Grace Isabel
          Colbron, tr.]
C17e.6   "The Lady with the Dagger: A Drama." *Reigen* [#L11.], 1933, p. 189-208.
          [Grace Isabel Colbron, tr.]

CRITICISM

C17x.1   Lorenz. Max. *Preussische Jahrbücher*, 108, i, Apr. 1902, S. 179-181.
C17x.2   Anon. "The Woman with the Dagger: First Act Follows the Second." *The
          Dramatist*, 3, iv, July, 1912, p. 15. [Brief analysis.]

C18.   DIE LETZTEN MASKEN: SCHAUSPIEL IN EINEM AKT
C18.1   – – *Lebendige Stunden* [#K3.], 1902, S. 71-106
C18.2   – – *Theaterstücke* [#J2.], 1912, Bd. II, S. 370-390.
C18.3   – – *Theaterstücke* [#J4.], 1922, Bd. II, S. 370-390.
C18.4   – – *Der grüne Kakadu* [#S1.], p. 87-110.
C18.5   – – *Theaterstücke* [#J6.], 1928, Bd. II, S. 370-390.
C18.6   – – *Dramatische Werke* [#J11.], 1962, Bd. I, S. 719-735.

ENGLISH TRANSLATIONS

C18e.1   "The Last Masks." *Living Hours* [#L2.], 1913. [Paul H. Grummann, tr.]
C18e.2   "Last Masks: A Drama." *Anatol* [#L5.], 1917, p. 137-155. [Grace Isabel Colbron,
          tr.]
C18e.3   "Last Masks." *Reigen* [#L11.], 1933, p. 209-228. [Grace Isabel Colbron, tr.]

FRENCH TRANSLATION

C18f.1   "Les derniers masques: Pièce en un acte." *Revue d'Allemagne*, 4, xxxiv, 15 août
          1930, p. 698-718. [Suzanne Clauser, tr.]
See Also: X39.

C19.   LITERATUR: LUSTSPIEL IN EINEM AKT
C19.1   – – *Lebendige Stunden* [#K3.], 1902, S. 107-159.
C19.2   – – *Theaterstücke* [#J2.], 1912, Bd. II, S. 391-420.

C19.3   --   *Theaterstücke* [#J4.], 1922, Bd. II, S. 391-420.
C19.4   --   *Der grüne Kakadu* [#S1.], 1928, p. 54-85.
C19.5   --   *Theaterstücke* [#J6.], 1928, Bd. II, S. 391-420.
C19.6   --   *Meisterdramen* [#J9.], 1955, S. 187-210.
C19.7   --   *Dramatische Werke* [#J11.], 1962, Bd. I, S. 735-757.

ENGLISH TRANSLATIONS

C19e.1   "Literature." *Living Hours* [#L2.], 1913. [Paul H. Grumman, tr.]
C19e.2   "Literature: A Comedy in One Act." *The German Classics: Masterpieces of German Literature Translated into English.* (Kuno Francke, ed.) New York: German Publication Society, 1914, Vol. XX, p. 332-359. [A. I. du P. Coleman, tr.]
C19e.3   "Literature." *International*, 9, ix, Nov., 1915, p. 330-336. [Pierre Loving, tr.]
C19e.4   "Literature: A Play in one Act." *Anatol* [#L5.], 1917, p. 152-182. [Grace Isabel Colbron, tr.]
C19e.5   "Literature: A Play in One Act." *Comedies of Words* [#L6.], 1917, p. 127-159. [Pierre Loving, tr.]
C19e.6   "Literature: A Comedy" *Fifty Contemporary One-Act Plays.* (Frank Shay & Pierre Loving, eds.) Cincinnati: Stewart & Kidd, 1920, p. 13-26. [Pierre Loving, tr. - Also: New York & London: D. Appleton, 1920.]
C19e.7   "Literature: A Comedy." *Reigen* [#L11.], 1933, p. 229-255. [Grace Isabel Colbron, tr.]

CRITICISM

C19x.1   Anon. *New York Dramatic Mirror*, 74, No. 1925, Nov. 13, 1915, p. 8.
C19x.2   Hamilton, Clayton. *The Bookman*, 42, vi, Feb., 1916, p. 650-651.
C19x.3   Zeydel, Edwin H. "Can We Rely On Translations?" *Modern Language Journal*, 25, v, Feb., 1941, p. 402-404. [Errors in the English translation by Pierre Loving.]
See Also: X131.

1903

C20.   DER PUPPENSPIELER: STUDIE IN EINEM AKT
C20.1   --   *Neue Freie Presse*, Nr. 13923, 31. Mai 1903. (Pfingstbeilage).
C20.2   --   *New Yorker Staats-Zeitung*, 12. Juli 1903.
C20.3   --   *Österreichische Dichter: Zum 60. Geburtstage Detlev von Liliencrons.* (Adolph Donath, ed.) Wien: Carl Konegen, 1904, S. 96-116.
C20.4   --   *Marionetten* [#K5.], 1906, S. 9-52.
C20.5   --   *Theaterstücke* [#J2.], 1912, Bd. III, S. 190-210.
C20.6   --   *Theaterstücke* [#J4.], 1922, Bd. III, S. 190-210.
C20.7   --   *Theaterstücke* [#J6.], 1928, Bd. III, S. 190-210.
C20.8   --   *Lust und Leid: Five One-Act Plays from Contemporary German Literature.* (William Diamond & Christel B. Schomaker, eds.) New York: Henry Holt, 1929, p. 23-47. [School edition.]
C20.9   --   *Stories and Plays* [#S3.], 1930, p. 128-149.
C20.10   *Altes und Neues.* Revised. (Robert O. Rösler & Wayne Wonderley, eds.) New York: Holt Rinehart & Winston, 1960, S. 55-75.
C20.11   --   *Dramatische Werke* [#J11.], 1962, Bd. I, S. 838-854.

CRITICISM

C20x.1   Poppenberg, Felix. "Puppen-und Menschenspieler." *Der Türmer*, 6, ii, Nov. 1903, S. 192-193.

C20x.2   Zieler, Gustav. *Das Literarische Echo*, 6, ii, 15. Okt. 1903, Sp. 135-136.
See Also: x33.

1904

C21.   DER EINSAME WEG: SCHAUSPIEL IN FÜNF AKTEN
C21.1   – – Berlin: S. Fischer, 1904, 166 S. [Auflagen:
         1. – 2.   1904
         3.   1905
         4.   1906
         5.   1910
         6.   1914
         8. – 9.   1921
         10. – 11. 1926]
C21.2   – – *Theaterstücke* [#J2.], 1912, Bd. III, S. 9-103.
C21.3   – – *Die Deutsche Literatur unserer Zeit: In Charakteristiken und Proben.*
         (Kurt Martens, ed.) München: Rösl, 1921, S. 137-146. [Selection.]
C21.4   – – *Theaterstücke* [#J4.], 1922, Bd. III, S. 9-103.
C21.5   – – *Theaterstücke* [#J6.], 1928, Bd. III, S. 9-103.
C21.6   – – *Meisterdramen* [#J9.], 1955, S. 211-287.
C21.7   – – *Dramatische Werke* [#J11.], 1962, Bd. I, S. 759-836.
C21.8   – – Stuttgart: Phillip Reclam jun., 1964, 95 S. (Reclams Universal Bibliothek,
         Nr. 8664). ["Nachwort," S. 93-95, signed "S."]

ENGLISH TRANSLATIONS

C21e.1   *The Lonely Way.* Boston: Little Brown, 1904. [Edwin Björkman, tr.]
C21e.2   "The Lonely Way: A Drama in Five Acts." *Lonely Way* [#L4.], 1915, p. 1-137.
          [Edwin Björkman, tr.]
C21e.3   "The Lonely Way." *Representative Continental Dramas: Revolutionary and Tran-
          sitional.* (Montrose J. Moses, ed.) Boston: Little, Brown, 1924, p. 59-101.
          [Edwin Björkman, tr.]
C21e.4   *The Lonely Way: Play in Five Acts.* New York: Rialto Service Bureau, 1931,
          various pagings. [Julian Leigh, tr. Typescript.]
C21e.5   *The Lonely Way: Play in Five Acts.* Acting Version by Philip Moeller. New
          York: Rialto Service Bureau, 1931, various pagings. [Typescript.]
C21e.6   "The Lonely Way: A Play in Five Acts." *Representative Modern Dramas.*
          (Charles H. Whitman, ed.) New York: MacMillan, 1936, p. 153-191. [Julian
          Leigh, tr.]

CRITICISM

C21x.1   Anon. *Der Regisseur*, 6, xii, 22. Feb. 1904.
C21x.2   Detleff, Ernst. *Der Kunstwart*, 17, xi, 1. März-H., 1904, S. 640-642.
C21x.3   Düsel, Friedrich. *Westermanns Monatshefte*, 48 (Bd. 96), dlxxi, Apr. 1904, S.
          151-154.
C21x.4   Frenzel, Karl. *Deutsche Rundschau*, 30 (Bd. 119), viii, Mai 1904, S. 293-294.
          [Fr. "Die Berliner Theater."]
C21x.5   Heilborn, Ernst. *Die Nation*, 21, xxi, 20. Feb. 1904, S. 333-334.
C21x.6   Kappstein, Theodor. *Deutschland*, 3, vi, März 1904, S. 795-797.
C21x.7   Kerr, Alfred. *Neue Rundschau*, 15, iv, Apr. 1904, S. 504-508.
C21x.8   Poppenberg, Felix. *Der Türmer*, 6, vii, Apr. 1904, S. 74-75. [Fr. "Hinter dem
          Schleier."]
C21x.9   Schmidt, P. Expeditus. *Literarische Warte*, 5, ix, 1. Juni 1904, S. 537-538.

61

C21x.10   Stümcke, Heinrich. *Bühne und Welt*, 6, xi, März 1904, S. 471-473.
C21x.11   Zieler, Gustav. *Das Literarische Echo*, 6, xii, 15. März 1904, Sp. 867-869.
C21x.12   Zieler, Gustav. *Schöne Literatur*, 5, v, 27. Feb. 1904, Sp. 79-80.
C21x.13   Anon. *Die Wage*, 21. Feb. 1914.
C21x.14   Polgar, Alfred. *Die Schaubühne*, 10, x, 5. März 1914, S. 271-275.
C21x.15   Jacobsohn, Siegfried. *Die Weltbühne*, 20, xlv, 4. Nov. 1924, S. 707-709.
C21x.16   Miller, Nellie Burget. "Arthur Schnitzler: The Drama of Disillusionment." *The Living Drama: Historical Development and Modern Movements Visualized. A Drama of the Drama.* New York & London: Century, 1924, p. 271-275. [Study-guide.]
C21x.17   Anon. *Deutsche Kritik*, 3, H. A39, 1. Mai 1926, S. 870. [Signed "W. Sch."]
C21x.18   Liptzin, Sol. "The Genesis of Schnitzler's 'Der einsame Weg'." *Journal of English and Germanic Philology*, 30, iii, July, 1931, p. 392-404. [Separation of material fr. "Professor Bernhardi;" account based on manuscript materials.]
See Also: x27, x149.

C22.   DER TAPFERE CASSIAN: PUPPENSPIEL IN EINEM AKT
C22.1   – – Burleske in einem Akt. *Neue Rundschau*, 15, ii, Feb. 1904, S. 227-247.
C22.2   – – *Marionetten* [#K5.], 1906, S. 53-96.
C22.3   "Lied des Martin aus dem tapferen Cassian: Mich treibt es in die Ferne . . ." *Die Woche* (Danzig), Sonderheft, 1910.
C22.4   – – Berlin: S. Fischer, 1910, 47 S. ["Buchdruckerei Roitzsch, Albert Schulze."]
C22.5   – – *Theaterstücke* [#J2.], 1912, Bd. III, S. 211-230.
C22.6   – – Wien, Leipzig: Karl Rönig, 1922, 37 S. ["Dieses Buch wurde mit Genehmigung des Verlages S. Fischer, Berlin, im Auftrage des Verlages Karl Rönig, Wien, in einer einmaligen numerierten Auflage von 800 Exemplaren hergestellt. Den Druck besorgte die Offizin Christoph Reisser's Söhne, Wien, im Frühling 1922. Die Nummern 1-50 auf Japan-Dokumentenpapier wurden vom Autor eigenhändig unterzeichnet und jede Lithographie von O. Laske handschriftlich signiert. Die Nummern 51-800 sind vom Künstler gefertigt."]
C22.7   – – *Theaterstücke* [#J4.], 1922, Bd. III, S. 211-230.
C22.8   – – *Theaterstücke* [#J6.], 1928, Bd. III, S. 211-230.
C22.9   – – *Dramatische Werke* [#J11.], 1962, Bd. I, S. 855-870.

ENGLISH TRANSLATIONS

C22e.1   *Gallant Cassian: A Puppet Play in One Act.* London & Glasgow: Gowans & Gray, 1914, 45 p. ["Glasgow: Printed at the University Press by Robert MacLehose & Co., Ltd." Adam L. Gowans, tr. – Also: Boston: Leroy Philipps, 1921, 45 p.; Girard, Kansas: Haldeman-Julius, 1914, 30 p. (Little Blue Books).]
C22e.2   "Gallant Cassian: A Puppet Play." *Poet Lore*, 33, iv, Dec., 1922, p. 507-520. [Moritz A. Jagendorf, tr.]
C22e.3   "Gallant Cassian." *Fifty One-Act Plays: Second Series.* (Constance Martin, ed.) London: Gollancz, 1940.

CRITICISM

C22x.1   Stümcke, Heinrich. *Bühne und Welt*, 7, vi, Dez. 1904, S. 253-254.
C22x.2   Zieler, Gustav. *Das Literarische Echo*, 7, vi, 15. Dez. 1904, Sp. 442.
C22x.3   Anon. *Athenaeum*, 1915-1, No. 4558, Mar. 6, 1915, p. 222.

1905

C23.   ZUM GROSSEN WURSTEL: BURLESKE IN EINEM AKT
C23.1   – – *Die Zeit*, 23. Apr. 1905. (Beilage to Nr. 926, Die Oster-Zeit).

C 23.2   – –   *Marionetten* [‡K5.], 1906, S. 98-148.
C23.3   – –   *Welthumor : Das lachende Deutschland.* (Roda Roda & Theodor Etzel, eds.) Berlin & Leipzig: Schuster & Löffler, 1910, S. 119-133.
C23.4   – –   *Theaterstücke* [‡J2.], 1912, Bd. III, S. 231-267.
C23.5   – –   *Theaterstücke* [‡J4.], 1922, Bd. III, S. 231-267.
C23.6   – –   *Theaterstücke* [‡J6.], 1928, Bd. III, S. 231-267.
C23.7   – –   *Dramatische Werke* [‡J11.], 1962, Bd. I, S. 871-894.
C23.8   – –   *Finale und Auftakt. Wien: 1898-1914. Literatur. Bildende Kunst. Musik.* (Otto Breicha & Gerhard Fritsch, eds.) Salzburg: Otto Müller, 1964, S. 44-70.

CRITICISM

C23x.1   Telmann, Fritz. *Das Literarische Echo*, 8, xv, 1. Mai 1906, Sp. 1106.
C23x.2   von Ende, Amelia. *Poet Lore*, 18, i, Spring, 1907, p. 128-129.

1906

C24.   DER RUF DES LEBENS: SCHAUSPIEL IN DREI AKTEN
C24.1   – –   Berlin: S. Fischer, 1906, 132 S. [Auflagen:
     1. – 2.   1906
     3.   1910
     4.   1913
     5.   1922 (Text of ‡J4., Bd. III, S. 271-347.)]
C24.2   – –   *Theaterstücke* [‡J2.], 1912, Bd. III, S. 269-347.
C24.3   – –   *Theaterstücke* [‡J4.], 1922, Bd. III, S. 269-347.
C24.4   – –   *Theaterstücke* [‡J6.], 1928, Bd. III, S. 269-347.
C24.5   – –   *Dramatische Werke* [‡J11.], 1962, Bd. I, S. 963-1027.

CRITICISM

C24x.1   Anon. *Die Gegenwart*, 35 (Bd. 69), ix, 3. März 1906, S. 142. [Signed "A. Hn."]
C24x.2   Anon. *Nord und Süd*, 117, Juni 1906, S. 441.
C24x.3   Anon. *Die Schaubühne*, 2, ix, 1. März 1906, S. 246-250.
C24x.4   Berg, Leo. *Das Literarische Echo*, 8, xiii, 1. Apr. 1906, Sp. 962-963.
C24x.5   Harden, Maximilan. *Die Zukunft*, 54, 3. März 1906, S. 356.
C24x.6   Heilborn, Ernst. *Die Nation*, 23, xxii, 3. März 1906, S. 346-348.
C24x.7   Kerr, Alfred. "Oedipus und der Ruf des Lebens." *Neue Rundschau*, 17, v. Mai 1906, S. 492-498.
C24x.8   Kienzl, Hermann. *Das Blaubuch*, 1, ix, 1906, S. 375-381.
C24x.9   Klaar, Alfred. *Österreichische Rundschau*, 6, lxxi, 1906, S. 271-273.
C24x.10   Poppenberg, Felix. *Der Türmer*, 8, vii, Apr. 1906, S. 114-116.
C24x.11   Stümcke, Heinrich. *Bühne und Welt*, 8, xii, 1906, S. 517-520.
C24x.12   Antropp, Theodor. *Österreichische Rundschau*, 21, vi, 15. Dez. 1909, S. 481-485.
C24x.13   Polgar, Alfred. *Die Schaubühne*, 5, liii, 30. Dez. 1909, S. 713-717.
C24x.14   Anon. *Velhagen & Klasings Monatshefte*, 24, Apr. 1910, S. 536.
C24x.15   Bromfield, Louis. *The Bookman*, 62, iv, Dec., 1925, p. 478-479.
C24x.16   Krutch, Joseph Wood. *The Nation*, 121, No. 3147, Oct. 28, 1925, p. 494-495.
C24x.17   Nathan, George Jean. "And the M. Schnitzler." *American Mercury*, 6, xxiv, Dec., 1925, p. 503-504.
C24x.18   Young, Stark. *New Republic*, 44, dlxix, Oct. 28, 1925, p. 255-256.
See Also: G6.1, x29., x149.

C25.   ZWISCHENSPIEL: KOMÖDIE IN DREI AKTEN
C25.1   – –   Berlin: S. Fischer, 1906, 139 S. ["Buchdruckerei Roitzsch." Auflagen:
     1. – 3.   1906
     4.   1909
     5.   1916
     6.   1922 (Text of ‡J4., Bd. III, S. 107-187.)]

C25.2   – – *Theaterstücke* [#J2.], 1912, Bd. III, S. 105-187.
C25.3   – – *Theaterstücke* [#J4.], 1922, Bd. III, S. 105-187.
C25.4   – – *Theaterstücke* [#J6.], 1928, Bd. III, S. 105-187.
C25.5   – – *Dramatische Werke* [#J11.], 1962, Bd. I, S. 895-961.
C25.6   – – *Du: Kulturelle Monatschrift*, 23, Apr. 1963, S. 25. [Selection.]

ENGLISH TRANSLATIONS

C25e.1   "Intermezzo: A Comedy in Three Acts." *Lonely Way* [#L4.], 1915, p. 139-259.
[Edwin Björkman, tr.]
C25e.2   "Intermezzo." *Plays from the Modern Theater.* (Harrison Ross Steeves, ed.)
Boston: D. C. Heath, 1931, p. 349-408. [Edwin Björkman, tr.]

CRITICISM

C25x.1   Anon. *Kritik*, Nr. 10, 1905.
C25x.2   Handl. Willi, "Schnitzler und sein 'Zwischenspiel'." *Die Schaubühne*, 1, vi,
12. Okt. 1905, S. 187-191.
C25x.3   Harden, Maximilan. *Die Zukunft*, 53, 9. Dez. 1905, S. 366-376.
C25x.4   Heilborn, Ernst. *Die Nation*, ix, 23, 2. Dez. 1905, S. 140-141.
C25x.5   Jacobsohn, Siegfried. *Die Schaubühne*, 1, xiii, 30. Nov. 1905, S. 358-361.
C25x.6   Minor, J. *Österreichische Rundschau*, 4, H. 50, 12. Okt. 1905, S. 542-546.
C25x.7   Seefeld, Carl. *Schöne Literatur*, 6, xxiii, 4. Nov. 1905, Sp. 413-415.
C25x.8   Servaes, Franz. *Der Kunstwart*, 19, iv, 2. Nov.-H., 1905, S. 220-222.
C25x.9   Telmann, Fritz. *Das Literarische Echo*, 8, vi, 1. Dez. 1905, Sp. 363.
C25x.10   Poppenberg, Felix. *Der Türmer*, 8, iv, Jan. 1906, S. 552-557.
See Also: x29., x33., x149.

1908

C26.   KOMTESSE MIZZI ODER DER FAMILIENTAG: KOMÖDIE
IN EINEM AKT
C26.1   – – *Neue Freie Presse*, Nr. 15684, 19. Apr. 1908, S. 31-35. (Osterbeilage.)
C26.2   – – Berlin: S. Fischer, 1909, 93 S. ["Buchdruckerei Roitzsch, Albert Schulze."
Auflagen:
1. – 3.   1909
4.   1917
5.   1922 (Text of #J4., Bd. IV, S. 11-49.)]
C26.3   – – *Theaterstücke* [#J2.], 1912, Bd. IV, S. 9-49.
C26.4   – – *Theaterstücke* [#J4.], 1922, Bd. IV, S. 9-49.
C26.5   – – *Theaterstücke* [#J6.], 1928, Bd. IV, S. 9-49.
C26.6   – – *Dramatische Werke* [#J11.], 1962, Bd. I, S. 1029-1061.

ENGLISH TRANSLATIONS

C26e.1   *Countess Mizzie*. Boston: Little, Brown, 1907. [Edwin Björkman, tr.]
C26e.2   "Countess Mizzie or the Family Reunion: A Comedy in One Act." *Lonely Way*
[#L4.], 1915, p. 261-323. [Edwin Björkman, tr.]
C26e.3   "Countess Mizzie or the Family Reunion: A Comedy in One Act." *Representa-
tive One-Act Plays by Continental Authors.* (Montrose J. Moses, ed.) Boston:
Little, Brown, 1922, p. 3-46. [Edwin Björkman, tr.]
C26e.4   "Countess Mizzie or the Family Reunion." *20 Non-Royalty One-Act Popular
Classics.* (Margaret Mayorga, ed.) New York: Greenberg, 1946, p. 203-238.
[Edwin Björkman, tr.]

C26x.1   Klinenberger, Ludwig. *Bühne und Welt*, 11-2, viii, Jan. 1909, S. 347.
C26x.2   Telmann, Fritz. *Das Literarische Echo*, 11, ix, 1. Feb. 1909, Sp. 671.
C26x.3   Anon. *Nord und Süd*, 140, Feb. 1912, S. 478.
C26x.4   Düsel, Friedrich. *Der Kunstwart*, 25, xii, 15. März 1912, S. 391-392.
C26x.5   Düsel, Friedrich. *Westermanns Monatshefte*, 112-1, dclxvii, März 1912, S. 133-134.
See *Also*: x69.

C27.   DIE VERWANDLUNGEN DES PIERROT: PANTOMIME IN
         EINEM VORSPIEL UND SECHS BILDERN
C27.1   − − *Die Zeit*, 19. Apr. 1908 (Nr. 2002, Beilage: "Die Oster-Zeit".)
C27.2   *Dramatische Werke* [#J11.], 1962, Bd. I, S. 1063-1078.

1909

C28.   DER TAPFERE KASSIAN: SINGSPIEL IN EINEM AUFZUGE
C28.1   − − Neu geschriebener Text in Versen. Musik von Oscar Straus. Leipzig,
         Wien: Ludwig Doblinger (Bernhard Herzmansky), 1909.
C28.2   − − *Dramatische Werke* [#J11.], 1962, Bd. II, S. 7-26.

C28x.1   Witkowski, Georg. *Zeitschrift für Bücherfreunde*, Beiblatt, 15, i, Jan./Feb. 1923,
         Sp. 29-30.

1910

C29.   DER JUNGE MEDARDUS: DRAMATISCHE HISTORIE IN
         EINEM VORSPIEL UND FÜNF AUFZÜGEN
C29.1   "Bastei Szene." *Neue Freie Presse*, Nr. 16378, 27. März 1910, S. 32-39.
C29.2   "Vorspiel zu einem Drama 'Der junge Medardus'." *Neue Rundschau*, 21 (Bd. 4),
         x, Okt. 1910, S. 1385-1415.
C29.3   − − Berlin: S. Fischer, 1910, 290 S. ["Druck der Spamerschen Buchdruckerei
         in Leipzig." Auflagen:

         1. – 5.   1910
         6. – 7.   1911
         8.   1919
         9. – 10.   1923 (Text of #J4., Bd. IV, S. 51-291.)]
C29.4   − − *Theaterstücke* [#J2.], 1912, Bd. IV, S. 51-291.
C29.5   − − *Theaterstücke* [#J4.], 1922, Bd. IV, S. 51-291.
C29.6   − − *Vom Rokoko bis zum Gegenwarts-Wien*. Wien: Deutscher Verlag für Jugend
         und Volk, 1922, S. 53-67. (Wiener Schicksale: Geschehnisse und Gestalten
         aus Wiens Werdegang. III. Bändchen.)
C29.7   − − *Theaterstücke* [#J6.], 1928, Bd. IV, S. 51-291.
C29.8   − − *Dramatische Werke* [#J11.], 1962, Bd. II, S. 27-215.

C29x.1   Graf, Max. *Der Merker*, 2, vi, 1910, S. 210-212.
C29x.2   Grossmann, Stefan. *Das Theater*, 2, 1910, S. 175-178.
C29x.3   Klinenberger, Ludwig. *Bühne und Welt*, 13-1, 1910, S. 259-262.
C29x.4   Minor, Jakob. *Österreichische Rundschau*, 25, v, 1. Dez. 1910, S. 387-394. [History
         and art not unified.]

C29x.5	Polgar, Alfred. *Die Schaubühne*, 6, xlix, 8. Dez. 1910, S. 1263-1268.
C29x.6	Prels. Max. *Ton und Wort*, 1. Dez. 1910, S. 17-19.
C29x.7	Seefeld, Carl. *Schöne Literatur*, 11, xxvi, 17. Dez. 1910, Sp. 487-488.
C29x.8	Zenker, E. V. *Die Wage*, 13, xlviii, 26. Nov. 1910, S. 1077-1081.
C29x.9	Anon. *The Nation*, 92, No. 2390, Apr. 20, 1911, p. 405.
C29x.10	Anon. *Velhagen & Klasings Monatshefte*, 25, März 1911, S. 408.
C29x.11	Antropp, Theodor. *Der Kunstwart*, 24, xi, 1. März-H. 1911, S. 330-333.
C29x.12	Eckhardt, Johannes. *Hochland*, 8, vii, Apr. 1911, S. 123-126.
C29x.13	Grossmann, Stefan. "Schnitzlers Massendramen." *Das Theater*, 2, ix, 1. Jan. 1911, S. 175-179.
C29x.14	Handl, Willi. "Medardus in Prag." *Die Schaubühne*, 7-1, xxiv/xxv, 22. Juni 1911, S. 636-641. [Only approaches being a great historical drama.]
C29x.15	Hoffmann, Camill. *Das Literarische Echo*, 13, vii, 1. Jan. 1911, Sp. 529-531.
C29x.16	Kienzel, Hermann. "Das Wiener Volk im Jungen Medardus." *Die Hilfe*, 17, vi, 9. Feb. 1911, S. 90-92. (Beiblatt).
C29x.17	Wyzewa, T. de. *Revue des deux mondes*, 18-1, iv, 15 fév. 1911, p. 935-939.
C29x.18	Schmid, F. O. *Alpen*, 5, 1911, S. 360-366.
C29x.19	Anon. *Die Schaubühne*, 10-2, xliii, 29. Okt. 1914, S. 314-316.
C29x.20	Bab, Julius. "Unzeitgemässes." *Die Gegenwart*, 43, xliv, 31. Okt. 1914, S. 691-693.
C29x.21	Anon. *Nord und Süd*, Jan. 1915, S. 124-127.
C29x.22	Brüll, Oswald. "Der junge Medardus." *Letztes Burgtheater: Requiem für das Österreichertum*. Leipzig. Wien, Zürich: Ilf., 1920, S. 15-20. [Best work, but too local to be exported.]
See Also:	x52., x120., x149.

C30.   DER SCHLEIER DER PIERRETTE: PANTOMIME IN DREI BILDERN

C30.1	– – Musik von Ernst von Dohnányi. Wien, Leipzig: L. Doblinger (Bernhard Herzmansky), 1910, 30 S. [Libretto.]
C30.2	– – Mit sechs Radierungen von Stefan Eggeler. Wien: Frisch, 1922, 63 S. ["Von diesem Buche wurden im Jahre 1922 vom Frisch & Co. Verlag (Inhaber Ernst Wilhartitz) dreihundert numerierte, vom Autor und vom Künstler signierte, in der eigenen Offizin des Verlages in Wien hergestellte Exemplare herausgegeben, von denen Nummer 1 bis 10 auf Japan-Dokumentenkarton gedruckt sind und von der unverstellten Platte abgezogene Radierungen enthalten."]
C30.3	– – *Dramatische Werke* [#J11.], 1962, Bd. II, S. 321-336.

CRITICISM

C30x.1	Adler, Felix. *Die Schaubühne*, 6, ix, 3. März 1910, S. 238-240.
C30x.2	Anon. *Die Wage*, 14, xxxviii, 23. Sept. 1911, S. 843-845.
C30x.3	Brandts-Buys, Jan. *Der Schleier der Pierrette, Pantomime in 3 Bildern.* Musik von Ernst von Dohnányi. Ein Führer durch das Werk. Wien: L. Doblinger, 1912, 18 S.
C30x.4	Düsel, Friedrich. *Der Kunstwart*, 26, xvi, 2. Mai-H., 1913, S. 284-285.
C30x.5	Düsel, Friedrich. *Westermanns Monatshefte*, 57 (Bd. 114-2), dclxxxii, Juni 1913, S. 634-635.
C30x.6	Polgar, Alfred. *Die Weltbühne*, 21, xxx, 28. Juli 1925, S. 138-139.
C30x.7	Sayler, Oliver M. *Saturday Review of Literature*, 4, xxx, Feb. 18, 1928, p. 611.
C30x.8	Young, Stark. *New Republic*, 54, dcxc, Feb. 22, 1928, p. 19.

C31.   DAS WEITE LAND: TRAGIKOMÖDIE IN FÜNF AKTEN

| C31.1 | – – *Österreichische Rundschau*, 25, i, 1. Okt. 1910, S. 30-48. [Selection.] |
| C31.2 | – – *Der Kunstwart*, 25, iv. 2. Nov.-H, 1911, S. 259-269. [Selection.] |

C31.3   – – Berlin: S. Fischer, 1911, 174 S. ["Buchdruckerei Roitzsch, Albert Schulze, Roitzsch." Auflagen:
    1. – 6.   1911
    7.   1916
    8. – 10. 1920]
C31.4   – – *Theaterstücke* [#J2.], 1912, Bd. IV, S. 293-419.
C31.5   – – *Theaterstücke* [#J4.], 1922, Bd. IV, S. 293-419.
C31.6   – – *Theaterstücke* [#J6.], 1928, Bd. IV, S. 293-419.
C31.7   – – *Meisterdramen* [#J9.], 1955, S. 289-391.
C31.8   – – *Dramatische Werke* [#J11.], 1962, Bd. II, S. 217-320.

ENGLISH TRANSLATION

C31e.1   "The Vast Domain: A Tragi-Comedy in Five Acts." *Poet Lore*, 34, iii, Sept., 1923, p. 317-407. [Edward Woticky & Alexander Caro, trs.]

CRITICISM

C31x.1   Anon. *Die Wage*, 14, xliv, 4. Nov. 1911, S. 1001-1004.
C31x.2   Düsel, Friedrich. *Westermanns Monatshefte*, 111-2, dclxiv, Dez. 1911, S. 637-638.
C31x.3   Eloesser, Arthur. *Das Literarische Echo*, 14, iii, 1. Nov. 1911, Sp. 204-206.
C31x.4   Elsner, Richard. *Arthur Schnitzler: Das Weite Land*. Berlin: Richard Elsner, 1911, 23 S. (Moderne Dramatik in kritischer Beleuchtung, H. 9).
C31x.5   Köhrer, Erich. "Schnitzler und Sudermann." *Das Theater*, 3, v, 1. Nov. 1911, S. 98-100.
C31x.6   Lautensack, Heinrich. *Schöne Literatur*, 12, xxiii, 4. Nov. 1911, Sp. 410.
C31x.7   Minor, J. *Österreichische Rundschau*, 29, iii, 1. Dez. 1911, S. 244-249.
C31x.8   Nidden, Ezard. *Der Kunstwart*, 25, iv. 2. Nov.-H., 1911, S. 256-259.
C31x.9   Stümcke, Heinrich. *Bühne und Welt*, 14-1, ii, Nov. 1911, S. 102-104.
C31x.10   Anon. *Velhagen & Klasings Monatshefte*, 26, März, 1912, S. 438-440.
C31x.11   Poppenberg, Felix. *Neue Rundschau*, 1912-2, S. 1323-1325.
C31x.12   Sprengler, Joseph. *Hochland*, 9, vi, März 1912, S. 773-776.
C31x.13   Furtmüller, Carl. "Schnitzler's Tragikomödie 'Das weite Land;' Ein Versuch psychologischer Literaturbetrachtung." *Zentralblatt für Psychoanalyse und Psychotherapie*." 4, i/ii, Okt. 1913, S. 28-40. [Diagnosis: inferiority complex, manifested in "der männliche Protest."]
C31x.14   Anon. *New Republic*, 4, xlix, Oct. 9, 1915, p. 263-264. [Signed "Q. K."]
C31x.15   Anon. *New York Dramatic Mirror*, 74, No. 1920, Oct. 6, 1915, p. 8.
C31x.16   Eloesser, Arthur. *Das Blaue Heft*, 3, x, 3. Dez. 1921, S. 272-273.
C31x.17   Liptzin, Sol. "The Genesis of Schnitzler's 'Das weite Land'." *PMLA*, 46, iii, Sept., 1931, p. 860-866. [Development from Novelle and tragicomedy; fatalism in the work. Valuable study.]
C31x.18   Romann, H. L. "Zu Arthur Schnitzlers Tragikomödie 'Das Weite Land.'" *Die Volksbühne*, 15, iv, 1964, S. 65.
See Also: x52., x69., x120., x149.

1912

C32.   PROFESSOR BERNHARDI: KOMÖDIE IN FÜNF AKTEN
C32.1   – – Berlin: S. Fischer, 1912, 255 S. [Auflagen:
    1. – 2.   1912
    6. – 14.   1913
    15. – 16. 1919
    20. – 25. 1925]
C32.2   "Professor Bernhardi: Der Schluss des letzten Aktes." *Das 27. Jahr*. Berlin: S. Fischer, 1913, S. 254-256.

C32.3   – – *Theaterstücke* [#J4.], 1922, Bd. V, S. 9-164.
C32.4   – – *Theaterstücke* [#J6.], 1928, Bd. V, S. 9-164.
C32.5   – – *Meisterdramen* [#J9.], 1955, S. 393-514.
C32.6   – – *Dramatische Werke* [#J11.], 1962, Bd. II, S. 337-463.

ENGLISH TRANSLATIONS

C32e.1   *Professor Bernhardi: A Comedy.* Adaptation in English by Mrs. Emil Pohli. San Francisco: Paul Elder, 1913, ix, 64 p. [Abridged.]
C32e.2   "Doctor and Priest: From 'Professor Bernhardi.' Act I." *The Warner Library: The World's Best Literature.* New York: Warner Library, 1917, Vol. XXI, p. 12922k-12922n.
C32e.3   *The Anti-Semites (Professor Bernhardi): A Play.* Girard, Kansas: Haldeman-Julius, 1920, 63 p. (Ten Cent Pocket Series No. 226).
C32e.4   *Professor Bernhardi: A Comedy in Five Acts.* London: Faber & Gwyer, 1927, 160 p. [Hetty Landstone, tr. – Also: New York: Simon & Schuster, 1928.]
C32e.5   "Professor Bernhardi." *Famous Plays of 1936.* London: Victor Gollancz, 1936, p. 11-118. [Louis Borell & Ronald Adam, trs.]
C32e.6   "Professor Bernhardi." *A Golden Treasury of Jewish Literature.* (Leo W. Schwarz, ed.) New York, Toronto: Farrar & Rinehart, 1937, p. 468-504. [Mrs. Emil Pohli, tr.]

CRITICISM

C32x.1   Anon. "Schnitzler und Brahm." *Die Schaubühne,* 8-2, xlix, 5. Dez. 1912, S. 601-603.
C32x.2   Anon. *Das Recht,* Nr. 13, Jan. 1913, S. 204-206.
C32x.3   Anon. "Arzt und Priester." *Die Wage,* 16, i, 4. Jan. 1913, S. 24-28.
C32x.4   Bab, Julius. *Deutsche Monatshefte,* 13, vii, Juli 1913, S. 270-271.
C32x.5   Bab, Julius. *Die Gegenwart,* 50, 1913, S. 795 ff.
C32x.6   Bianquis, Geneviève. "Une pièce interdite en Autriche." *La grande revue,* 17 (t. 81), vii, 10 sept., 1913, p. 156-160.
C32x.7   Düsel, Friedrich. *Der Kunstwart,* 26, vii, 1. Jan.-H., 1913, S. 57-58.
C32x.8   Düsel, Friedrich. *Westermanns Monatshefte,* 57 (Bd. 113-2), dclxxvii, Jan. 1913, S. 804-805.
C32x.9   Eloesser, Arthur. "Schnitzler und Sohn." *Das Literarische Echo,* 15, vii, 1. Jan. 1913, Sp. 475-478.
C32x.10 Elsner, Richard. *Arthur Schnitzlers Professor Bernhardi.* Berlin: Richard Elsner, 1913, 23 S. (Moderne Dramatik in kritischer Beleuchtung, H. 16).
C32x.11 Finckh, Ludwig. *Deutsche Medizinische Wochenschrift,* 39, xiii, 27. März 1913, S. 613.
C32x.12 Frenzel, Karl. *Deutsche Rundschau,* 39 (Bd. 156), x, Juli 1913, S. 152-153.
C32x.13 Halbert, A. "Die Tragikomödie des Starrsinns: Zu Arthur Schnitzlers 'Professor Bernhardi'." *Die Wage,* 16, xvi, 19. Apr. 1913, S. 385-387.
C32x.14 Lautensack, Heinrich. *Schöne Literatur,* 14, i, 1. Jan. 1913, Sp. 9-10.
C32x.15 Nathan, George Jean. *Smart Set,* 41, i, Sept. 1913, S. 148-149.
C32x.16 Rauscher, Ulrich. *Süddeutsche Monatshefte,* 10, v, Feb. 1913, S. 746-752. [Fr. "Vom Berliner Theater."]
C32x.17 Roderich-Stoltheim, P. *Hammer,* 12, cclviii, 15. März 1913, S. 159-163.
C32x.18 Stümcke, Heinrich. *Bühne und Welt,* 15-1, vii, Jan. 1913, S. 298-300.
C32x.19 Trog, Hans. *Wissen und Leben,* 13 i, 1. Okt. 1913, S. 57-58.
C32x.20 Wymetal, Wilhelm von. *März,* 7 (Bd. 2), xiv, 5. Apr. 1913, S.31-33.
C32x.21 Anon. "Arthur Schnitzler Writes a Play Without a Woman In It." *Current Opinion,* 56, iii, Mar., 1914, p. 193-194.
C32x.22 Rethy, J. B. *International,* 8, iii, Mar., 1914, p. 92.
C32x.23 Huneker, James Gibbons. *Ivory Apes and Peacocks.* New York: Charles Scribner,

1915, p. 210-217. [Fr. "New Plays by Hauptmann, Sudermann and Schnitzler." – Play lacks dramatic movement.]

C32X.24 Naumburg, Bernhard. "Schnitzler's 'Professor Bernhardi'." *The Judaeans*, 2, 1917, p. 119-126. [Vol. 2 title: "Judaean Addresses: Selected 1900-1917." – Bernhardi not a modern Nathan.]

C32X.25 Kronfeld, Curt. *Wiener Medizinische Wochenschrift*, 69, ix, 22. Feb. 1919, Sp. 462-463.

C32X.26 Anon. *Feuerreiter*, Feb. 1923, S. 60-63.

C32X.27 Jacobsohn, Siegfried. *Die Weltbühne*, 19, x, 8. März 1923, S. 275-277.

C32X.28 Ould, Hermon. "Schnitzler and Somerset Maugham." *The Bookman* (London), 73, cdxxxviii, Mar., 1928, p. 330.

C32X.29 Pinski, David. "A Tragedy of the Jew." *Book League Monthly*, 1, i, Nov., 1928, p. 349-350.

C32X.30 Belázs, Béla. *Die Weltbühne*, 26, vii, 11. Feb. 1930, S. 257-258.

C32X.31 Jungmann, E. *C. V. Zeitung*, 9, 1930, S. 55.

C32X.32 Liptzin, Sol. "The Genesis of Schnitzler's 'Professor Bernhardi'." *Philological Quarterly*, 10, iv, Oct., 1931, p. 348-355. [Accounts for the all-male cast; based on unpublished notes and manuscript materials.]

C32X.33 MacCarthy, Desmond. "Greatly to Find a Quarrel in a Straw?" *New Statesman and Nation*, 12, cclxxxvii, Aug. 22, 1936, p. 255-256.

C32X.34 Walker-Smith, Derek. *English Review*, 63, iii, Sept., 1936, p. 275.

C32X.35 Melchinger, Siegfried. "Das Jüdische in 'Professor Bernhardi.'" *Theater heute*, 5, xii, 1964, S. 32-35.

See Also: FI1.1, X120., Y18.

1915

C33. DAS BACCHUSFEST
C33.1 – – *Komödie der Worte* [#K9.], 1915, S. 139-194.
C33.2 – – *Theaterstücke* [#J4.], 1922, Bd. V, S. 249-279.
C33.3 – – *Theaterstücke* [#J6.], 1928, Bd. V, S. 249-279.
C33.4 – – *Dramatische Werke* [#J11.], 1962, Bd. II, S. 530-554.

ENGLISH TRANSLATIONS

C33e.1 "The Festival of Bacchus." *International*, 10, i, Oct., 1916, p. 303-310. [Pierre Loving, tr.]

C33e.2 "The Festival of Bacchus: A Comedy of Words." *Comedies of Words* [#L6.], 1917, p. 91-124. [Pierre Loving, tr.]

C33e.3 "The Festival of Bacchus: A Comedy of Words." *Twenty-Five Short Plays: International*. (Frank Shay, ed.) New York & London: D. Appleton, 1925, p. 15-34. [Pierre Loving, tr.]

C34. GROSSE SZENE
C34.1 – – *Komödie der Worte* [#K9.], 1915, S. 63-138.
C34.2 – – *Theaterstücke* [#J4.], 1922, Bd. V, S. 201-247.
C34.3 – – *Theaterstücke* [#J6.], 1928, Bd. V, S. 201-247.
C34.4 – – *Stories and Plays* [#S3.], 1930, p. 150-198. [School edition.]
C34.5 – – *Grosse Szene* [#K14.], 1959, S. 61-115.
C34.6 – – *Dramatische Werke* [#J11.], 1962, Bd. II, S. 491-529.

ENGLISH TRANSLATION

C34e.1 "The Big Scene: A Play in One Act." *Comedies of Words* [#L6.], 1917, p. 37-90. [Pierre Loving, tr.]

c35.   STUNDE DES ERKENNENS
c35.1   — — *Komödie der Worte* [#K9.], 1915, S. 7-62.
c35.2   — — *Theaterstücke* [#J4.], 1922, Bd. V, S. 167-199.
c35.3   — — *Theaterstücke* [#J6.], 1928, Bd. V, S. 167-199.
c35.4   — — *Dramatische Werke* [#J11.], 1962, Bd. II, S. 466-491.

                        ENGLISH TRANSLATIONS

c35e.1 "The Hour of Recognition." *International,* 10, vi, June, 1916, p. 167-174.
        [Pierre Loving, tr.]
c35e.2 "The Hour of Recognition: A Comedy of Words." *Comedies of Words* [#L6.],
        1917, p. 1-36. [Pierre Loving, tr.]

                              1917

c36.   FINK UND FLIEDERBUSCH: KOMÖDIE IN DREI AKTEN
c36.1   — — Berlin: S. Fischer, 1917, 156 S. ["Druck der Spamerschen Buchdruckerei
        in Leipzig." 1. – 6. Aufl.]
c36.2   — — *Theaterstücke* [#J4.], 1922, Bd. V, S. 281-397.
c36.3   — — *Theaterstücke* [#J6.], 1928, Bd. V, S. 281-397.
c36.4   — — *Dramatische Werke* [#J11.], 1962, Bd. 11, S. 555-649.

                             CRITICISM

c36x.1 Anon. *Der Merker,* 15. Dez. 1917, S. 847-850.
c36x.2 Anon. *Die Schaubühne,* 13-2, Nr. 50, 13. Dez. 1917, S. 569-571.
c36x.3 Körner, Josef. *Donauland,* 1, 1917, S. 1244.
c36x.4 Kohlhaas, M. "Der neue Schmock: Bemerkungen zu Schnitzlers Journalisten-
        komödie." *Die Glocke,* 3-2, xxxvii, 15. Dez. 1917, S. 432-436. [Sociological
        review.]
c36x.5 Heynen, Walter. "Journalistenkomödien." *Deutsche Rundschau,* 45 (Bd. 177),
        i, Okt. 1918, S. 160-163.
c36x.6 Weilen, Alexander von. *Das Literarische Echo,* 20, vii, 1. Jan. 1918, Sp. 402-403.
c36x.7 Witkowski, Georg. *Zeitschrift für Bücherfreunde,* Beiblatt, 10-1, i/ii, Apr./Mai,
        1918, Sp. 80-81.
c36x.8 Ludwig, Albert. "Fliederbusch der Unsterbliche." *Das Literarische Echo,* 22,
        xxii, 15. Aug. 1920, Sp. 1398-1400.
c36x.9 Tessmer, Hans. *Das Literarische Echo,* 23, ii, 15. Okt. 1920, Sp. 71-73. [Fr. "Der
        Redakteur in der modernen Literatur."]

                              1919

c37.   DIE SCHWESTERN ODER CASANOVA IN SPA: EIN LUST-
        SPIEL IN VERSEN. DREI AKTE IN EINEM
c37.1   — — *Deutsche Rundschau,* 46 (Bd. 181), i, Okt. 1919, S. 1-66.
c37.2   — — Berlin: S. Fischer, 1919, 109 S. ["Druck der Spamerschen Buchdruckerei."
        Auflagen:
        1. – 6.   1919
        7.   1922]
c37.3   — — *Theaterstücke* [#J4.], 1922, Bd. V. S. 399-515.
c37.4   "Casanova." *Almanach 1925.* Berlin: S. Fischer, 1924, S. 96-98. [Selection.]
c37.5   — — *Theaterstücke* [#J6.], 1928, Bd. V, S. 399-515.
c37.6   — — *Dramatische Werke* [#J11.], 1962, Bd. II, S. 651-737.

70

CRITICISM

C37x.1 Antropp, Theodor. *Österreichische Rundschau*, 63, i, 1. Apr. 1920, S. 45-46.
C37x.2 Arnold, Robert F. *Das Literarische Echo*, 22, xv, 1. Mai 1920, Sp. 924-926.
C37x.3 Feld, Leo. *Das Deutsche Drama*, 3, iii, 1. Mai 1920, S. 153-155.
C37x.4 Polgar, Alfred. *Die Weltbühne*, 16, xv, 8. Apr. 1920, S. 404-405.

1924

C38.   KOMÖDIE DER VERFÜHRUNG: IN DREI AKTEN
C38.1   – – *Neue Freie Presse*, Nr. 21412, 20. Apr. 1924, S. 31-39. (Osterbeilage.)
         [Selection.]
C38.2   – – Berlin: S. Fischer, 1924, 264 S. ["Druck der Spamerschen Buchdruckerei
         in Leipzig." 1. – 5. Aufl.]
C38.3   "Karnevalsfest." *Almanach 1926*. Berlin: S. Fischer, 1925, S. 125-130.
C38.4   – – *Dramatische Werke* [#J11.], 1962, Bd. II, S. 845-974.

CRITICISM

C38x.1 Arnold, Robert F. *Die Literatur*, 27, iii, Dez. 1924, S. 173.
C38x.2 Lehner, Fritz. *Schöne Literatur*, 25, xi, 15. Nov. 1924, S. 441-442.
C38x.3 Stranik, Erwin. *Universum*, 41, v, 30. Okt. 1924, S. 97-98.
See Also: Y21.

1926

C39.   DER GANG ZUM WEIHER: DRAMATISCHE DICHTUNG IN
        FÜNF AUFZÜGEN
C39.1   – – Berlin: S. Fischer, 1926, 164 S. ["Spamersche Buchdruckerei, Leipzig."
         1. – 5. Aufl.]
C39.2   – – *Dramatische Werke* [#J11.], 1962, Bd. II, S. 739-843.

CRITICISM

C39x.1 Witkowski, Georg. *Zeitschrift für Bücherfreunde*, Beiblatt, 19, iv, Juli/Aug. 1927,
       Sp. 177.
C39x.2 Anon. *Das Deutsche Drama in Geschichte und Gegenwart*, 3, 1931, S. 255-257.
       [Reprints fr. newspapers.]
C39x.3 Arnold, Robert F. *Die Literatur*, 33, vii, Apr. 1931, S. 406.
C39x.4 Auernheimer, Raoul. *Theater Arts Monthly*, 15, v, May, 1931, p. 407-409.
C39x.5 Lehner, Fritz. *Schöne Literatur*, 32, iv, Apr. 1931, S. 198-199.
See Also: X258., Y21.

1930

C40.   IM SPIEL DER SOMMERLÜFTE: IN DREI AUFZÜGEN
C40.1   – – *Kunst und Volk*, 4, v, Jan. 1930, S. 148-152. [Selection.]
C40.2   – – Berlin: S. Fischer, 1930, 85 S. ["Druck: Bibliographisches Institut,
         Leipzig." 1. – 5. Aufl.]
C40.3   – – *Dramatische Werke* [#J11.], 1962, Bd. II, S. 975-1034.

CRITICISM

C40x.1 Anon. *Das Deutsche Drama in Geschichte und Gegenwart*, 2, 1930, S. 250-252.
       [Reprints fr. newspapers.]

C40x.2 Arnold, Robert F. *Die Literatur*, 32, v, Feb. 1930, S. 290.
C40x.3 Lehner, Fritz. *Schöne Literatur*, 31, ii, Feb. 1930, S. 104-105.
C40x.4 Thyriot, Hans. *Die Literatur*, 33, ix, Juni 1931, S. 514.
C40x.5 Zucker, A. E. *Germanic Review*, 6, i, Jan., 1931, p. 91-93.
See Also: x258.

1932

C41. ANATOLS GRÖSSENWAHN: EIN AKT
C41.1 – – Berlin: S. Fischer, 1932, 26 S. [Stage manuscript.]
C41.2 – – *Meisterdramen* [#J9.], 1955, S. 585-603.
C41.3 – – *Dramatische Werke* [#J11.], 1962, Bd. I, S. 105-123.
C41.4 – – *Anatol* [#C4.22], 1964, S. 97-117.
See Also: x238.

C42. DIE GLEITENDEN: EIN AKT
C42.1 – – Berlin: S. Fischer, 1932, 34 S. [Stage manuscript.]
See Also: x238.

C43. DIE MÖRDERIN: TRAGISCHE POSSE (SKETSCH) IN EINEM
AKT
C43.1 – – Berlin: S. Fischer, 1932, 36 S. [Stage manuscript.]
See Also: x238.

PART D: PHILOSOPHICAL REFLECTIONS

DI.I   *Buch der Sprüche und Bedenken : Aphorismen und Fragmente.* Wien: Phaidon, 235 S.
[(Vorwort). 1. Sprüche in Versen. 2. Ahnungen und Fragen. 3. Schicksal und
Wille. 4. Verantwortung und Gewissen. 5. Beziehungen und Einsamkeiten.
6. Wunder und Gesetze. 7. Tageswirren, Gang der Zeiten. 8. Werk und
Widerhall. 9. Kleine Sprüche. – Motto: "Tiefsinn hat nie ein Ding erhellt;
Klarsinn schaut tiefer in die Welt." "Druck: Record-Office, Wien VIII."]

DI.2   "Kleine Sprüche." *Deutsch für Erwachsene.* II. Teil. Vollständige umgearbeitete
Ausgabe. Berlin: M. D. Berlitz, 1929. [School edition. – Selections.]

DI.3   "Zur Ermutigung." *Twentieth-Century German Verse.* A Selection translated
by Herman Salinger. Princeton, N. J.: Princeton University Press, 1952, as
motto facing title page. [English translation of the same below with the title
"Encouragement."]

ENGLISH TRANSLATIONS

DIe.I   "Aphorisms: From an Unpublished Book 'Proverbs and Reflections'." *Plain
Talk*, 2, v, May, 1928, p. 590; 3, iv, Oct., 1928, p. 419; 3, vi, Dec., 1928, p. 733.
[Dorothy Alden, tr.]

CRITICISM

DIX.I   Anon. *Menorah*, 6, 1928, p. 255.
DIX.2   Lothar, Ernst. *Literarische Welt*, 17, Feb. 1928.
DIX.3   Hutschneider, Josef. "Arthur Schnitzler als Aphoristiker: Bemerkungen zu
seinem Buch 'Buch der Sprüche und Bedenken'." *JIASRA*, 4, ii, Summer,
1965, p. 4-19. [AS's dialectic, humility and "Ethos der Wirklichkeit."]
See Also: x248.

D2.I   *Der Geist im Wort und der Geist in der Tat.* Vorläufige Bemerkungen zu zwei
Diagrammen. Berlin: S. Fischer, 60 S. (& 2 diagrams). [(Vorwort). I. Der Geist
im Wort. II. Ein Zwischenkapitel über Begabungen und Seelenzustände. III.
Der Geist in der Tat. Erstes Diagram: Der Geist im Wort. Zweites Diagram:
Der Geist in der Tat. – "Spamersche Buchdruckerei in Leipzig." 1. – 3. Aufl.]

D2.2   "– – –" *Menorah*, 10, v/vi, Mai/Juni 1932, S. 187-202. [Repr. of ‡D2.1 without
chapter III.]

CRITICISM

D2X.I   Anon. *Books Abroad*, 1, iv, Oct., 1927, p. 46. [Signed "W. A. W."]
D2X.2   Allers, Rudolf. "Ein philosophischer Versuch Arthur Schnitzlers." *Wiener
Medizinische Wochenschrift*, 77, xxxi, 30. Juli 1927, S. 1020-1021.

D2x.3   Loving, Pierre. "The Spirit Diagrammed." *Saturday Review of Literature*, 4, i, July 30, 1927, p. 10.
D2x.4   Lucka, Emil. "Arthur Schnitzler als Charakterologe." *Die Literatur*, 29, viii, Mai 1927, S. 455-457.
D2x.5   York-Steiner, Heinrich. *Menorah*, 5, iii, März 1927, S. 201-202.
D2x.6   Zuckerkandl, Viktor. *Neue Rundschau*, 38, iv, Apr. 1927, S. 423-426.
See *Also*: x248., x375.

1939

D3.1   *Über Krieg und Frieden.* Stockholm: Bermann-Fischer, 46 S. (Schriftenreihe "Ausblicke"). [Prefatory note: "Die hier veröffentlichten Aufzeichnungen Arthur Schnitzlers aus der Zeit des Weltkriegs fanden sich, in einer besonderen Mappe zusammengefasst, im Nachlass des Dichters. Die Mappe trägt die Aufschrift: 'Und einmal wird der Friede wiederkommen'." – "Druck: N.V. Drukkerij G. J. Thieme, Nijmegen."]
D3.2   "Aufzeichungen aus der Kriegszeit. Aus dem Nachlass." *Neue Rundschau*, 43, v, Mai 1932, S. 678-681. [At end: "Geschrieben im Jahre 1915." – Except for one paragraph a partial pre-printing of ‡D3.1.]
D3.3   "Über Krieg und Frieden. Aus dem gleichnamigen Werk." *Zehnjahrbuch 1938-1948.* (Friedrich Torberg, ed.) Wien/Stockholm: Bermann-Fischer, 1948, S. 77-79. [Selections from ‡D3.1.]

ENGLISH TRANSLATION

D3e.1   "Notes on War and Peace: 1915-1919." *Twice A Year*, Nos. 3/4, Spring/ Summer, 1940, p. 18-31. [Christl Ritter, tr. – Selections.]

PART E: APHORISMS, ETC.

1886

E1.   "Aphorismen." *Deutsche Wochenschrift*, 4, xlix, 5. Dez., S. 625.

1888

E2.   "Sprüche in Versen." *Deutsche Wochenschrift*, 6, xxi, S. 8.

1891

E3.   "Sprüche in Versen." *An der schönen blauen Donau*, 6, ii, S. 39.

1896

E4.   "Anmerkungen." *Wiener Allgemeine Zeitung.*

1906

E5.   "Bemerkungen." *Österreichische Rundschau*, 5, lx/lxi, Jan., S. 395-396.

1927

E6.   "Kleine Sprüche." *Buch der Sprüche und Bedenken* [‡D1.1], S. 221-235.
E7.   "Sprüche in Versen." *Buch der Sprüche und Bedenken* [‡D1.1], S. 13-27. [Zur Ermutigung. Wahlspruch. Wort und Wahrheit. Einem Philosophen ins Stammbuch. Frühling im Herbst. Die feinen Gaumen. Treib weit hinaus. Von Ferne zu Ferne. Einladung. Der Exakte spricht. Ewige Wahrheit. Freund und Feind. An ein Mädchen. Vergebliche Flucht. Der neue Duft. Wortspirale. Klarheit. Heb dich hinweg. Frohe Ahnung. Freudenfest. An einen Rezensenten. Recht hattest du. Arme-Leut-Stücke. Porträt. Maske. Beethovenfeier. Nachwelt. Distichen. Unsterblichkeit. Schiller-Feier. Umgläubige Distichen. Widmung in die Zukunft. In eigner Sache.]

1928

E8.   "Bemerkungen (Bisher Ungedruckt)." *Österreichische Dichtergabe.* Ungedrucktes von Hugo von Hofmannsthal, Max Mell, Arthur Schnitzler, Karl Schönherr, Anton Wildgans. Wien: Wiener Bibliophilen-Gesellschaft, S. 43-47.

1932

E9.   "Gedanken über Kunst: Aus dem Nachlass." *Neue Rundschau*, 43, i, Jan.,
       S. 37-39.

1933

E10.   "Gedanken über Schriftstellerei." *Das 47. Jahr.* Berlin: S. Fischer, S. 109-111.
       [Repr. of ♯E9.]

1956

E11.   "Bemerkungen zum Thema 'Kunst und Kritik'." *Almanach: Das siebzigste
       Jahr 1886-1956.* Frankfurt a.M.: S. Fischer, S. 83-84. ["Aus 'Die Neue Rund-
       schau' 1921."]

1962

E12.   "Bemerkungen: Aus dem Nachlass." *Neue Rundschau*, 73, ii/iii, S. 347-357.
E13.   "Kritisches: Aus dem Nachlass." *Neue Rundschau*, ii/iii, S. 203-228. [Notes on
       Tolstoi, Ibsen, Hauptmann, H. Mann, Kraus, Wassermann, Salten, Barbusse,
       Kerr, Hofmannsthal and Werfel, as well as "Aufführung von Hervieu im
       Théâtre Français."]
E14.   "Notizen über Politik." *Forum* (Wien), 9, ci, Mai, S. 222. ["Aus dem Nachlass."]

PART F: ESSAYS, SKETCHES, ETC.

1879

F1.   "Von Amsterdam nach Ymuiden: Reiseeindrücke." *Wiener Medizinische Presse*, 20, xxxviii, 21. Sept., Sp. 1219-1221. [Not signed. Travel impressions of an international medical congress in Amsterdam. AS's first publication.]

1880

F2.   "Über den Patriotismus." *Der Freie Landesbote*, 15. Nov. [Essay.]

1888

F3.   "Londoner Briefe." *Internationale Klinische Rundschau*, 2, xxvii, 1. Juli, Sp. 1067-1069; 2, xxix, 15. Juli, Sp. 1164-1166; 2, xxxi, 29. Juli, Sp. 1237-1239.

1889

F4.   "Sylvesterbetrachtungen." *Internationale Klinische Rundschau*, 3, i, 6. Jan., Sp. 35-36. [Signed "A. S." Pessimistic thoughts on the new year.]

F4.1 – – *Almanach. Das achtundsiebzigste Jahr*. Frankfurt a.M.: S. Fischer, 1964, S. 143-146.

1891

F5.   "[Four book reviews]." *Moderne Rundschau*, 3, S. 84, 86, 243.

F6.   "64. Versammlung der Gesellschaft deutscher Naturforscher und Ärzte in Halle a. S. 22. September 1891." *Internationale Klinische Rundschau*, 5, xxxix, 27. Sept., Sp. 1520-1521. [Signed "A.S."]

1893

F7.   "Spaziergang." *Deutsche Zeitung* (Wien), 6. Dez. [In the series "Wiener Spiegel."]

1894

F8.   "[Letter on "Das Märchen"]." *Neues Wiener Journal*, 3. Apr.

F9.   "Der Fall Jacobsohn." *Die Zukunft*, 49, 17. Dez., S. 401-404. [AS defends Siegfried Jacobsohn against a charge of plagiarism.]

F10.   "[Contribution]." *Die Bücher zum wirklichen Leben. Nebst Briefen von . . . Dr. Artur Schnitzler.* (Hermann Bahr). Wien: Hugo Heller. [AS's ten favorite works, including as one item "Jeder beliebige Band Maupassant, Novellen." – Repr. in: *Jahrbuch deutscher Bibliophilen und Literaturfreunden*, 16/17, 1931, S. 124-125.]

F11.   "Zum 'Professor Bernhardi'." *Der Merker*, 4, iv, S. 135. [Letter to the editors in reference to Brandes' article; Bernhardi not patterned after AS's father.]

F12.   "Protest." *Forum* (München), 1, ix, Dez., S. 489-491. [Repr. of an article published "in einem Schweizer Blatt" wherein AS disclaims any nationalistic critical views because of the war. – Repr. in: *Georg Brandes und Arthur Schnitzler* [#G8.], 1956, S. 206-208.]

F13.   "Berichtigung: Ein paar Worte zum Gutachten Maximilian Hardens über den 'Reigen'." *Neues Wiener Journal*, 30. Jan.

F14.   "[Tribute to Gerhart Hauptmann]." *Festschrift zum 60. Geburtstag Gerhart Hauptmanns: Im Auftrage der Genossenschaft deutscher Bühnenangehöriger.* (Felix Hollaender, ed.) Berlin: Rudolf Mosse, S. 4.

F15.   "An Thomas Manns 50. Geburtstag." *Berliner Tageblatt*, Nr. 266, 7. Juni, 6. Beiblatt.

F16.   "Zur Physiologie des Schaffens: Die Entstehung des 'Schleier der Beatrice'." *Neue Freie Presse*, Nr. 24168, 25. Dez., S. 38-39. ["Aus dem Nachlass."]

F17.   "Gespräch, welches in der Kaffeehausecke nach Vorlesung der 'Elixiere' geführt wird. 31./VIII 90. & 15./IX 90." *Jahrbuch deutscher Bibliophilen und Literaturfreunde*, 18/19, S. 91-93. ["Unveröffentlichtes aus dem Nachlass."]

1942

F18. "Meine Stellung zum Zionismus." *Aufbau*, 8, xix, 9. Mai, S. 17.

1956

F19. "Nicht gehaltene Festrede für Georg Brandes." *Georg Brandes und Arthur Schnitzler* [‡G8.], 1956, S. 157-162. [Brandes compared with Voltaire.]

1964

F20. "Gespräch zwischen einem neuen und einem alten Kritiker." *Neue Rundschau*, 75, ii, S. 303-308. (Robert O. Weiss, ed.) [Fr. the Nachlass, written about 1902. Attacks literary critics and asserts literary validity of the one-act play.]

1965

F21. "Ansätze zu Parabeln." *Almanach: Das neunundsiebzigste Jahr*. (J. Hellmut Freund & Gerda Niedieck, eds.) Frankfurt a.M.: S. Fischer, S. 151-154. [Includes "Legende vom ewigen Funken." – Items dated 1890-1921.]

ENGLISH TRANSLATIONS

1926

Fe.1 "The Jew in Me and My Works: Confessions of Literary Luminaries on their Intimate Attitude toward the Jewish Complex. I Spurn the Dodge of Baptism." *American Hebrew*, 119, xv, Aug. 20, p. 407. ["I regard Zionism as the worst affliction that has ever burst upon the Jews."]

1931

Fe.2 "[Letter.]" *New York Herald Tribune Books*, 8, vi, Oct. 18, p. 9. [Appears in the article "The Writer & His Daily Bread" by Roy Temple House. AS argues for reform of the copyright laws.]

PART G: CORRESPONDENCE

GI.   **THEODOR HERZL**
GI.I   "Brief an Theodor Herzl vom 5. August 1892." *Jüdischer Almanach*, 1900, S. 102-103.

G2.   **HUGO VON HOFMANNSTHAL**
G2.1   "Briefe an Arthur Schnitzler." *Neue Rundschau*, 41, iv, Apr. 1930, S. 512-514. [Fr. "Briefe an Freunde." Two letters of 1892.]
G2.2   "Briefe an Arthur Schnitzler." *Neue Rundschau*, 65, iii/iv, 1954, S. 390-396. [Eight letters from the period 1911-1927.]
G2.3   "Aus dem Briefwechsel." *Almanach: Das vierundsiebzigste Jahr*. Frankfurt a.M.: S. Fischer, 1960, S. 21-23. [Three letters of 1900.]
G2.4   "Hugo von Hofmannsthal an Arthur Schnitzler." *Almanach: Das sechsundsiebzigste Jahr*. Frankfurt a.M.: S. Fischer, 1962, S. 9-11. [Letter of 1912.]
G2.5   *Hugo von Hofmannsthal – Arthur Schnitzler Briefwechsel*. Herausgegeben von Therese Nickl und Heinrich Schnitzler. Frankfurt a.M.: S. Fischer, 1964, 411 S. [Period 1890-1929. With annotations, "Werkregister" and "Personenregister."]

CRITICISM

G2.5x   LoCicero, Vincent. *JIASRA*, 4, ii, Summer, 1965, p. 32-33.

G3.   **MAX BURCKHARD**
G3.1   "Schnitzlers Einzug ins Burgtheater." *Wiener Studien und Dokumente*. (Karl Glossy). Wien: Steyrermühl, 1933, S. 166-168. [Four letters from AS to Burckhard with two replies concerning the submission of "Alkandis Lied," "Anatol," and "Liebelei."]

G4.   **ERNST BERNHARD**
G4.1   *Die Inspiration: Unveröffentlichte Briefe von Hofmannsthal, Schnitzler, Dehmel, Liliencron, Lagerlöf, u.a.* (Ernst Bernhard, ed.) Herrliberg, Zürich: Bühl, 1946, S. 8-9. (Bühl Verlag Blätter 9). [One letter.]

G5.   **OTTO BRAHM**
G5.1   *Der Briefwechsel Arthur Schnitzler – Otto Brahm*. Herausgegeben und eingeleitet von Oskar Seidlin. Berlin: Gesellschaft für Theatergeschichte, 1953, 266 S. (Schriften der Gesellschaft für Theatergeschichte, Bd. 57). [Period 1894-1913. Index includes personal names and literary works. Valuable for material on the genesis of the dramas and AS's attitudes towards members of the Brahm ensemble.]
G5.2   "Unveröffentlichte Briefe Schnitzlers an Brahm: Ein Nachtrag zu Band 57 der 'Schriften'." (Heinrich Schnitzler, ed.) *Kleine Schriften der Gesellschaft für Theatergeschichte*, H. 16, 1958, S. 44-55. [Fourteen letters of the period 1896-1910 with annotations. – Also as a separate reprint, 1958, 12 S.]

G5.1x1   Beharriell, Frederick. *Monatshefte für deutschen Unterricht*, 46, v, Oct., 1954, p. 288-289.
G5.1x2   Heun, Hans Georg. *Deutsche Literaturzeitung für Kritik der internationalen Wissenschaft*, 75, xi, Nov. 1954, Sp. 707-710.
G5.1x3   Plant, Richard. *Germanic Review*, 29, iv. Dec., 1954, p. 298-299.
G5.1x4   Hatfield, Henry. *Modern Language Quarterly*, 16, ii, June, 1955, p. 181.
G5.1x5   Lucas, W. I. *Modern Language Review*, 50, i, Jan. 1955, p. 103-104.
G5.1x6   Zucker, A. *Modern Language Notes*, 70, viii, Dec., 1955, p. 625-627.
G5.1x7   Lange, Victor. *Journal of English and Germanic Philology*, 55, i, Jan., 1956, p. 187-189.
See Also: Y39.

G6.   DR. FROMM
G6.1   "Patriotismus und Schauspielkunst: Zwei Briefe aus dem Nachlass von Arthur Schnitzler." (Henry Schnitzler, ed.) *Kleine Schriften der Gesellschaft für Theatergeschichte*, H. 11, 1953, S. 20-26. [One letter each from Fromm and AS on the question of patriotism in "Der Ruf des Lebens."]

G7..   SIGMUND FREUD
G7.1   "Briefe an Arthur Schnitzler." *Neue Rundschau*, 66, i, 1955, S. 95-106. [Ten letters of 1906-1931. Detailed notes by Henry Schnitzler.]
G7.2   "Sigmund Freud an Arthur Schnitzler." (Werner Rudolf). *Medizinische Klinik*, 53, i, 3. Jan. 1958, S. 32-33. [Letter of 14. Mai 1922.]
G7.3   *Sigmund Freud: Briefe 1873-1939*. Ausgewählt und herausgegeben von Ernst L. Freud. Frankfurt a.M.: S. Fischer, 1960, S. 249-250; 338-340. [Two letters, dated 8. Mai 1906 and 14. Mai 1922.]
G7.4   "Sigmund Freud an Arthur Schnitzler (8. Mai 1906)." *Du*, 23, Apr. 1963, S. 25.

G7e.1   *The Life and Works of Sigmund Freud*. (Ernest Jones). New York: Basic Books, 1957, Vol. 3, p. 443-444. [Letter from Freud of May 14, 1922. Abridged.]
See Also: X320.

G8.   GEORG BRANDES
G8.1   *Georg Brandes und Arthur Schnitzler: Ein Briefwechsel*. Herausgegeben von Kurt Bergel. Bern: Francke, 1956, 240 S. [Period 1894-1926. Notes, index of names and index of publications. Illuminating document of AS's debt to Brandes; useful for AS's comments on his own works. – Also: Berkeley & Los Angeles: University of California Press, 1956. (University of California Publications in Modern Philology, Vol. 46).]

G8.1x1   Beharriell, Fred J. *Monatshefte für deutschen Unterricht*, 50, vi, Nov., 1958, p. 322-323.
G8.1x2   Heun, Hans Georg. *Deutsche Literaturzeitung für Kritik der internationalen Wissenschaften*, 79, vi, Juni 1958, Sp. 510-511.
G8.1x3   Politzer, Heinz. *Modern Language Notes*, 73, iv. Apr., 1958, p. 317-319.
See Also: Y18.

G9.   VARIOUS
G9.1   "Briefe." *Neue Rundschau*, 68, i, 1957, S. 88-101. [Thirteen letters, edited by Heinrich Schnitzler: three to Richard Beer-Hofmann (1892-1904), four to

Hugo von Hofmannsthal (1892-1925), one each to Hermann Bahr (1901), Alfred von Berger (1907), Hans Henning (1914), Alfred Kerr (1918), Heinrich Mann (1919) and Jakob Wassermann (1924).]

G10.   **RAINER MARIA RILKE**
G10.1   "Rainer Maria Rilke und Arthur Schnitzler. Ihr Briefwechsel. Mit Anmerkungen versehen und veröffentlicht von Heinrich Schnitzler." *Wort und Wahrheit*, 13, iv. Apr. 1958, S. 283-298. [Period 1896-1902.]

G11.   **EGON FRIEDELL**
G11.1   *Egon Friedell: Briefe.* Ausgewählt und herausgegeben von Walter Schneider. Wien: Georg Prachner, 1959, S. 39. [Letter of 17. Mai 1920; request by AS for an Altenberg letter.]

G12.   **S. FISCHER**
G12.1   *Neue Rundschau*, 72, iii, 1961, S. 547-548; 559-568. [Fr. "Aus der Werkstatt der neuen Rundschau 1890-1917." Two letters from AS (1907) and nine from S. Fischer (1898-1915).]
G12.2   "Zur Geschichte des 'Reigen': Aus dem Briefwechsel zwischen Arthur Schnitzler und S. Fischer." (Peter de Mendelssohn). *Almanach: Das sechsundsiebzigste Jahr.* Frankfurt a.M.: S. Fischer, 1962, S. 18-35. [Excerpts from the correspondence and a history of the printing of the work.]

G13.   **GERHART HAUPTMANN**
G13.1   "Arthur Schnitzler an Gerhart Hauptmann." *Programm des Volkstheaters* (Wien), H. 7, 1962/1963, S. 2 & 5. [Fr. the Nachlass, dated 17. März 1922; not known wheter the letter was actually sent.]

* * *

See Also: s1., x207., y22.

PART H: MEDICAL WRITINGS AND REVIEWS

1886

H1. "[Rev. of] Anatomische, pathologische und klinische Studien über Hyperplasie der Rachentonsille, sowie chirurgische Behandlung der Hyperplasie zur Verhütung von Erkrankungen des Gehörorgans. Von Dr. F. Trautmann. Berlin: August Hirschwald, 1886." *Wiener Medizinische Presse*, 27, xli, 10. Okt., Sp. 1341. [Not signed.]

H2. "[Rev. of] Das chlorsaure Kali, seine physiologischen, toxischen und therapeutischen Wirkungen. Von Dr. J. von Mering. Berlin: August Hirschwald, 1885." *Wiener Medizinische Presse*, 27, li, 19. Dez., Sp. 1666-1669. [Signed "Dr. A. Sch."]

H3. "[Rev. of] Grundriss der medizinischen Elektrizitätslehre für Aerzte und Studirende. Von Dr. Konrad Rieger. Jena: Gustav Koch, 1886." *Wiener Medizinische Presse*, 27, xx, 16. Mai. Sp. 652. [Signed "Dr. A-r."]

H4. "[Rev. of] Handbuch der speziellen Pathologie und Therapie für praktische Aerzte und Studirende. Von Dr. Hermann Eichhorst. 2. Aufl., Wien & Leipzig: Urban & Schwarzenberg, 1885." *Wiener Medizinische Presse*, 27, v, 31. Jan., Sp. 153-154. [Not signed. – "Uns will es bedünken, dass der Autor die Abschnitte über Herzkrankheiten und in zweiter Linie die über Erkrankung der Niere und des Nervensystems mit der grössten Liebe behandelt hat."]

H5. "[Rev. of] Niemeyer's Lehrbuch der speziellen Pathologie und Therapie mit besonderer Rücksicht auf Physiologie und pathologische Anatomie. Neu bearbeitet von Dr. Eugen Seitz. 11. Aufl., Berlin: August Hirschwald, 1885." *Wiener Medizinische Presse*, 27, xliii, 24. Okt., Sp. 1410. [Not signed.]

H6. "[Rev. of] Taschenbuch der medizinisch und klinischen Diagnostik. Von Dr. Otto Seifert & Dr. Fr. Müller. 2. Aufl., Wiesbaden: Bergmann, 1886." *Wiener Medizinische Presse*, 27, xxxi, 1. Aug., Sp. 1020-1021. [Signed "Dr. A."]

1887

H7. "[Rev. of] Die Behandlung gewisser Formen von Neurasthenie und Hysterie. Von Dr. Weier Mitchels. Berlin: Hirschwald, 1887." *Internationale Klinische Rundschau*, 1, vi, 6. Feb., Sp. 185-188. [Signed "Dr. A. Sch."]

H8. "[Rev. of] Handwörterbuch der gesammten Medizin. Herausgegeben von Dr. A. Villaret. 2 Bde. Stuttgart: Ferdinand Enke, 1887." *Internationale Klinische Rundschau*, 1, xxxii, 7. Aug., Sp. 1023; 1, xxxvi, 4. Sept., Sp. 1155; 1, xlviii, 27. Nov., Sp. 1551. [None of these signed.]

H9. "[Rev. of] Neue Vorlesungen über die Krankheiten des Nervensystems, insbesondere über Hysterie. Von J. M. Charcot. Autorisirte deutsche Ausgabe von Dr. Sigmund Freud. Leipzig & Wien: Toeplitz & Deuticke, 1886." *Internationale Klinische Rundschau*, 1, i, 2. Jan., Sp. 19-20.

H9.1 – – *Almanach. Das achtundsiebzigste Jahr.* Frankfurt a.M.: S. Fischer, 1964, S. 135-138.

HIO.   "[Rev. of] Die syphilitischen Erkrankungen des Nervensystems. Von Dr. Theodor Rumpf. Wiesbaden: J. F. Bergmann, 1887." *Internationale Klinische Rundschau*, 1, xxxi, 31. Juli, Sp. 989-991.

HII.   "[Rev. of] Über multiple inselförmige Sklerose des Zentralnervensystems im Kindesalter: Eine pediatrisch-klinische Studie. Von Dr. D. Unger. Wien: Toeplitz & Deuticke, 1887." *Internationale Klinische Rundschau*, 1, xv, 10. Apr., Sp. 469-470. [Signed "A. S."]

1888

HI2.   "[Rev. of] Therapeutisches Hilfsbuch zur rationellen Behandlung in der internen Praxis: Für Aerzte und Studirende. Von J. Milner Fothergill. Autorisirte Uebersetzung von Dr. J. Krakauer. Wien & Leipzig: Urban & Schwarzenberg, 1888." *Internationale Klinische Rundschau*, 2, xlii, 14. Okt., Sp. 1659-1662.

1889

HI3.   "Über funktionelle Aphonie und deren Behandlung durch Hypnose und Suggestion." *Internationale Klinische Rundschau*, 3, x, 10. März, Sp. 405-408; 3, xi, 17. März, Sp. 457-461; 3, xii, 24. März, Sp. 494-499; 3, xiv, 7. Apr., Sp. 583-586. [Repr.: Wien: Wilhelm Braumüller, 1889, 30 S.]

HI4.   "[Rev. of] Die Suggestion und ihre Heilwirkung. Von Dr. H. Bernheim. Autorisirte deutsche Ausgabe von Dr. Sigmund Freud. Leipzig & Wien: Deuticke, 1888-89." *Internationale Klinische Rundschau*, 3, xxi, 26. Mai, Sp. 891-893.

1890

HI5.   "[Rev. of] Die Frage des Übergangs gutartiger Kehlkopfgeschwülste in bösartige, speziell nach intralaringealen Operationen. Von Felix Semon. Berlin: August Hirschwald, 1889." *Internationale Klinische Rundschau*, 4, v, Sp. 203-205.

HI6.   "[Rev. of] Die sexuelle Hygiene und ihre ethischen Konsequenzen: Drei Vorlesungen von Dr. med. Seved Ribbing. Deutsch von Dr. med. Oskar Reyner. Leipzig: Hobbing, 1890." *Internationale Klinische Rundschau*, 4, 23. Nov., Sp. 1937-1939.

HI6.1   – – *Almanach. Das achtundsiebzigste Jahr.* Frankfurt a.M.: S. Fischer, 1964, S. 138-143.

HI7.   "[Rev. of] Über psychische Therapie innerer Krankheiten. Von Prof. Dr. Rosenbach. Berlin: Fischer, 1890." *Internationale Klinische Rundschau*, 4, xxx, 27. Juli, Sp. 1248-1249. [Signed "Dr. A. S."]

1891

HI8.   *Klinischer Atlas der Laryngologie und Rhinologie, nebst Anleitung zur Diagnose und Therapie der Krankheiten des Kehlkopfes und der Luftröhre.* Herausgegeben von Dr. Johann Schnitzler unter Mitwirkung von Dr. M. Hajek und Dr. A. Schnitzler. Wien & Leipzig: Wilhelm Braumüller, 1891-1895. [O. P. Schinnerer: "AS behauptete, dass er irrtümlicherweise als Mitarbeiter genannt wurde, da er so gut wie gar nichts zu dem Atlas beigetragen habe. Professor Dr. Hajek hat dies bestätigt."]

HI9.   "[Rev. of] Die Behandlung der Hysterie, der Neurasthenie und ähnlicher allgemeiner funktioneller Neurosen. Von Dr. V. Holst. 3. Aufl., Stuttgart: Ferdinand Enke, 1891." *Internationale Klinische Rundschau*, 5, xxix, 19. Juli, Sp. 1111. [Signed "A.S."]

84

H20. "[Rev. of] Der geniale Mensch. Von Cesare Lombroso. Autorisirte Über-
setzung von Dr. H. O. Fraenkel. Hamburg: Verlagsanstalt, 1890." *Internationale
Klinische Rundschau,* 5, i, 4. Jan., Sp. 21-24.

H21. "[Rev. of] Klinische Vorlesungen über Psychiatrie: Auf wissenschaftlichen
Grundlagen für Studierende und Aerzte, Juristen und Psychologen. Von
Hofrath Prof. Dr. Theodor Meynert. Wien: Wilhelm Braumüller, 1890."
Internationale Klinische Rundschau, 5, iv, 25. Jan., Sp. 162. [Not signed.]

H22. "[Rev. of] Neue Forschungen auf dem Gebiete der Psychopatia sexualis: Eine
medizinisch-psychologische Studie. Von Dr. R. von Krafft-Ebing. Stuttgart:
Ferdinand Enke, 1890." *Internationale Klinische Rundschau,* 5, ii, 11. Jan., Sp.
69-70. [Signed "Dr. A. S."]

1892

H23. "[Rev. of] Cesare Lombroso und die Naturgeschichte des Verbrechers. Von
Dr. H. Kurella. Hamburg: J. F. Richter, 1892." *Internationale Klinische Rundschau,* 6, xxix, 17. Juli, Sp. 1191. [Signed "A. S."]

H24. "[Rev. of] Der Hypnotismus in gemeinfasslicher Darstellung. Von Dr. Hans
Schmidkunz. Stuttgart: A. Zimmer (E. Mohrmann), 1892." *Internationale
Klinische Rundschau,* 6, xlviii, 27. Nov., Sp. 1959-1961. [Signed "A. S."]

H25. "[Rev. of] Neue Studien über Hypnotismus, Suggestion und Psychotherapie.
Von H. Bernheim. Übersetzt von Dr. Sigmund Freud. Leipzig & Wien:
Franz Deuticke, 1892." *Internationale Klinische Rundschau,* 6, lii, 25. Dez., Sp.
2133. [Not signed.]

H26. "[Rev. of] Poliklinische Vorträge. Von Prof. J. M. Charcot. Übersetzt von
Dr. Sigmund Freud. Leipzig & Wien: Franz Stuhlich." *Internationale Klinische
Rundschau,* 6, xlvi, 13. Nov., Sp. 1887. [Signed "A. S."]

PART J: COLLECTED WORKS

JI.   *Erzählende Schriften.* Berlin: S. Fischer, 3 Bde., 317 S., 386 S., 460 S. (Gesammelte
       Werke in zwei Abteilungen: Erste Abteilung). [Bd. I (Novellen): Sterben.
       Blumen. Ein Abschied. Die Frau des Weisen. Der Ehrentag. Die Toten
       schweigen. Andreas Thameyers letzter Brief. Der blinde Geronimo und sein
       Bruder. Leutnant Gustl. Die griechische Tänzerin. – Bd. II (Novellen): Frau
       Berta Garlan. Das Schicksal des Freiherrn von Leisenbohg. Die Fremde. Die
       Weissagung. Das neue Lied. Der Tod des Junggesellen. Der tote Gabriel.
       Das Tagebuch der Redegonda. Der Mörder. Die dreifache Warnung. Die
       Hirtenflöte. – Bd. III: Der Weg ins Freie. – "Entwurf des Einbands von
       Erich Mende. Das Porträt nach einer Originalzeichnung von Emma Löwen-
       stamm. Druck der Spamerschen Buchdruckerei in Leipzig." Auflagen:
       1. – 6. Tsd.   1912
       6. – 9.   1913
       10. – 13.   1914
       19. – 33.   1918]

CRITICISM

JIX.I Anon. *Westermanns Monatshefte*, 112-2, dclxxi, Juli 1912, S. 780.

J2.   *Die Theaterstücke.* Berlin: S. Fischer, 4 Bde., 439 S., 420 S., 347 S., 423 S.
       (Gesammelte Werke in zwei Abteilungen: Zweite Abteilung). [Bd. I: Anatol.
       Das Märchen. Liebelei. Freiwild. Das Vermächtnis. – Bd. II: Paracelsus. Die
       Gefährtin. Der grüne Kakadu. Der Schleier der Beatrice. Lebendige Stunden.
       Die Frau mit dem Dolche. Die letzten Masken. Literatur. – Bd. III: Der einsame
       Weg. Zwischenspiel. Der Puppenspieler. Der tapfere Cassian. Zum grossen
       Wurstel. Der Ruf des Lebens. – Bd. IV: Komtesse Mizzi oder Der Familientag.
       Der junge Medardus. Das weite Land. – "Spamersche Buchdruckerei in
       Leipzig." Auflagen:
       1. – 5. Tsd.   1912
       6. – 8.   1913
       9. – 10.   1915
       15. – 18.   1918]

J3.   *Erzählende Schriften.* [#JI with the addition of one volume.] Bd. IV, 375 S.
       [("Ergänzungsband IV" in some printings.) (Novellen). Frau Beate und ihr
       Sohn. Doktor Gräsler, Badearzt. Casanovas Heimfahrt. – "Druck vom Biblio-
       graphischen Institut in Leipzig." 34. – 37. Aufl. of #JI.]

J4.   *Die Theaterstücke.* [#J2 with the addition of one volume.] Bd. V, 519 S. [("Er-
       gänzungsband V" in some printings.) Professor Bernhardi. Stunde des Er-

kennens. Grosse Szene. Das Bacchusfest. Fink und Fliederbusch. Die Schwestern oder Casanova in Spa. – "Druck vom Bibliographischen Institut in Leipzig." 27. – 30. Aufl. of. ≠J2.]

1928

J5.   *Erzählende Schriften.* [≠J3 with the addition of two volumes and with new subtitles.] Bd. V, 392 S., Bd. VI, 281 S. (Gesammelte Schriften). [Bd. I: "Sterben und andere Novellen." Bd. II: "Frau Bertha Garlan und andere Novellen." Bd. IV: "Die Alternden." – Bd. V: Therese, Chronik eines Frauenlebens. – Bd. VI (Die Erwachenden: Novellen): Fräulein Else. Die Frau des Richters. Traumnovelle. – Above volumes also published separately without the series title. "Druck: Bibliographisches Institut A. G. in Leipzig." – Bd. V, 21. – 35. Aufl.; Bd. VI, 1. – 5. Aufl.]

J6.   *Die Theaterstücke.* [≠J4 with new series title.] (Gesammelte Schriften.)

1932

J7.   *Die kleine Komödie: Frühe Novellen.* Mit einem Nachwort von Otto P. Schinnerer. Berlin: S. Fischer, 335 S. [Amerika. Er wartet auf den vazierenden Gott. Der Witwer. Der Andere. Welch eine Melodie. Der Empfindsame. Ein Erfolg. Geschichte eines Genies. Legende (Fragment). Um eine Stunde. Wohltaten, still und rein gegeben. Die Braut. Die grüne Krawatte. Exzentrik. Mein Freund Ypsilon. Die drei Elixire. Der Fürst ist im Hause. Erbschaft. Der Sohn. Komödiantinnen: Helene, Fritzi. Reichtum. Die Nächste. Die kleine Komödie. (Nachwort. Bibliographie und Zeittafel). – "Druck: Bibliographisches Institut AG. in Leipzig." 1. – 5. Aufl.]

CRITICISM

J7x.1   Kutzleb, Hjalmar. *Neue Literatur*, 34, iii, März 1933, S. 144.

1950

J8.   *Ausgewählte Erzählungen.* Frankfurt a.M.: S. Fischer, 591 S. (Gesammelte Werke in Einzelbänden). [Sterben. Blumen. Ein Abschied. Die Frau des Weisen. Die Toten schweigen. Der letzte Brief eines Literaten. Andreas Thameyers letzter Brief. Der blinde Geronimo und sein Bruder. Leutnant Gustl. Die griechische Tänzerin. Das Schicksal des Freiherrn von Leisenbohg. Die Fremde. Der Tod des Junggesellen. Das Tagebuch der Redegonda. Der Mörder. Die dreifache Warnung. Die Hirtenflöte. Die Frau des Richters. Spiel im Morgengrauen. Casanovas Heimfahrt. Fräulein Else. – "Druck: Carl Überreuter in Wien."]

1955

J9.   *Meisterdramen.* Frankfurt a.M.: S. Fischer, 604 S. [Anatol. Liebelei. Der grüne Kakadu. Lebendige Stunden. Literatur. Der einsame Weg. Das weite Land. Professor Bernhardi. Reigen. Anatols Grössenwahn. – "Gesamtherstellung: W. Büxenstein GmbH., Berlin."]

1961

J10.   *Die erzählenden Schriften.* Frankfurt a.M.: S. Fischer, 2 Bde., 1013 S., 997 S. (Gesammelte Werke). [Bd. I: Welch eine Melodie. Er wartet auf den vazierenden Gott. Amerika. Erbschaft. Der Fürst ist im Hause. Mein Freund Ypsilon. Der Andere. Reichtum. Die drei Elixire. Die Braut. Der Sohn. Sterben. Die kleine Komödie. Komödiantinnen: Helene, Fritzi. Blumen. Der Witwer. Ein Abschied. Der Empfindsame. Die Frau des Weisen. Der Ehrentag. Die Toten schweigen. Um eine Stunde. Die Nächste. Leutnant Gustl. Der blinde Geronimo und sein Bruder. Frau Berta Garlan. Andreas Thameyers letzter Brief. Wohltaten, still und rein gegeben. Ein Erfolg. Legende. Boxeraufstand. Die grüne Krawatte. Die Fremde. Exzentrik. Die griechische Tänzerin. Das Schicksal des Freiherrn von Leisenbohg. Die Weissagung. Das neue Lied. Der Weg ins Freie. Geschichte eines Genies. Der Tod des Junggesellen. Der tote Gabriel. Das Tagebuch der Redegonda. Der Mörder. – Bd. II: Die dreifache Warnung. Die Hirtenflöte. Frau Beate und ihr Sohn. Doktor Gräsler, Badearzt. Der letzte Brief eines Literaten. Casanovas Heimfahrt. Fräulein Else. Die Frau des Richters. Traumnovelle. Spiel in Morgengrauen. Abenteuernovelle. Therese. Der Sekundant. Flucht in die Finsternis. (Nachwort, Bibliographisches Verzeichnis). – "Gesamtherstellung: Friedrich Pustet in Regensburg. Gedruckt auf Persia Dünndruck der Papierfabrik Schoeller & Hoesch in Gernsbach/Baden. Typographie und Ausstattung, Hermann Zapf, Frankfurt am Main."]

CRITICISM

J10X.1   Binger, Norman H. *JIASRA*, 1, iv/v, Autumn/Winter, 1962, p. 17-18.
J10X.2   Kreuzer, Helmut. *Germanistik*, 3, iii, Juli 1962, S. 463.
J10X.3   Beharriell, Frederick J. *German Quarterly*, 37, ii, 1964, p. 170-172.
See Also: x387.

1962

J11.   *Die dramatischen Werke.* Frankfurt a.M.: S. Fischer, 2 Bde., 1080 S., 1045 S. (Gesammelte Werke). [Bd. I: Alkandi's Lied. Anatol. Anatols Grössenwahn. Das Märchen. Die überspannte Person. Halbzwei. Liebelei. Freiwild. Reigen. Das Vermächtnis. Paracelsus. Die Gefährtin. Der grüne Kakadu. Der Schleier der Beatrice. Sylvesternacht. Lebendige Stunden. Die Frau mit dem Dolche. Die letzten Masken. Literatur. Der einsame Weg. Der Puppenspieler. Der tapfere Cassian. Zum grossen Wurstel. Zwischenspiel. Der Ruf des Lebens. Komtesse Mizzi oder Der Familientag. Die Verwandlung des Pierrot. – Bd. II: Der tapfere Kassian (Singspiel). Der junge Medardus. Das weite Land. Der Schleier der Pierrette. Professor Bernhardi. Stunde des Erkennens. Grosse Szene. Das Bacchusfest. Fink und Fliederbusch. Die Schwestern oder Casanova in Spa. Der Gang zum Weiher. Komödie der Verführung. Im Spiel der Sommerlüfte. (Nachwort und bibliographisches Verzeichnis mit Uraufführungsdaten). – "Gesamtherstellung" as in #J10.]

See Also: x387.

PART K: ANTHOLOGIES – GERMAN

1898

K1.   *Die Frau des Weisen: Novelletten.* Berlin: S. Fischer, 171 S. [Die Frau des Weisen.
       Ein Abschied. Der Ehrentag. Blumen. Die Toten schweigen. – Auflagen:
       1. – 2.   1898
       3.   1902
       5. – 6.   1906
       9.   1922 (Text of #J3, S. 118-219)
       10. – 11. 1926]

CRITICISM

K1X.1   Anon. *Velhagen & Klasings Monatshefte,* 2, 1898, S. 11.
K1X.2   Blum, Walther. W. *Zeit und Geist,* 2, xi, 1898, S. 377-380.
K1X.3   Eloesser, Arthur. *Neue Deutsche Rundschau,* 9, viii, Aug. 1898, S. 818-819.
K1X.4   Fred, W. *Magazin für Litteratur,* 67, xxxiii, 20. Aug. 1898, Sp. 775-776.
K1X.5   Geiger, Albert. *Die Nation,* 16, viii, 19. Nov. 1898, S. 112-113.
K1X.6   Lothar, Rudolf. *Die Wage,* 1, 1898, S. 39-40.
K1X.7   Ubell, Hermann. *Die Zeit* (Wien), 17, ccxi, 15. Okt. 1898, S. 41-42.

1899

K2.   *Der grüne Kakadu. Paracelsus. Die Gefährtin. Drei Einakter.* Berlin: S. Fischer,
       178 S. (Werke von Arthur Schnitzler). ["Druck von A. Seydel & Cie., G.m.b.H.,
       Berlin S.W." Auflagen:
       1. – 2.   1899
       3.   1900
       4.   1905
       5.   1908
       6. – 7.   1911
       8.   1918
       9. – 11.   1922]

CRITICISM

K2X.1   Anon. *Die Fackel,* Nr. 1, Anfang Apr. 1899, S. 24-25.
K2X.2   Anon. *Die Gegenwart,* 28 (Bd. 55), xviii, 6. Mai 1899, S. 287.
K2X.3   Anon. *Der Kunstwart,* 12, xvii, 1. Juniheft, 1899, S. 163-164.
K2X.4   Burckhard, Max. *Die Zeit* (Wien), 17, xxiii, 1899, S. 140-141.
K2X.5   Hirschfeld, Leo. "Schnitzlers Einakter-Abend." *Dramaturgische Blätter,* 2, xi,
         18. März 1899, Sp. 85-87.
K2X.6   Jellinek, Arthur L. *Das Literarische Echo,* 1, xiii, 1. Apr. 1899, Sp. 862-863.

K2x.7	Lothar, Rudolf. *Die Wage*, 2, 1899, S. 162-163.
K2x.8	Lublinski, S. *Das Literarische Echo*, 2, iv, 15. Nov. 1899, Sp. 227.
K2x.9	Steiner, Rudolf. *Magazin für Litteratur*, 68, xviii, 6. Mai 1899, Sp. 425-427.
K2x.10	Wilhelm, Paul. *Die Gesellschaft*, 15 (Bd. 2), v, 1899, S. 336-339.
K2x.11	Zieler, Gustav. *Das Literarische Echo*, 1, xvii, 1. Juni 1899, Sp. 1114.

1902

K3. *Lebendige Stunden: Vier Einakter.* Berlin: S. Fischer, 159 S. [Lebendige Stunden. Die Frau mit dem Dolche. Die letzten Masken. Literatur. – Auflagen:

    1. – 4.   1902
    5.   1903
    6.   1906
    7.   1909
    8. – 9.   1912
    10. – 12.   1922]

CRITICISM

K3x.1	Anon. *Die Gegenwart*, 31 (Bd. 61), ii, 11. Jan. 1902, S. 30.
K3x.2	Burckhard, Max. *Die Zeit* (Wien), 31, cccxcvii, 10. Mai 1902, S. 90-91.
K3x.3	Franzos, Karl Emil. *Deutsche Dichtung*, 32, i, Apr. 1902, S. 47-56.
K3x.4	Frenzel, Karl. *Deutsche Rundschau*, 28 (Bd. 111), viii, Mai 1902, S. 300.
K3x.5	Harden, Maximilan. *Die Zukunft*, 38, 29. März 1902, S. 535-540.
K3x.6	Heilborn, Ernst. *Die Nation*, 19, xv, 11. Jan. 1902, S. 237-238.
K3x.7	Kalkschmidt, Erich. *Der Kunstwart*, 15, viii, 2. Jan.-heft, 1902, S. 395-396.
K3x.8	Kerr, Alfred. *Neue Deutsche Rundschau*, 13, v, 1902, S. 551-553.
K3x.9	Lorenz, Max. *Preussische Jahrbücher*, 107, ii, Feb. 1902, S. 373-376.
K3x.10	Martersteig, Max. *Deutsche Monatsschrift*, 1, iv, Jan. 1902, S. 790-791.
K3x.11	Poppenberg, Felix. "Schicksalsminaturen." *Der Türmer*, 4, v, Feb. 1902, S. 555-561.
K3x.12	Stümcke, Heinrich. *Bühne und Welt*, 4-1, viii, Jan. 1902, S. 346-347.
K3x.13	Zieler, Gustav. *Das Literarische Echo*, 4, ix, Feb. 1902, Sp. 631-633.
K3x.14	Bahr, Hermann. *Rezensionen: Wiener Theater 1901 bis 1903.* Berlin: S. Fischer, 1903, S. 252-268; 390-396. [Two separate reviews.]
K3x.15	Detleff, Ernst. *Der Kunstwart*, 17, ii, 2. Okt.-heft, 1903, S. 100.

See Also: X17.

1905

K4. *Die griechische Tänzerin: Novellen.* Wien & Leipzig: Wiener Verlag, 131 S. (Bibliothek moderner deutscher Autoren, Bd. I), [Der blinde Geronimo und sein Bruder. Andreas Thameyers letzter Brief. Exzentrik. Die griechische Tänzerin. – "Umschlag von J. Engelhart." Auflagen:

    1.   1905
    2.   "Neue Auflage" 1907 (Without "Andreas Thameyers letzter Brief.")]

CRITICISM

| K4x.1 | Busse, C. *Velhagen & Klasings Monatshefte*, Apr. 1905, S. 225. |
| K4x.2 | Ubell, Hermann. *Das Literarische Echo*, 8, i, 1. Okt. 1905, Sp. 12-13. |

1906

K5. *Marionetten: Drei Einakter.* Berlin: S. Fischer, 148 S. [Der Puppenspieler.

Der tapfere Cassian. Zum grossen Wurstel. – "Buchdruckerei Roitzsch,
G.m.b.H., Roitzsch." Auflagen:
1.–2. 1906
3.   1911
4.   1922 (Text of #J4, Bd. III, S. 191-267)]

CRITICISM

K5x.1   Handl, Willi. *Die Schaubühne*, 2-1, xxi, 24. Mai 1906, S. 609-613.
K5x.2   Friedemann, H. "Schattenspiele." *Ost und West*, 6, 1907, S. 112.

1907

K6.   *Dämmerseelen: Novellen*. Berlin: S. Fischer, 132 S. [Das Schicksal des Freiherrn
von Leisenbohg. Die Weissagung. Das neue Lied. Die Fremde. Andreas
Thameyers letzter Brief. – "Von diesem Buch sind 25 Exemplare auf hand-
geschöpftem Büttenpapier abgezogen, numeriert und in Ganzleder gebunden.
Sie sind zum Preise von 10 Mark für das Exemplar direkt vom Verlage zu
beziehen." Auflagen:
1.–10. 1907
12.   1911
13.   1918
14.–15. 1920
16.–18. 1922]

CRITICISM

K6x.1   Anon. *Der Kunstwart*, 21, Nov. 1907, S. 181.
K6x.2   Anon. *Velhagen & Klasings Monatshefte*, 22, Juni 1907, S. 489.
K6x.3   Presber, Rudolf. *Das Literarische Echo*, 10, i, 1. Okt. 1907, Sp. 56-57.
K6x.4   Stössl, Otto. *Österreichische Rundschau*, 13, ii, 2. Okt.-Heft, 1907, S. 147-148.
K6x.5   Wassermann, Jakob. *Neue Rundschau*, 18-2, vii, Juli 1907, S. 889-890.

1912

K7.   *Masken und Wunder: Novellen*. Berlin: Fischer, 190 S. [Die Hirtenflöte. Der
Tod des Junggesellen. Der Mörder. Der tote Gabriel. Das Tagebuch der
Redegonda. Die dreifache Warnung. – "Entwurf des Umschlags von Erich
Mende. Druck der Spamerschen Buchdruckerei." Auflagen:
1.–10. 1912
13.–14. 1917
15.–16. 1920
17.–18. 1922]

CRITICISM

K7x.1   Anon. *Velhagen & Klasings Monatshefte*, 26, Juli 1912, S. 472.
K7x.2   Heilborn, Ernst. *Das Literarische Echo*, 14, xxiv, 15. Sept. 1912, Sp. 1737-1738.
K7x.3   Poppenberg, Felix. *Neue Rundschau*, 1912 (Bd. 2), S. 1320.
K7x.4   Ratislav. Josef Karl. *Die Quelle*, 5. Sept. 1912.
K7x.5   Stadler, Ernst. *Die Aktion*, 2, xxvii, 3. Juli 1912, Sp. 844-846.

1914

K8.   *Die griechische Tänzerin und andere Novellen*. Berlin: S. Fischer, 177 S. (Fischers
Bibliothek zeitgenössischer Romane, 6. Reihe, Band I). [Der blinde Geronimo

und sein Bruder. Die Toten schweigen. Die Weissagung. Das neue Lied. Die griechische Tänzerin. – "Druck der Spamerschen Buchdruckerei in Leipzig." Auflagen:

   1.   1914
   56. – 61. 1921 (without series title)
   62. – 65. 1924]

1915

K9.   *Komödie der Worte: Drei Einakter.* Berlin: S. Fischer, 193 S. [Stunde des Erkennens. Grosse Szene. Das Bacchusfest. – "Druck der Spamerschen Buchdruckerei in Leipzig." Auflagen:

   1. – 6. 1915
   7.   1918
   8. – 9. 1922 (Text of #J4, Bd. V, S. 169-279)]

CRITICISM

K9x.1   Seefeld, Carl. *Schöne Literatur*, 16, xxiii, 6. Nov. 1915, Sp. 316-319.
K9x.2   Weilen, Alexander von. *Das Literarische Echo*, 18, iv, 15. Nov. 1915, Sp. 230-233.
K9x.3   Kienzl, Hermann. *Der Türmer*, 18, viii, 2. Jan.-Heft, 1916, S. 553-554.
K9x.4   Eloesser, Arthur. *Das Blaue Heft*, 5, ix, 1. Juni 1924, S. 63-65.
K9x.5   Jacobsohn, Siegfried. *Die Weltbühne*, 20, xx, 15. Mai 1924, S. 665-667.
K9x.6   Marcel, Gabriel. "Le spectacle du Studio allemand de Paris." *L'Europe nouvelle*, 14, dcxcviii, 27 juin 1931, p. 887-888.

1924

K10.   *Die dreifache Warnung: Novellen.* Mit einem Nachwort von Oswald Brüll. Leipzig: Phillip Reclam jun., 74 S. (Universal-Bibliothek, Nr. 6458). [Die Frau des Weisens. Die dreifache Warnung. Der blinde Geronimo und sein Bruder. – "Druck von Philipp Reclam jun., Leipzig. Auf holzfreies Papier gedruckt." Repr., 1948, 69 S.]

1931

K11.   *Traum und Schicksal: Sieben Novellen.* Berlin: S. Fischer, 448 S. [Traumnovelle. Spiel im Morgengrauen. Frau Beate und ihr Sohn. Der blinde Geronimo und sein Bruder. Die Hirtenflöte. Die Fremde. Das Schicksal des Freiherrn von Leisenbohg. – "Einband und Schutzumschlag von Georg Salter. Druck: Bibliographisches Institut AG, Leipzig." Auflagen:

   1. – 50. 1931
   61. – 70. 1932]

See Also: x233.

1939

K12.   *Flucht in die Finsternis und andere Erzählungen.* Forum deutscher Dichter. Gemeinschaftsproduction der Verlage Bermann-Fischer, Stockholm; Allert de Lange, Amsterdam; Querido, Amsterdam, 350 S. (Forum Bücher). [Spiel im

Morgengrauen. Traumnovelle. Flucht in die Finsternis. – "Druck: N.V. Drukkerij G. J. Thieme, Nijmegen (Holland)."]

1948

K13.   *Traumnovelle. Flucht in die Finsternis. Zwei Novellen.* Amsterdam: Bermann-Fischer/Querido Verlag N.V., 226 S. (Bermann-Fischer Roman-Bibliothek). ["Druck: Holdert & Co. N.V., Amsterdam. Einband: Fa. J. Brandt & Zoon, Amsterdam. Schutzumschlag: Fritz Neugebauer."]

1959

K14.   *Grosse Szene.* Eingeleitet und ausgewählt von Herbert Foltinek. Graz & Wien: Stiasny, 128 S. (Stiasny-Bücherei, Bd. 53). [Die Fremde. Der Ehrentag. Grosse Szene. Aphorismen (fr. ♯D1. and ♯D3.). Mein Kritiker. (Lebenstafel, Bibliographie). – "Umschlagentwurf von Liselotte Bayer-Schindler. Druck: Heinrich Stiasny's Söhne, Graz."]

1960

K15.   *Liebelei. Reigen.* Mit einem Nachwort von Richard Alewyn. Frankfurt a.m. & Hamburg: Fischer Bücherei, 160 S. (Fischer Bücherei, Bd. 361). ["Umschlagentwurf: Gerhard M. Hotop. Gesamtherstellung: Hanseatische Druckanstalt G.m.b.H., Hamburg-Wandsbek."]

1965

K16.   *Erzählungen.* Frankfurt a.M.: Suhrkamp, 221 S. (Bd. 149 der Bibliothek Suhrkamp). [Der Andere. Sterben. Der blinde Geronimo und sein Bruder. Fräulein Else. – "Satz und Druck in Linotype Garamond von Buchdruckerei Georg Wagner, Nördlingen. Bindearbeiten Hanz Klotz, Augsburg." 1. – 5. Tsd.]

K17.   *Spiel im Morgengrauen und acht andere Erzählungen.* Auswahl und Einleitung von Hans Weigel. Reproduktionen nach Zeichnungen von Gustav Klimt. Zürich: Diogenes, 438 S. (Diogenes Erzähler Bibliothek). [(Vorwort). Der Sohn. Der Witwer. Der Ehrentag. Die Toten schweigen. Leutnant Gustl. Die Fremde. Das Tagebuch der Redegonda. Spiel in Morgengrauen. Der Sekundant. – "Druck Benziger & Co. AG. Einband W. Eibert." Twelve sketches by Klimt.]

PART L: ANTHOLOGIES – ENGLISH

1913

L1. *The Green Cockatoo and Other Plays.* Translated into English by Horace B. Samuel. Chicago: A. C. McClurg, ix, 124 p. [(Introduction). "The Green Cockatoo: A Grotesque in One Act" (Der grüne Kakadu). "The Mate: A Play in One Act" (Die Gefährtin). "Paracelsus: A Play in Verse in One Act." – "Printed by Hazell, Watson & Viney, Ltd., London & Aylesbury, Eng." – Also: London & Edinburgh: Gay & Hancock.]

CRITICISM

L1X.1 Anon. *The Athenaeum*, No. 4466, May 31, 1913, p. 599.

L2. *Living Hours: Four One-Act Plays.* Boston: Badger. (Vienna Edition). [P. H. Grummann, tr. – "Living Hours" (Lebendige Stunden). "The Lady with the Dagger" (Die Frau mit dem Dolche). "Last Masks" (Die letzten Masken). "Literature" (Literatur).]

L3. *Viennese Idylls.* Boston: John W. Luce, ix, 182 p. [Frederick Eisemann, tr. – (Introduction). "Flowers" (Blumen). "The Sage's Wife" (Die Frau des Weisen). "Blind Geronimo and His Brother" (Der blinde Geronimo und sein Bruder). "Andreas Thameyer's Last Letter" (Andreas Thameyers letzter Brief). "The Farewell" (Ein Abschied). "The Dead Are Silent" (Die Toten schweigen).]

1915

L4. *The Lonely Way. Intermezzo. Countess Mizzie. Three Plays.* Translated from the German with an Introduction by Edwin Björkman. New York: Mitchell Kennerley, xliii, 323 p. (The Modern Drama Series). [(Introduction, Preface to Anatol by Hugo von Hofmannsthal. Chronological List of Plays and First Performances). "The Lonely Way: A Drama in Five Acts" (Der einsame Weg). "Intermezzo: A Comedy in Three Acts" (Zwischenspiel). "Countess Mizzie or the Family Renion" (Komtesse Mizzie oder der Familientag). – Also: Boston: Little, Brown, 1922.]

CRITICISM

L4X.1 Anon. "A Great Austrian Dramatist." *American Review of Reviews*, 52, ii, Aug., 1915, p. 243-244.
L4X.2 Soule, George. "Ironies." *New Republic*, 4, No. 50, Oct. 16, 1915, p. 290.
L4X.3 Towse, J. Ranken. "Modern Vienna: Three Plays." *The Nation*, 101, No. 2632, Oct. 7, 1915, p. 442-443.

L5. *Anatol. Living Hours. The Green Cockatoo.* Translated by Grace Isabel Colbron. Introduction by Ashley Dukes. New York: Boni & Liveright, xiii, 226 p. (The Modern Library of the World's Best Books, No. 32). [(Introduction, Introduction to Anatol by Hugo von Hofmannsthal). "Anatol." "Living Hours" (Lebendige Stunden). "The Lady with the Dagger" (Die Frau mit dem Dolche). "Last Masks: A Drama (Die letzten Masken). "Literature: A Comedy" (Literatur). "The Green Cockatoo: Grotesquery in One Act" (Der grüne Kakadu). – Also: New York: The Modern Library, 1925.]

CRITICISM

L5x.1 Anon. *New York Times Book Review*, March 3, 1918, p. 88.

L6. *Comedies of Words and Other Plays.* Englished from the German with an Introduction by Pierre Loving. Cincinnati: Stewart & Kidd, xxx, 182 p. [(Introduction). "The Hour of Recognition: A Comedy of Words" (Stunde des Erkennens). "The Big Scene: A Play in One Act" (Grosse Szene). "The Festival of Bacchus: A Comedy of Words" (Das Bacchusfest). "Literature: A Play in One Act." (Literatur). "His Helpmate" (Die Gefährtin). – Printings:
1. – 2. 1917
3. 1923]

CRITICISM

L6x.1 Anon. "Books and Things." *New Republic*, 11, cxli, July 14, 1917, p. 308. [Signed "P. L."]
L6x.2 Anon. *American Review of Reviews*, 56, iv, Oct., 1917, p. 444.
L6x.3 Anon. "Schnitzler's Experiments." *The Nation*, 105, No. 2722, Aug. 30, 1917, p. 225-226.
L6x.4 Haynes, Williams. "The Dramatist of Psycho-Analysis." *The Dial*, 63, dccxlvi, July 19, 1917, p. 63-64.

1922

L7. *The Shepherd's Pipe and Other Stories.* Authorized Translation from the German by O. F. Theis. New York: Nicholas L. Brown, 169 p. (The Sea Gull Library, Vol. 3). [(Introduction). "The Shepherd's Pipe" (Die Hirtenflöte). "The Murderer" (Der Mörder). "The Blind Geronimo and His Brother" (Der blinde Geronimo und sein Bruder). – Later edition: New York: Frank-Maurice.]

1926

L8. *Beatrice and Other Stories.* London: T. Werner Laurie, vii, 247 p. [Agnes Jacques and Elsie M. Lang, trs. – "Beatrice" (Frau Beate und ihr Sohn). "Flowers" (Blumen). "A Farewell" (Ein Abschied). "The Wife of the Wise Man" (Die Frau des Weisen). "The Hour of Fame" (Der Ehrentag). "The Dead Are Silent" (Die Toten schweigen). (The first tr. by Jacques, the rest by Lang). – Repr. in 1930.]

CRITICISM

L8x.1 Lloyd, J. A. T. *Fortnightly Review*, 128, dccxxix, Sept. 1, 1927, p. 431.

L9.   *Little Novels*. Translated from the German by Eric Sutton. New York: Simon & Schuster, 279 p. ["The Fate of the Baron" (Das Schicksal des Freiherrn von Leisenbohg). "The Stranger" (Die Fremde). "The Greek Dancing-Girl" (Die griechische Tänzerin). "The Prophecy" (Die Weissagung). "Blind Geronimo and His Brother" (Der blinde Geronimo und sein Bruder). "Andreas Thameyer's Last Letter" (Andreas Thameyers letzter Brief). "Redegonda's Diary" (Das Tagebuch der Redegonda). "Dead Gabriel" (Der tote Gabriel). "The Murderer" (Der Mörder). "The Death of a Bachelor" (Der Tod des Junggesellen). – Also: London: Constable, 1932, 216 p.]

CRITICISM

L9X.1   Anon. *The Bookman* (New York), 70, i, Sept., 1929, p. xiv.
L9X.2   Anon. *New Republic*, 61, dcclxxxiv, Dec. 11, 1929, p. 76. [Signed "H. G."]
L9X.3   Anon. *New Statesman*, 33, dccclvi, Sept. 21, 1929, p. 712-713. [Signed "E. S."]
L9X.4   Anon. *Times Literary Supplement*, No. 1437, Aug. 15, 1929, p. 635.
L9X.5   Shirley, Mary. *Outlook and Independent*, 153, i, Sept. 4, 1929, p. 28-29.
L9X.6   Endore, S. Guy. "The Uses of Melodrama." *Menorah Journal*, 18, ii, Feb., 1930, p. 193-194.

L10.   *Viennese Novelettes*. With Illustrations by Kurt Wiese. New York: Simon & Schuster, xlv, 433 p. [(Introduction by Otto P. Schinnerer). "Daybreak" (Spiel im Morgengrauen, William A. Drake, tr.). "Fräulein Else" (Robert A. Simon, tr.). "Rhapsody" (Traumnovelle, Otto P. Schinnerer, tr.). "Beatrice" (Frau Beate und ihr Sohn, Agnes Jacques, tr.). "None but the Brave" (Leutnant Gustl, Richard L. Simon, tr.).]

L11.   *Reigen, The Affairs of Anatol and Other Plays*. Translated by Marya Mannes and Grace Isabel Colbron. Introduction by Ashley Dukes. New York: The Modern Library, xv, 301 p. (The Modern Library of the World's Best Books). [(Introduction, Introduction to Anatol by Hugo von Hofmannsthal). "Reigen (Hands Around): Ten Dialogues." "The Affairs of Anatol." "Living Hours" (Lebendige Stunden). "The Lady with the Dagger: A Drama" (Die Frau mit dem Dolche). "Last Masks: A Drama" (Die letzten Masken). "Literature: A Comedy" (Literatur). "The Green Cockatoo: Grotesquery in One Act." (Der grüne Kakadu). (The first translated by Mannes, the rest by Colbron).]

PART M: ANTHOLOGIES – FRENCH

1913

M1.   *Anatole, suivi de La Compagne.* Traductions de Maurice Rémon et Maurice Vaucaire. Paris: P. V. Stock, 275 p. (Bibliothèque cosmopolite, no. 60). ["Anatole" (Anatol, Rémon, tr.). "La Compagne" (Die Gefährtin, Vaucaire, tr.).]

CRITICISM

M1X.1   Praviei, Armand. *Polybiblion*, 128 (2⁰ sér., t. 78), 1913, p. 130-131.

1929

M2.   *La pénombre des âmes.* Nouvelles traduites de l'allemand par Suzanne Clauser. Paris: Stock (Delemain et Boutelleau), 250 p. (Le cabinet cosmopolite, no. 41). [(Préface par Félix Bertaux). "Le destin du baron de Leisenbohg" (Das Schicksal des Freiherrn von Leisenbohg). "Fleurs" (Blumen). "Géronimo l'aveugle et son frère" (Der blinde Geronimo und sein Bruder). "Le journal de Radegonde" (Das Tagebuch der Redegonda). "La mort du vieux garçon" (Der Tod des Junggesellen). "L'assassin" (Der Mörder). "L'ombre de Gabriel" (Der tote Gabriel). "L'apothéose" (Der Ehrentag). "La femme d'un sage" (Die Frau des Weisen). "Les morts se taisent" (Die Toten schweigen).]

CRITICISM

M2X.1   Buenzod, E. *Bibliothèque universelle et Revue de Genève*, 1930-1, p. 390.
M2X.2   Ségur, N. *Revue mondiale*, 196/197, 1930, p. 84-89.

1932

M3.   *L'Appel des ténèbres, suivi de la Flûte du pâtre et de le Lieutenant Gustel.* Paris: Stock, Delemain et Boutelleau, xii, 209 p. (Le cabinet cosmopolite, no. 64). [Suzanne Clauser, tr. – (Préface par Paul Géraldy). "L'appel des ténèbres" (Flucht in die Finsternis). "La flûte de pâtre" (Die Hirtenflöte). "Le Lieutenant Gustel" (Leutnant Gustl).]

CRITICISM

M3X.1   Cahuet, A. *L'Illustration*, 184, 1932, p. 124.

M4.   *Mademoiselle Else, suivie de plusiers nouvelles traduites de l'allemand.* Paris: Librairie Stock (Delamain et Boutelleau), 251 p. (Le roman cosmopolite). ["Mademoiselle Else" (Fräulein Else). "Le destin du baron de Leisenbohg" (Das Schicksal des

97

Freiherrn von Leisenbohg). "Fleurs" (Blumen). "Géronimo l'aveugle et son frère" (Der blinde Geronimo und sein Bruder). "L'assassin" (Der Mörder). "L'apothéose" (Der Ehrentag). "Les morts se taisent" (Die Toten schweigen). (The first translated by Clara Pollaczek, the rest by Suzanne Clauser).]

1953

M5.   *Les dernières cartes*. Traduit de l'allemand par Dominique Auclères. Paris: Calmann-Lévy, 279 p. (Collection "Traduit de"). ["Les dernières cartes" (Spiel im Morgengrauen). (Traumnovelle).]

PART S: SCHOOL EDITIONS

1928

S1. *Der grüne Kakadu. Literatur. Die letzten Masken.* Edited with an Introduction, Notes, and Vocabulary by Otto P. Schinnerer. New York: Alfred A. Knopf, xiv, 169 p. (Borzoi German Texts). [Facsimile letter from AS to Schinnerer on p. v. – Also: New York: F. S. Crofts, 1930; New York: Appleton-Century-Crofts, 1956.]

CRITICISM

S1X.1 Kurath, William. *German Quarterly*, 2, i, Jan., 1929, p. 26.
S1X.2 Vos, B. J. *Monatshefte der deutschen Freunde*, 21, 1930, p. 86.

1929

S2. *Zwei Tiroler Novellen.* i. Der blinde Geronimo und sein Bruder. ii. Die Weissagung. Edited with Questions, Notes, Exercises and Reproductions by A. S. Macpherson. London: G. Bell, viii, 177 p. (Bell's Modern Language Texts). [Revised edition, 1931. Repr., 1936.]

1930

S3. *Stories and Plays.* Edited with Introduction, Notes, and Vocabulary by Allen W. Porterfield. Boston: D. C. Heath, xxix, 306 p. (Heath's Modern Language Series). [Introduction]. Der blinde Geronimo und sein Bruder. Der Ehrentag. Die Weissagung. Blumen. Leutnant Gustl. Der Puppenspieler. Grosse Szene. – Also: London: George G. Harrap, 1934.]

CRITICISM

S3X.1 Schroetter, Erich von. *Modern Language Journal*, 15, vi, March, 1931, p. 468-472.

1956

S4. *Der blinde Geronimo und sein Bruder. Die Hirtenflöte. Zwei Erzählungen.* Nachwort von Fritz Martini. Berlin & Frankfurt a.M.: S. Fischer, 80 S. (S. Fischer Schulausgaben Moderner Autoren). ["Druck: Hanseatische Druckanstalt GmbH, Hamburg." 1. – 10. Tsd.]

55.   *Drei Szenen aus Anatol und zwei Erzählungen.* Selected and Edited by Harlan
      P. Hanson. New York: W. W. Norton, viii, 86 p. (General Editor: Jack Stein).
      [(Introduction). Die Frage an das Schicksal. Episode. Abschiedssouper. Die
      Fremde. Die dreifache Warnung.]

See also: B6.4, B7.9, B10.3, B14.9, B17.13, B17.17, B17.19, B17.23, B18.6, B18.11, B18.14,
      B32.9, B35.7, C4.14, C4.15, C4.16, C4.18a, C5.8, C8.2, C11.9, C14.6, C20.8, C20.10,
      D1.2.

PART X: GENERAL CRITICISM ON SCHNITZLER

1894

X1.   Bahr, Hermann. *Studien zur Kritik der Moderne.* Frankfurt a.M.: Literarische Anstalt (Rütten & Loening), S. 82-83. [Fr. "Das junge Österreich." Not what AS says, but how he says it is important.]

1896

X2.   Heubaum, A. "Zwei Dramen von Arthur Schnitzler." *Die Wahrheit,* 7, lxxvii, 1. Dez., S. 155-157. [Negative reviews of "Freiwild" and "Liebelei."]

X3.   Kerr, Alfred. "Arthur Schnitzler." *Neue Deutsche Rundschau,* 7, iii, März, S. 287-292. [Enthusiastic praise for "Anatol." – Repr. in *Die Welt im Drama.* Berlin, S. Fischer, 1917, Bd. I: "Das Neue Drama," S. 119-127.]

X4.   Reichmann, A. "Arthur Schnitzler." *Internationale Literaturberichte,* 3, S. 164.

1897

X5.   Schaeffer, Emil. "Arthur Schnitzler: eine Studie." *Die Gesellschaft,* 13-2, iv, Apr., S. 22-33. [AS understands the stage; never offends or compromises.]

X6.   Stoessl, Otto. *Neue Deutsche Rundschau,* 8, ii, S. 205. [Fr. "Ein Wiener Brief."]

1898

X7.   Benzmann, Hans. "Arthur Schnitzler." *Nord und Süd,* 86, cclvii, Aug., S. 177-191. [AS most talented of the young Austrian dramatists; his sphere is limited, but well-controlled. "Liebelei" without flaw.]

X8.   Fuchs, O. *Die Wage,* 1, S. 120-121.

X9.   Necker, Moritz. *Deutsche Litteraturzeitung,* 19, xvii, 30. Apr., Sp. 681-683. [Revs. of "Anatol" and "Freiwild."]

1899

X10.   Bahr, Hermann. "Zehn Jahre." *Die Zeit,* 20, S. 91-92.

X11.   Speidel, S. "Arthur Schnitzler." *Das Neue Jahrhundert,* 5. März.

1900

X12.   Sieven, Paul. "Arthur Schnitzler." *Das Neue Jahrhundert,* 3, v.

x13.   Ettlinger, Joseph. *Das Literarische Echo*, 3, xxi, Aug., Sp. 1500-1501. [Rev. of "Frau Bertha Garlan" and "Leutnant Gustl."]

x14.   Koch, Max. "Neueste Dichtungen von Arthur Schnitzler." *Die Zeit*, 28, ccclxi, 31. Aug., S. 137-138. [Rev. of "Der Schleier der Beatrice," "Frau Bertha Garlan," and "Leutnant Gustl."]

x15.   Lorenz, Max. *Preussische Jahrbücher*, 105, i, Juli, S. 165-169. [Rev. of "Der Schleier der Beatrice," "Frau Bertha Garlan" and "Leutnant Gustl."]

x16.   Pollack, P. "Neue Belletristik." *Umschau*, 5, S. 911-913.

x17.   Kerr, Alfred. *Neue Deutsche Rundschau*, 13, v. S. 551-553. [Rev. of "Lebendige Stunden" (cycle) and "Der grüne Kakadu."]

x18.   Lothar, Rudolf. *Das Literarische Echo*, 4, viii, Jan., Sp. 514-515. [Fr. "Litteraturbilder aus deutschen Einzelgauen: Wien." Praise for AS's lyrical power and sensitivity.]

x19.   Schoeppl, Hugo. "Arthur Schnitzler: Eine literarische Portraitstudie." *Der Autor*, Nr. 8, Aug., S. 1-4.

x20.   Brandes, Georg Morris Cohen. "Arthur Schnitzler." *Gestalten und Gedanken: Essays*. München: Albert Langen, S. 35-40. [Special praise for "Die Toten schweigen" and "Der Schleier der Beatrice."]

x21.   Charmatz, Richard. "Wiener Literatur I: Arthur Schnitzler, Hugo von Hofmannsthal, E. E. delle Grazie." *Die Zeit* (Berlin), 2, xiv, 1. Jan., S. 436-440.

x22.   Halbert-Charlottenburg, A. "Schnitzlers Lebenskunst." *Magazin für Litteratur*, 72, 2. Dez.-H., S. 534-535. [Paraphrased aphorisms.]

x23.   Landsberg, Hans. *Arthur Schnitzler*. Berlin: Gose & Tetzlaff, 42 S. (Moderne Essays, Heft 33). [Primarily on the dramas. AS a psychological impressionist, whose real forte, in spite of his excellent dialogue technique, is the narrative. (!)]

x24.   Limé, Ernst. "Arthur Schnitzler." *Das Literarische Deutsch-Österreich*, 4, iv, Apr., S. 1-4 bis 5-4. [On AS's greatness, not discounting his failures.]

x25.   Stümcke, Heinrich. *Die vierte Wand: Theatralische Eindrücke und Studien*. Leipzig: Georg Wigand. [Section on AS.]

x26.   Anon. "Arthur Schnitzler, the Austrian Hauptmann." *Current Literature*, 39, v, Nov., p. 552.

x27.   Goldmann, Paul. *Aus dem dramatischen Irrgarten: Polemische Aufsätze über Berliner Theateraufführungen*. Frankfurt a.M.: Literarische Anstalt (Rütten & Loening), S. 109-124; 185-195. [On "Der Schleier der Beatrice" and "Der einsame Weg" respectively. Characters not sufficiently tragic and lacking in motivation.]

x28.   Herrmann, Helene. "Probleme in Arthur Schnitzlers Dichtungen." *Westermanns Monatshefte*, 97, dlxxxi, Feb., S. 686-694. [Ibsen influence, problems of the artist and reality, ethical-aesthetic approach.]

x29. Frenzel, Karl. *Deutsche Rundschau*, 32 (Bd. 127), viii, Mai, S. 299. [Fr. "Die Berliner Theater." Rev. of "Zwischenspiel" and "Der Ruf des Lebens."]

x30. Friedemann, H. "Schattenspiele: Noch ein Wort über Schnitzler." *Ost und West*, 6, xii, Dez., Sp. 815-816. [The *Jung Wien* school's feeling for the unreal.]

x31. Klemperer, Victor. "Arthur Schnitzler." *Ost und West*, 6, v/vi, Mai/Juni, Sp. 371-378. ["Der Schleier der Beatrice" AS's best. Subjective criticism.]

x32. Land, H. *Universum*, (Beilage: Weltrundschau), S. 159-161.

x33. Bahr, Hermann. *Glossen: Zum Wiener Theater (1903-06)*. Berlin: S. Fischer, S. 84-93; 196-202; 227-228; 440-449. [Revs. of "Zwischenspiel," "Freiwild," "Der grüne Kakadu" and "Der Puppenspieler" respectively.]

x34. Lothar, Rudolf. *Septett: Ein Leben in Liebesgeschichten*. Berlin-Charlottenburg: Vita, 201 S. [Novel dealing with AS.]

x35. Salkind, Alexander. *Arthur Schnitzler: Eine kritische Studie über seine hervorragendsten Werke*. Berlin-Leipzig: Modernes Verlagsbureau (Curt Wigand), 130 S. [Treats works appearing in book-form up to 1907. Brief, uneven synopses and criticism. Contemporary critics cited, individual characters discussed. AS a *konsequenter Naturalist* who unites lyricism with realism. Superficial, but suggestive of some useful literary problems.]

x36. Strobl, Karl Hans. "Arthur Schnitzler." *Das Literarische Echo*, 9, viii, 15. Jan., Sp. 576-587. [AS-themes and the recurrent *leichtsinniger Melancholiker*.]

x37. Stümcke, Heinrich. *Modernes Theater: Studien und Eindrücke*. Berlin: Deutsche Bücherei. [Section on AS.]

x38. Auernheimer, Raoul. "Der Umschwung." *Das Literarische Echo*, 10, x, 1. März, Sp. 778. [Repr. fr. *Neue Freie Presse*. AS and Gerhart Hauptmann.]

x39. Mamroth, Fedor. *Aus der Frankfurter Theaterchronik (1889-1907)*. Berlin: Egon Fleischel. Bd. I, S. 237-241; 247; 320-322; Bd. II, S. 192. [Revs. of "Liebelei," "Abschiedssouper," "Das Vermächtnis" and "Die letzten Masken" respectively.]

x40. Muret, Maurice. "Un Parisien de Vienne: M. Arthur Schnitzler." *Nouvelle Revue*, 3. Série, 4, 1er août, p. 339-354. [AS excels in psychological analysis; more French than German in spirit and grace.]

x41. Johnson, Fannie. "Arthur Schnitzler." *New Quarterly*, 2. viii, p. 587-597.

x42. Schmid, F. O. "A. Schnitzler und die Jung-Wiener Schule." *Berner Rundschau*, 4, iii, 15. Sept., S. 63-74.

x43. Tibal, André. "Arthur Schnitzler." *Revue de Paris*, 16-3, xii, 15. juin, p. 813-830. [AS's universe tragic, but always delicate and discreet.]

x44. Birnbaum, Martin. "Arthur Schnitzler." *The Bookman*, 30, v, Jan., p. 502-503. [Fr. "Some Contemporary German Tendencies."]

x45. Czinner, Paul. "Arthur Schnitzler." *Der Merker*, 2, v, 10. Dez., S. 203-209. [A masterful artist of mood; "Der junge Medardus" his best.]

x46. Samuel, Horace B. "Arthur Schnitzler." *Fortnightly Review*, 93, dxix, Mar. 1, p. 447-462. [AS successful writer of problem plays; his peculiar excellence the subordination of plot to atmosphere. Fails in "Der einsame Weg."]

1911

x47. Anon. "Arthur Schnitzler, Dramatist of the Twilight Soul." *Current Literature* 51, vi, Dec., p. 670-672.

x48. Bab, Julius. *Neue Wege zum Drama*. Berlin: Oesterheld, S. 69-71. [Repr. in *Die Chronik des deutschen Dramas*. Berlin: Oesterheld, 1922, Teil I: "1900-1906," S. 68-70. – AS lacking in passionate interest.]

x49. Carney, Felix Trent. *The Bookman*, 33, vi, Aug., p. 623-624. [Fr. "The Immortals of Yesterday and of Tomorrow."]

x50. Dukes, Ashley. "Arthur Schnitzler." *Modern Dramatists*. London: Frank Palmer, p. 151-159. [Also: Chicago: Charles H. Sergel, 1912, p. 151-159. – All of AS's dramas dependent upon a crisis in the lives of two people.]

x51. Feigl. Leo. *Arthur Schnitzler und Wien: Eine Studie*. Wien: Paul Knepler, 32 S. [Vienna traced through AS's works; "Der Weg ins Freie" his crowning achievement. Rambling survey.]

x52. Kerr. Alfred. *Neue Rundschau*, 22, xii, Dez., S. 1771-1775. [Fr. "Dramatiker." Rev. of "Der junge Medardus" and "Das weite Land."]

x53. Klemperer, Victor. "Arthur Schnitzler." *Bühne und Welt*, 13-1, ix, 1. Feb., S. 355-368. [Tragic traits in AS's character; his forte the *Menschendrama*, not the problem play. Basic dichotomy in his works: *Tatenmensch* and *Grübler*.]

x54. Klemperer, Victor. "Arthur Schnitzler." *Jahrbuch für jüdische Geschichte und Literatur*, 14, S. 139-208. [Comprehensive survey. AS always on both sides of every issue, unable to take a stand; as a *seltsamer Grübler* he is essentially Jewish. "Der Weg ins Freie" lacking in unity.]

x55. Menkes, Hermann. *Das Literarische Echo*, 13, vii, 1. Jan., Sp. 511. [Summary of an interview appearing in the *Neues Wiener Journal*, 1910.]

x56. Pollard, Percival. "Vienna's Essence: Schnitzler." *Masks and Minstrels of New Germany*. Boston: John W. Luce, p. 265- 283. [AS has a philandering mind, whose charm makes him morally dangerous.]

x57. Ratislav, Josef Karl. *Arthur Schnitzler: Eine Studie*. Hamburg: Verlagsgesellschaft Hamburg, 43 S. [Works divided into seven groups and treated accordingly. Ratislav hopes that AS will turn to comedy, the beginnings of which are already evident.]

1912

x58. Anon. *Nord und Süd*, 141, Juni, S. 396-399.

x59. Anon. *Velhagen & Klasings Monatshefte*, 26, Juli S. 471-472.

x60. Anon. "Der Schnitzler-Tag." *Bühne und Welt*, 14-2, xvii. [Signed "H. St." Birthday tribute.]

x61. Bab, Julius. "Arthur Schnitzler." *Die Gegenwart*, 41 (Bd. 81), xx, 18. Mai, S. 313-315.

x62. Bäumer, Gertrud. "Das Werk Arthur Schnitzlers." *Die Hilfe*, 18, xl.

x63. Bahr, Hermann. "Glückwunsch." *Der Merker*, 3, ix, Mai, S. 334-337. ["Werde, was du bist!"]

x64. Benn, Joachim. "Arthur Schnitzlers episches Werk." *Die Rheinlande*, 12, viii, S. 273-276. [Weakness of the earlier works, profundity of "Die Fremde" and "Der Weg ins Freie" and more recent falling off. Early attempt to trace AS's literary development.]

x65. Brandes, Georg. "Schnitzler-Medaillon." *Der Merker*, 3, ix, 1. Mai, S. 337.
x66. Dörmann, Felix. "An Arthur Schnitzler." *Der Merker*, 3, ix, 1. Mai, S. 337. [Poem.]
x67. Dünwald, Willi. "Der Spieler Paracelsus: Zu Schnitzler fünfzigstem Geburtstag." *Die Schaubühne*, 8-1, xx, 16. Mai, S. 553-558. [AS the reincarnation of his historical character.]
x68. Düsel, Friedrich. *Westermanns Monatshefte*, 112-2, dclxx, Juni, S. 624. [On AS's fiftieth birthday.]
x69. Frenzel, Karl. *Deutsche Rundschau*, 38 (Bd. 151), ix, Juni, S. 470-471. [Fr. "Die Berliner Theater." Rev. of "Das Weite Land" and "Komtesse Mizzie."]
x70. Gregori, Ferdinand. "Schnitzler und Hauptmann." *Der Merker*, 3, ix, 1. Mai S. 338-339. [They speak to everyone.]
x71. Grummann, Paul H. "Arthur Schnitzler." *Poet Lore*, 23, i, Jan./Feb., p. 25-41. [Plot summaries with questionable interpretations. AS should not be living in Vienna, but Germany, "a joy to any poet."]
x72. Henderson, Archibald. "Arthur Schnitzler." *North American Review*, 196, v, Nov., p. 635-645. [AS's spirit of melancholy reflection, his genius in the one-act play and his sympathy for *das süsse Mädel* (the real heroine of his dramas).]
x73. Hirschfeld, Georg. "Maitage." *Der Merker*, 3, ix, 1. Mai, S. 339-340.
x74. Kapp, Julius. *Arthur Schnitzler*. Leipzig: Xenien, 178 S. [Introductory section on AS and *Jung-Österreich*. Discussions of the individual works including some of the pre-"Anatol" writings, showing AS's development. Essentially laudatory, but points out weaknesses.]
x75. Kienzl, Hermann. "Arthur Schnitzler zu seinem 50. Geburtstag, 15. Mai 1912." *Das Theater*, 3, xviii, 11. Mai, S. 346-348.
x76. König, Otto. "Terzinen." *Der Merker*, 3, ix, 1. Mai, S. 340-341. [Poem.]
x77. Lessing, O. E. *Das Literarische Echo*, 15, iv, 15. Nov., Sp. 280-281. [Fr. "Amerikanischer Brief." Survey of a "Schnitzler-mode" in America.]
x78. Lothar, Ernst. "Der Führer." *Der Merker*, 3, ix, 1. Mai, S. 341-343. [AS's characters real people.]
x79. Lugné-Poe. "Une lettre." *Der Merker*, 3, ix, 1. Mai, S. 343. [Tribute.]
x80. Mann, Heinrich. "Der Romancier des Theaters." *Der Merker*, ix, 1. Mai, S. 343-344.
x81. Mann, Thomas. "Dank." *Der Merker*, 3, ix, 1. Mai, S. 344-345.
x82. Molo, Walter von. "Tagebuchblatt." *Der Merker*, 3, ix, 1. Mai, S. 345-346.
x83. Morgan, Bayard Quincy. "Arthur Schnitzler." *The Drama*, No. 7, Aug., p. 3-13. [Classes AS with the naturalists; his genius is the one-act play, his art not monumental enough for larger works.]
x84. Nowack, K. F. "Arthur Schnitzler: Zu seinem 50. Geburtstag." *Reclams Universum*, (Beilage: Weltrundschau), 28, S. 209-212.
x85. Ratislav, Josef Karl. "Arthur Schnitzler." *Heimgarten*, 37, iii, Dez., S. 195-200. [Survey of the works.]
x86. Reik, Theodor. "Arthur Schnitzler vor dem 'Anatol': Psychoanalytisches." *Pan*, 2, xxxii, 27. Juni, S. 899-905. ["Alkandis Lied" the most significant of these early works.]
x87. Reik, Theodor. "Der kleine Anti-Schnitzler." *Pan*, 2, S. 1118. [On Karl Kraus' attack on AS.]
x88. Rittner, Thaddäus. "Seelische Geographie." *Der Merker*, 3, ix, 1. Mai, S. 346.
x89. Salten, Felix. "Arthur Schnitzler." *Neue Rundschau*, 23, v, Mai, S. 635-639. [Also in *S. F. V.: Das 26. Jahr*. Berlin: S. Fischer, 1912, S. 15-21. – Organic unity of AS's personality and works.]
x90. Salten, Felix. "Schnitzler." *Der Merker*, 3, ix, 1. Mai, S. 324-330. [AS's future lies in the comedy and novel.]
x91. Schmidtbonn, Wilhelm. "Zwei Städte." *Der Merker*, 3, ix, 1. Mai, S. 346. [Berlin and Vienna.]
x92. Schönherr, Karl. "Brief." *Der Merker*, 3, ix, 1. Mai, S. 347. [Tribute.]

x93. Specht, Richard. "Schnitzler-Glossen." *Der Merker*, 3, ix, 1. Mai, S. 351-356.
[AS's diversity of theme and development.]

x94. Wassermann, Jakob. "Silhouette." *Der Merker*, 3, ix, 1. Mai, S. 348-349.

x95. Weilen, Alexander von. "Arthur Schnitzler (Zum fünfzigsten Geburtstage)."
Österreichische Rundschau, 31, iv, 15. Mai, S. 294-300. [AS's world narrowly
limited, but completely controlled; his characters never truly in love.]

x96. Zweig, Stephan. "Schnitzler und die Jugend." *Der Merker*, 3, ix, 1. Mai, S.
349-350. [Repr. in *Blätter der Internationalen Stefan Zweig Gesellschaft*, 13/14,
Apr. 1962, S. 10-12.]

1913

x97. Brandes, Georg, "Theater und Schauspiel in Deutschland." *Der Merker*, 4,
iii, S. 95-99.

x98. Henderson, Archibald. "Arthur Schnitzler (1862-   ): A Bibliography.
Translations, Productions and Criticism in English." *Bulletin of Bibliography
and Quarterly Dramatic Index*, 7, vii, Oct., p. 155-156. [Repr. with slight revision
in *Modern Drama and Opera: Reading Lists on the Works of Various Authors*.
Boston: Boston Book Co., 1915, Vol. 2, p. 103-108. – Biographical note,
works, portraits, productions and criticism with excerpts from reviews.]

x99. Marcel, Gabriel. "Le Théâtre de Schnitzler." *Grande Revue*, 81, 10 oct., p.
513-530. [Dramas surveyed. For AS tragedy the clash of *destinées étrangères*.]

x100. Palmer, John. "A Schnitzler Matinee." *Saturday Review*, 115, No. 2994, 15.
Mar., p. 326-327. [AS's morality.]

x101. Reik, Theodor. "Die 'Allmacht der Gedanken' bei Arthur Schnitzler." *Imago*,
2, iii, Juni, S. 319-335. [The first chapter of ♯x102.]

x102. Reik, Theodor. *Arthur Schnitzler als Psycholog*. Minden, Westfalen: J. C. C.
Bruns, 303 S. ["Meinem verehrten Lehrer Professor Dr. Sigmund Freud in
Dankbarkeit gewidmet." – Treats AS's characters as real people, subjecting
them to psychoanalysis. Diagnoses interesting, even if some seemed forced to
the layman. The cornerstone of the "psychoanalytic school" of AS-criticism.]

x103. Reik, Theodor. "Das Geschlechterverhältnis bei Arthur Schnitzler." *Neue
Generation*, 9, iii, 14. März, S. 128-135.

x104. Roseeu, Robert. *Arthur Schnitzler*. Berlin: Wilhelm Borngräber (Neues Leben),
57 S. (Der moderne Dichter, Bd. 9). [Excellent brief treatment: comparison
with Hauptmann, the Viennese milieu, characters and basic themes. AS's forte
the novelle and one-act play, his genius dialogue and *Andeutungskunst*.]

x105. Sachs, Hanns. "Die Motivgestaltung bei Schnitzler." *Imago*, 2, iii, Juni, S.
302-318. [Recurrence of such motifs as the unsuccessful assassination attempt
on a tyrant.]

x106. Salten, Felix. "Arthur Schnitzler." *Gestalten und Erscheinungen*. Berlin: S. Fischer,
S. 49-63. [Reflections on AS's works and their excellences.]

x107. Samuel, Horace. "Arthur Schnitzler." *Modernities*. London: Kegan Paul,
Trench, Trübner, p. 161-195. [Also: New York: E. P. Dutton, 1914. – An
expansion of ♯x46.]

x108. Wessely, Jary. "Arthur Schnitzler." *Neues Frauenleben*, 15, ii, Feb., S. 47-51.

1914

x109. Chandler, Frank Wadleigh. *Aspects of Modern Drama*. New York: Macmillan,
p. 177-178; 279-287; 327-328. [AS an Austrian Sterne.]

x110. Jenney, Florence G. "The Plays of Arthur Schnitzler." *The Colonnade*, 8, iii,
Sept., p. 99-110. [AS attracted by the "prostitute-psyche." Clash of man's
intellectual perception with his self-will a recurrent thesis.]

XIII.　Moderwell, Hiram Kelly. *The Theatre of Today.* New York & London: John Lane; Toronto: Bell & Cockburn, p. 208-211. [Also: New York: Dodd, Mead, 1927. – Fr. "The Literary Forces: Dramatists of the Germanic Nations."]

XII2.　Petsch, Robert. *Zeitschrift für deutschen Unterricht*, 28, iv, S. 326-327. [Fr. "Hauptströmungen im Drama der Gegenwart."]

XII3.　Reik, Theodor. "Schnitzler als Psycholog." *Die Persönlichkeit*, 1, iv, Apr., S. 312-313. [Rev. of #x102. by its author.]

XII4.　Storer, Edward. "The Art of Arthur Schnitzler." *The Academy*, 86, No. 2175, Jan. 10, p. 37-38.

XII5.　Von Ende, Amelia. *The German Classics.* (Kuno Francke, ed.) New York: German Publication Society, Vol. 20, p. 103-105. [Fr. "The Contemporary German Drama."]

1915

XII6.　Björkman, Edwin. "Introduction." *The Lonely Way* [#L4.], p. vii-xxxiv. [Survey of the dramas.]

XII7.　Lewisohn, Ludwig. *The Modern Drama: An Essay in Interpretation.* New York: B. W. Huebsch, p. 154-163. [Fr. "The Naturalistic Drama in Germany." – AS's art an extraordinary and complex product.]

XII8.　McAfee, Helen, *Yale Review*, 5, i, Oct., p. 192-197. [Various dramas reviewed.]

XII9.　Smith, Winifred. "A Viennese Playwright in English." *The Dial*, 59, dccii, Sept. 30, p. 267-269. [Various dramas reviewed.]

XI20.　Stümcke, Heinrich. *Vor der Rampe: Dramaturgische Blätter.* Oldenburg & Leipzig: Schulz, S. 127-138. [Revs. of "Das weite Land," "Professor Bernhardi" and "Der junge Medardus."]

1916

XI21.　Buck, Philo M., Jr. "Naturalism and Fiction: Arthur Schnitzler." *The Nation*, 103, No. 2676, Oct. 12, p. 342-344.

XI22.　Fröhlich, Otto. "Arthur Schnitzlers künstlerische Entwicklung (Ein kritischer Versuch)." *Der Merker*, 7, vii, S. 250-256. [AS's psychological development and his genius.]

XI23.　Lewisohn, Ludwig. *The Spirit of Modern German Literature: Lectures Delivered Before the University of Wisconsin.* New York: B. W. Huebsch, p. 52-55.

XI24.　Walzel, Oskar. "Jungösterreichische Dichtung." *Internationale Monatsschrift*, 10, ix, 1. Juni, Sp. 1116-1121.

1917

XI25.　Dukes, Ashley. "Introduction." *Anatol* [#L5.], p. ix-xiii. [AS essentially a comic writer.]

XI26.　Kerr, Alfred. *Die Welt im Drama.* Berlin: S. Fischer, Bd. I, S. 119-142; Bd. II, S. 275-309; Bd. IV, S. 33-34. (Gesammelte Schriften in zwei Reihen: Erste Reihe). [Various dramas reviewed.]

XI27.　Körner, Josef. "Arthur Schnitzler und Sigmund Freud." *Das Literarische Echo*, 19, xiii, 1. Apr., Sp. 802-805. [Rev. of #x102.]

XI28.　Lewisohn, Ludwig. "Arthur Schnitzler (1862-　　　)." *The Warner Library: The World's Best Literature.* (John W. Cunliffe & Ashley H. Thorndike, eds.) New York: Warner Library, Vol. 21, p. 12922a-12922c.

XI29.　Loving, Pierre. "Introduction." *Comedies of Words* [#L6.], p. vii-xxx. [AS a Viennese satirist with a tragic Weltanschauung.]

1918

X130. Henderson, Archibald. "Arthur Schnitzler." *European Dramatists*. Cincinnati: Stewart & Kidd, p. 399-429. [Treats one-act plays only, where AS at his best.]
X131. Jacobsohn, Siegfried. "Arthur Schnitzler Abend." *Das Jahr der Bühne*, Berlin: Oesterheld, Bd. VI, S. 187-189. [Rev. of scenes fr. "Anatol" and "Literatur."]
X132. Körner, Josef. "Arthur Schnitzlers Gestalten und Probleme." *Donauland*, 2, ix, Nov., S. 997-1008. [AS's works *Märchen;* ideas here more fully developed in ‡x146.]
X133. Walzel, Oskar. "Arthur Schnitzler." *Der Zwinger*, 2, vi, 1. Juni, S. 215-220. [Defense of AS against critics who call him out-dated; he has resurrected romantic irony.]

1920

X134. Bailey, Joseph W. "Arthur Schnitzler's Dramatic Work." *Texas Review*, 5, iv, July, p. 294-307. [AS a great writer, but with limitations such as the narrow Viennese-aristocratic-artistic range of his subject matter.]
X135. Edschmid, Kasimir. "Schnitzler oder der psychologische Roman." *Das Feuer*, 1, v, S. 338-343. [Highly rarefied praise for AS, who, like Keyserling, unites *Zeit* and *Volk*.]
X136. Jameson, Storm. *Modern Drama in Europe*. London: W. Collins, p. 166-170. [AS supreme in terms of grace and sanity.]

1921

X137. "An Arthur Schnitzler: Kundgebungen Österreichischer Zeitgenossen." *Moderne Welt*, 3, xii, S. 10-15. [Notices by Anton Bettelheim, Josef Jarno, Leopold Kramer, Max Mell, Hans Müller, Roda Roda, Moriz Rosenthal, Felix Salten, Otto Tressler, Paul Wertheimer, Felix Weingartner, Anton Wildgans, Stefan Zweig.]
X138. "Arthur Schnitzler im Urteil des Auslandes." *Moderne Welt*, 3, xii, S. 19-23. [Notices by Ferdinand Gregori, Gustav Linden, August Brunius, Karl Laurin, Ejnar Smith, Sven Söderman, Heinrich Mann, Henry Moritz, Scofield Thayer, Stella & Edmond Visser, Louis de Vries.]
X139. Anon. *The Nation*, 112, No. 2915, May 18, p. 703. [Editorial on AS, whose art is wronged by all translations.]
X140. Auernheimer, Raoul. "Arthur Schnitzler und das Wiener Theater." *Moderne Welt*, 3, xii, S. 7-9.
X141. Bahr, Hermann. "Brief an Arthur Schnitzler." *Moderne Welt*, 3, xii, S. 3-6.
X142. Grabowski, A. "Dostojewski und Schnitzler." *Das Neue Deutschland*, 10, iii/iv, Nov., S. 60-62.
X143. Grossmann, Stefan. "Schnitzler." *Das Tagebuch*, 2, xiii, 2. Apr., S. 402-404.
X144. Jacobsohn Siegfried. *Die Weltbühne*, 17, iii, 20. Jan., S. 72-74. [AS and Hofmannsthal.]
X145. Jacobsohn, Siegfried. "Schnitzler und Lautensack." *Die Weltbühne*, 17-2, xlviii, 1. Dez., S. 552-557.
X146. Körner, Josef. *Arthur Schnitzlers Gestalten und Probleme*. Zürich, Leipzig, Wien: Amalthea, 228 S. (Amalthea-Bücherei, Bd. 23). [Three periods in AS's writings, with the use of problem or *Fall* the starting point in all the works. AS's *Märchenwelt* atmosphere and recurring characters and motifs traced. A basic and monumental piece of criticism.]
X147. Oberholzer, Otto. *Richard Beer-Hofmann: Werk und Weltbild des Dichters*. Bern: A. Francke, S. 15-18. [Fr. "Das Wesen der Wiener Dekadenz." Citations fr. AS, Hofmannsthal, Beer-Hofmann and Schaukal compared.]

x148. Rosenthal, Friedrich. "Arthur Schnitzler als Regisseur." *Moderne Welt*, 3, xii, S. 24.

x149. Salten, Felix. *Schauen und Spielen: Studien zur Kritik des modernen Theaters*. Wien & Leipzig: WILA, Bd. I: Ergebnisse: Erlebnisse, S. 163-203. [Revs. of "Der Ruf des Lebens," "Der einsame Weg," "Zwischenspiel," "Das weite Land" and "Der junge Medardus."]

x150. Seligmann, A. F. "Kunst und Erotik." *Moderne Welt*, 3, xii, S. 16-18. [AS not an erotic writer, but an artist.]

1922

x151. "Arthur Schnitzler zu seinem sechzigsten Geburtstag (15. Mai 1922)." *Neue Rundschau*, 33, v, Mai, S. 498-513. [Notices by Oskar Bie, Raoul Auernheimer, Hermann Bahr, Franz Blei, S. Fischer, Otto Flake, Egon Friedell, Gerhart Hauptmann, Hugo von Hofmannsthal, Felix Hollaender, Alfred Kerr, Heinrich Mann, Thomas Mann, Jakob Wassermann, Franz Werfel, Stefan Zweig. – Hofmannsthal contribution repr. as "Arthur Schnitzler: Zum 60. Geburtstag" in *Die Berührung der Sphären*, Berlin: S. Fischer, 1931, S. 308-309, and in *Prosa*, Frankfurt a.M.: S. Fischer, 1955, Bd. IV, S. 99-100. (Gesammelte Werke in Einzelausgaben). Zweig contribution repr. as "Arthur Schnitzler: Zum 60. Geburtstag" in *Europäische Erbe*, Frankfurt a.M.: S. Fischer, 1960, S. 183-186. – "Den Sinn für Schnitzler, heisst Kultur besitzen, und sich von Schnitzler angezogen fühlen, heisst die Kultur suchen." Gerhart Hauptmann.]

x152. Auernheimer, Raoul. "Arthur Schnitzler zum 60. Geburtstag." *Baden-Baden Bühnenblatt*, 2, lxi/lxii, 26. Mai, S. 1-3.

x153. Bahr, Hermann. *London Mercury*, 7, xxxviii, Dec., p. 194-195. [Fr. "A Letter from Germany." AS at sixty.]

x154. Faesi, Robert. "Hauptmann und Schnitzler, die Sechzigjährigen." *Der Lesezirkel*, 9, xii.

x155. Hofmannsthal, Hugo von. *The Dial*, 73, ii, Aug., p. 207-209. [Fr. "Vienna Letter." Shorter works best.]

x156. Kappstein, Theodor. *Arthur Schnitzler und seine besten Bühnenwerke: Eine Einführung*. Berlin & Leipzig: Franz Schneider, 100 S. (Schneiders Bühnenführer). [For AS danger of the *bon mot* being substituted for reality; one-act plays his best productions. Plot summaries of the major plays.]

x157. Körner, Josef. "Arthur Schnitzler: Der Dichter und sein Werk." *Die Scene*, 12, vi, Juni, S. 93-96. [Selection from ‡x146. with a footnote review by F. Gregori.]

x158. Lewy, Walter. "Arthur Schnitzler." *Der Kritiker*, 6, ii, 1/2. Mai-H., S. 1-2.

x159. Mann, W. "Arthur Schnitzler." *Juden in der deutschen Literatur: Essays über zeitgenössische Schriftsteller*. (Gustav Krojanker, ed.) Berlin: Welt-Verlag, S. 207-218. [AS's characters all Jewish *Literaten*-types who perceive their own unimportance and express hope for next generation. Perceptive analysis.]

x160. Rychner, Max. "Ein anderer Jubilar." *Wissen und Leben*, 15, xv, 15. Juni, S. 746-747. [On the sixtieth birthday celebration.]

x161. Schumann, Wolfgang. "Arthur Schnitzler: Zu seinem sechzigsten Geburtstag." *Der Kunstwart*, 35, viii, Mai, S. 68-72. [AS not lacking in profundity.]

x162. Specht, Richard. "Arthur Schnitzler." *The Dial*, 73, iii, Sept., p. 241-245. [Kenneth Burke, tr. Fr. ‡x163. Less effective in English.]

x163. Specht, Richard. "Arthur Schnitzler." *Neue Rundschau*, 33, v, Mai, S. 488-498. [Printing of part of the first two sections of ‡x164. prior to its publication.]

x164. Specht, Richard. *Arthur Schnitzler: Der Dichter und sein Werk. Eine Studie.* Berlin, S. Fischer, 349 S. [A highly literary, somewhat casual and disorganized treatment in which Specht tries to rival AS in style. Subjective, yet of considerable biographical and literary-critical value.]

x165. Stefan, Paul. "Arthur Schnitzler: Zum sechzigsten Geburtstag." *Das Literari-sche Echo*, 24, xix, 1. Juli, Sp. 1178-1179. [Repr. fr. article in the *Neue Zürcher Zeitung*.]

x166. Wallisch, Friedrich. "Arthur Schnitzler: Zu seinem 60. Geburtstag am 15. Mai." *Das Deutsche Drama*, 5, iv, 1. Okt., S. 148-151. [Includes remarks by AS.]

1923

x167. Koehler, Selma. "The Question of Moral Responsibility in the Dramatic Works of Arthur Schnitzler." *Journal of English and Germanic Philology*, 22, iii, July, p. 376-411. [AS's characters not morally responsible for their conduct. Rigid division of the dramas into three groups; some questionable literary judgments.]

x168. Marcuse, Ludwig. "Arthur Schnitzler." *Die Welt der Tragödie*. Berlin, usw.: Franz Schneider, S. 153-157. [General observations on AS's characters and a discussion of death, the ultimate reality, in his works.]

x169. Rittenberg, Louis. "Arthur Schnitzler – The Shaw of Vienna." *American Hebrew*, 113, xii, Aug. 3, p. 244 & 253. [AS the exposer of Viennese moral laxity.]

1924

x170. Bernstein, Herman. "Arthur Schnitzler." *Celebrities of Our Time: Interviews.* New York: Joseph Lawren, p. 318-325. [Interview on war.]

x171. Brüll, Oswald. "Nachwort." *Die dreifache Warnung* [♯K10.], S. 70-73. [AS's narratives avoid *die grosse Welt*.]

x172. Palm, Carla L. "Schnitzleresque: A Satire in One Act." *Drama Magazine*, 14, vi, Mar./Apr., p. 210-212; 238. [Recaptures some of the characteristics of AS's dialogue technique.]

x173. Witkop, Philipp, "Arthur Schnitzler." *Deutsche Dichtung der Gegenwart*. Leipzig: H. Haessel, S. 134-137.

1925

x174. Bab, Julius. *Das deutsche Drama*. (Robert F. Arnold, ed.) München: C. H. Beck, S. 726-735. [Fr. "Die Lebenden." – "Anatol" the basis for AS's later develop-ment; a number of incisive observations.]

x175. Berger, Alfred von. "Arthur Schnitzler." *Burgtheater Almanach*. (Nikolaus Hovorka, ed.) Wien-Berlin: Reinhold, 1. Jg., S. 16-22. [AS's preoccupation with love, death and *Komödiespielen*. His debt to Paris.]

x176. Helbling, Carl. "Arthur Schnitzler." *Der Lesezirkel*, 12, v, Jan., S. 57-62.

x177. Körner, Josef, "Arthur Schnitzler." *Baden-Baden Bühnenblatt*, 5, iii, 9. Jan.

x178. Stefan, Paul. "Arthur Schnitzler und Arnold Schönberg: Zwei Widmungs-blätter aus Wien." *Jahrbuch der literarischen Vereinigung Winterthur*, 10. Gabe, S. 52-55. [Two separate appreciations; AS. 52-53.]

x179. Wertheimer, Paul. "Begegnung mit Arthur Schnitzler." *Brüder im Geiste*. Wien: Deutsch-Österreichischer Verlag, S. 88-94. [Repr. fr. the *Neue Zürcher Zeitung*.]

1926

x180. Anon. "Arthur Schnitzler." *Zürcher Student*, 3, vii, Jan., S. 99-102.

x181. Bab, Julius. "Neues von Schnitzler." *Die Chronik des Deutschen Dramas*. Berlin: Oesterheld, Bd. V: Deutschlands Dramatische Produktion 1919-1926, S. 265-269. [Negative reaction to theatrical works.]

x182. Bianquis, Geneviève. *La poésie autrichienne de Hofmannsthal à Rilke*. Paris: Les Presses universitaires de France, p. 4-6; 11-13.

x183. Henderson, Archibald. "Arthur Schnitzler." *European Dramatists*. New York, London: D. Appleton, p. 407-465. [AS uses "romantic impressionism;" he is the dramatist of character rather than of action.]

x184. Mahrholz, Werner. *Deutsche Literatur der Gegenwart: Probleme, Ergebnisse, Gestalten*. Berlin: Wegweiser, S. 82-86. [AS the artist of Eros.]

x185. Mann, W. "Arthur Schnitzler zum 60. Geburtstag." *Jüdische Rundschau*, 27, S. 262.

x186. Monahan, Michael. "Amourettes." *Nemesis*. New York: Frank-Maurice, p. 238-242. [AS unlike Maupassant.]

1927

x187. Anon. "Arthur Schnitzler: Bemerkungen." *Das Tagebuch*, 8-2, xlvii, 19. Nov., 1879-1881.

x188. Hutten, Leonhard. "65 Jahre und doch noch jung. Arthur Schnitzler an der Pensionsgrenze." *Deutscher Journalistenspiegel*, 3, xvi, 20. Mai, S. 481-482.

x189. Körner, Josef. "Arthur Schnitzlers Spätwerk." *Preussische Jahrbücher*, 208, i, Apr., S. 53-83; 208, ii, Mai, S. 153-163. [Supplement to #x146. AS's new directions in post-World War I works and his aesthetic preference for the narrative form.]

1928

x190. Anon. *Arthur Schnitzler: A Short Note about the Man and His Work*. New York: Simon & Schuster, 7 p. [Notes on AS's working habits and the late prose works.]

x191. Bertaux, Félix. *Panorama de la littérature allemande contemporaine*. Paris: KRA, p. 112-114. [Also: *A Panorama of German Literature: From 1871 to 1931*. New York: Whittlesey House (McGraw-Hill), 1935, p. 93-94. Tr. by John J. Trounstine.]

x192. Lewisohn, Ludwig. "Arthur Schnitzler." *Columbia University Course in Literature*. New York: Columbia University Press, Vol. IX: The German Mind, p. 559-561.

x193. March, I. George. "The World of Arthur Schnitzler." *Poet Lore*, 39, iv, Dec., p. 573-581. ["Liebelei" extolled; AS the quintessence of the Austrian spirit and landscape, but his Vienna gone and little can be expected of him in the future.]

x194. Quadt, Max. "Arthur Schnitzler als Erzähler." *Germanic Review*, 3, i, Jan., p. 34-45. [AS as the subtle dissector of human souls; aspects of his narrative technique and its development into more traditional forms (emergence of the objective world).]

x195. Rieger, Erwin. *Ewiges Österreich*. Wien: Manzscher, S. 25-74. [Section on AS.]

x196. Schinnerer, Otto P. "Introduction." *Der grüne Kakadu* [#s1.], p. ix-xiv. [Brief survey.]

x197. Wassermann, Jakob. "Einige Bemerkungen über Arthur Schnitzler." *Lebensdienst: Gesammelte Studien, Erfahrungen und Reden aus drei Jahrzehnten*. Leipzig, Zürich: Grethlein, S. 294-295. [Praise in general terms.]

1929

x198. Bertaux, Félix. "Préface." *La pénombre des âmes* [#M2.], p. 1-5.

x199. Diamond, William. "Arthur Schnitzler." *Monatshefte für deutschen Unterricht*, 21, i, Jan., p. 6-10. [AS one of the subtlest and most creative of modern writers; "Der Weg ins Freie" and "Professor Bernhardi" especially effective.]

x200. Mertens, Heinz. *Unheldenhafte und heldenhafte Menschen bei den Wiener Dichtern um 1900.* Bonn: Ludwig Röhrscheid, 192 S. (Mnemosyne: Arbeiten zur Erforschung von Sprache und Dichtung. Heft 2). [Of the various Viennese writers discussed AS given the most emphasis.]

x201. Schinnerer, Otto P. "The Early Works of Arthur Schnitzler." *Germanic Review*, 4, ii, Apr., p. 153-197. [Scrutiny of the works published before 1895 and their foreshadowing of the later works. A basic study.]

1930

x202. Clauser, Suzanne. "Arthur Schnitzler." *Revue d'Allemagne*, 4, xxxiv, 15. août, p. 719-731. [AS transcends Vienna and the limited range usually attributed to him.]

x203. Ewen, David. "Anti-Semitism: A Healthy Influence. As Told in Interview with David Ewen. Written by Arthur Schnitzler for the 'Jewish Exponent'." *Jewish Exponent*, 87, i, Sept. 26, p. 1; 10.

x204. Phillips, Henry Albert. "Why He Wears Whiskers." *The Spur*, 45, i, Jan. 1, p. 40; 99. [Interview; journalistic.]

x205. Porterfield, Allen W. "Introduction." *Stories and Plays* [#s3.], p. vii-xxix. [AS's four literary periods. A number of questionable value-judgments.]

x206. Schinnerer, Otto P. "The Literary Apprenticeship of Arthur Schnitzler." *Germanic Review*, 5, i, Jan., p. 58-82. [Supplements #x201. Discussion of the medical writings and additional biographical information, especially AS's association with Viennese journals.]

x207. Schinnerer, Otto P. "Schnitzler and the Military Censorship: Unpublished Correspondence." *Germanic Review*, 5, iii, July, p. 238-246. [Account of the consequences following publication of "Leutnant Gustl;" correspondence with the military, excerpts from reviews.]

x208. Viereck, George Sylvester. "The World of Arthur Schnitzler." *Glimpses of the Great.* New York: Macaulay, p. 395-409. [Also: London: Duckworth. – Interview with AS wherein he claims to have anticipated Freud's theory of dreams.]

x209. Wendt, H. G. *German Quarterly*, 3, iii, May, p. 107-111. [Rev. of two school editions: #s3. and #b17.13.]

1931

x210. Anon. *Die Literatur*, 34, iii, Dez., S. 146-148. [Fr. "Echo der Zeitungen." Excerpts fr. articles by Eduard Korrodi, Arnold Hoellriegel, Monty Jacobs, Bernhard Diebold, Hugo Kubsch, Max Hochdorf, and Alfred Kerr.]

x211. Anon. "Dr. Arthur Schnitzler." *Wiener Medizinische Wochenschrift*, 81, xliv, 31. Okt., S. 1451-1452. [Obituary.]

x212. Anon. "Dr. Arthur Schnitzler: Beobachtetes und Erlebtes." *Menorah*, 9, xi/xii, Nov./Dez., S. 491-497; 499. [AS's temperament, his Jewishness and interest in copyrights.]

x213. Anon. "Fame and a Playwright." *Theatre Arts Monthly*, 15, xii, Dec., p. 965-966. [AS did not write a single great play.]

x214. Anon. *Publisher's Weekly*, 120, xviii, Oct. 31, p. 2034. [Obituary.]

x215. "Persönliche Erinnerungen an Arthur Schnitzler." *Literarische Welt*, 7, xlv, 6. Nov. [Tributes by Hermann Bahr, Felix Salten, and Stefan Zweig.]

x216. Bab, Julius. "Arthur Schnitzler." *Die Hilfe*, 37, xliv, 31. Okt., S. 1059-1063.

x217. Bauer, Ludwig. "Schnitzler." *Das Tagebuch*, 12-2, xliv, 31. Okt., S. 1704-1707.

x218. Behl, C. F. W. "Arthur Schnitzler." *Der Heimatdienst*, 11, S. 337.

X219. Breitner, Burghard. "Dr. Arthur Schnitzler." *Wiener Medizinische Wochenschrift*, 81, xliv, 31. Okt., S. 1451. [Tribute to the physician.]

X220. Chandler, Frank Wadleigh. *Modern Continental Playwrights*. New York & London: Harper, p. 345-355. [AS shows no development.]

X221. Clauser, Suzanne. "La mort d'Arthur Schnitzler." *Revue d'Allemagne*, 5, no. 50, 15 déc., p. 1057-1061. [Eulogy.]

X222. Ewen, David. "Arthur Schnitzler: Man of Genius. An Interview." *B'nai B'rith Magazine*, 46, iii, Dec., p. 73-74. [Purportedly last interview with AS; interesting notes on his writing habits.]

X223. Fontana, Oskar M. "Das Begräbnis." *Das Tagebuch*, 12-2, xliv, 31. Okt., S. 1707-1709.

X224. Goldberg, Isaac. "Arthur Schnitzler: Man of Genius. An Appreciation." *B'nai B'rith Magazine*, 46, iii, Dec., p. 72.

X225. Nabl. Franz. "Gedächtnisworte für Arthur Schnitzler." *Die Literatur*, 34, iii, Dez., S. 176-178. ["Gedenkblätter XXXIX."]

X226. Olden, Rudolf. "Zu Schnitzlers Tod." *Die Weltbühne*, 27-2, xliii, 27. Okt., S. 648-650.

X227. Poeppig, Fred. "Von der Welt Arthur Schnitzlers (Zum Tode des Dichters)." *Goetheanum*, 10, xlv, 8. Nov., S. 361.

X228. Polgar, Alfred. "Der Theaterdichter Schnitzler." *Die Weltbühne*, 27-2, xliv, 3. Nov., S. 679-680.

X229. Sander, E. "In Memoriam Arthur Schnitzler." *Der Kreis*, 8, xi, Nov., S. 648-650.

X230. Schinnerer, Otto P. "Introduction." *Viennese Novelettes* [#L10.], p. vii-xlv. [Biographical and literary survey. AS achieved perfection within his limits.]

X231. Schinnerer, Otto P. "Schnitzler: A Man Who Loved Life." *The Nation*, 133, No. 3462, Nov. 11. 516-517. [Valuable biographical notes.]

X232. Urzidil, J. "Erinnerungen an Arthur Schnitzler." *Hochschulwissen*, 8, S. 679.

X233. Walter. *Jüdische Rundschau*, 36, S. 402. [Rev. of "Der Weg ins Freie" and #K11.]

X234. Wiegler, Paul. "Arthur Schnitzlers Tod." *Literarische Welt*, 7, xlv, 6. Nov.

X235. Wilson, Edmund. "Schnitzler and Philip Barry." *New Republic*, 65, dcccxliv, Feb. 4, p. 322-323. [Repr. in *The Shores of Light: A Literary Chronicle of the Twenties and Thirties*. New York: Farrar, Straus & Young, 1952, p. 504-508. – AS a foil for Barry.]

1932

X236. Anon. "How Schnitzler Wrote." *Living Age*, 342, No. 4386, Mar., p. 81-82. [Translation of some of AS's notes on the origins of inspiration; detailed account of the genesis of "Der Schleier der Beatrice."]

X237. "Schnitzler Symposium." *Books Abroad*, 6, i, Jan., p. 95-99; 6, ii, Apr., p. 244-247. [Notices by Carl van Doren, Stark Young, Channing Pollock, Burns Mantle, Joseph Wood Krutch, F. W. Kaufmann, A. E. Zucker, Clifton Fadiman, Isaac Goldberg, John S. Nollen, Arpad Steiner, Edward Franklin Hauch, Otto P. Schinnerer, Gustav Mueller, Allen W. Porterfield, Jakob Wassermann, G. Bernard Shaw, Ernst Zahn, A. Busse, B. J. Vos, Bayard Q. Morgan, Julius Bab.]

X238. Arnold, R. F. *Die Literatur*, 34, ix, Juni, S. 518. [Rev. of "Die Gleitenden," "Anatols Grössenwahn," "Die Mörderin," "Eine überspannte Person" and "Halb Zwei."]

X239. Auernheimer, Raoul. "Arthur Schnitzler philosophe." *Revue d'Allemagne*, 6, lv, 15 mai, p. 424-430. [Suzanne Clauser, tr.]

X240. Beer-Hofmann, Richard. "Der einsame Weg." *Corona*, 2, iv, Jan., S. 476-477. [Repr. in *Verse*. Stockholm & New York: Bermann-Fischer, 1941, S. 16-17. – Poem. Handwritten facsimile.]

X241. Bertaux, Félix. "Arthur Schnitzler." *Revue mondiale*, 43, (T. 208), 15 mai, p. 139-141.

X242. Burkhard, Arthur. "Schnitzler, Symbol of Austria's Past." *Books Abroad*, 6, i, Jan., p. 20-21.

X243. Dehorn, W. *Germanic Review*, 7, iii, July, p. 255-260. [Fr. "Psychoanalyse und neuere Dichtung." – AS a psychoanalyst who considers man a *Geschlechtswesen*.]

X244. Dunan, Marcel. "Schnitzler et la France: Souvenirs personnels." Revue d'Allemagne, 6, lv, 15 mai, p. 419-423. [General reflections on AS.]

X245. Geraldy, Paul. "Amitiés Viennoises: Schnitzler et Hofmannsthal." *Annuaire politique et littéraire*, 98, p. 77-78.

X246. Gillet, Louis. "Image de Schnitzler." *Revue d'Allemagne*, 6, lx, 15 mai, p. 375-386.

X247. Goldschmidt, K. W. "Schnitzler zu 70. Geburtstag." *Die Sendung*, 9, S. 404.

X248. Hofacker, Emil. "Schnitzler the Scientist." *Books Abroad*, 6, ii, Apr., p. 159-160. [Citations fr. "Das Buch der Sprüche und Bedenken."]

X249. Jakob, Heinrich Eduard. "Der Kämpfer Arthur Schnitzler." *Die Weltbühne*, 28-2, xv, 12. Apr., S. 572-573. [Notes on AS's persecution by his Austrian contemporaries.]

X250. Kayser, Rudolf. "Arthur Schnitzler." *Neue Rundschau*, 43, v, Mai, S. 719. [Brief tribute.]

X251. Kerr, Alfred. "L'auteur dramatique." *Revue d'Allemagne*, 6, lv, 15 mai, p. 407-409. [Suzanne Clauser, tr.]

X252. Koganowsky, Maximilian Georg. "Das philosophische Weltbild der Dichtung Arthur Schnitzlers." *Gral*, 26, S. 386-388. [AS an agnostic pessimist.]

X253. Liptzin, Sol. "Arthur Schnitzler." *Books Abroad*, 6, i, Jan., p. 16-17. [Neat summing up of AS's philosophy.]

X254. Liptzin, Sol. *Arthur Schnitzler*. New York: Prentice Hall, 275 p. [Only book-length study of AS in English. Three of the chapters are reworkings of #C21X.18, #C31X.17 and #C32X.32. Major themes – life, death, love and fate – are treated, and the works are surveyed in a topical fashion.]

X255. Liptzin, Sol. "The Call of Death and the Lure of Love: A Study in Schnitzler." *German Quarterly*, 5, i, Jan., p. 21-36. [Death a predominant theme in AS's works with a number of *morituri* living under its shadow. Anatol-type the epitome of life.]

X256. Loving, Pierre. "Schnitzler and Interior Monologue." *Books Abroad*, 6, i, Jan., p. 18-19. [AS's style fine and musical.]

X257. Marschik, H. *Monatsschrift für Ohrenheilkunde und Laryngo-Rhinologie*, 66, iv, Apr., S. 482. [Tribute to AS, the laryngologist.]

X258. Randall, A. W. G. "Arthur Schnitzler." *Saturday Review of Literature*, 8, xlvii, June 11, p. 787. [Rev. of "Flucht in die Finsternis," "Der Gang zum Weiher" and "Im Spiel der Sommerlüfte."]

X259. Reinhardt, Kurt F. "In memoriam Arthur Schnitzler (1862-1931)." *Books Abroad*, 6, ii, Apr., p. 163-164. [AS passé.]

X260. Salten, Felix. "Aus den Anfängen: Erinnerungsskizzen." *Jahrbuch deutscher Bibliophilen und Literaturfreunde*, 18/19, S. 31-46. [Dr. AS as hypnotist.]

X261. Salten, Félix. "L'interrogation du destin." *Revue d'Allemagne*, 6, lv, 15 mai, p. 410-412. [Suzanne Clauser, tr.]

X262. Schaukal, Richard von. "Arthur Schnitzler Apotheose." *Deutschlands Erneuerung*, 16, ii, Feb., S. 111-113. "Repr. in *Neue Literatur*, 33, iii, März, 1932, S. 136-138. – Quotations from obituaries and tributes.]

X263. Schaukal, Richard von. "Arthur Schnitzler und die Seinen: Ein Nachwort zu den Wiener Nachrufen." *Deutsches Volkstum*, 1. Halbjahr, ii, Feb., S. 118-122. [Satirical and anti-Semitic account of the *Todesfeier*.]

X264. Schinnerer, Otto P. "Nachwort." *Die kleine Komödie* [#J7.], S. 322-332. [Brief history of the pre-"Anatol" publications; anticipation of later motifs in the early works.]

X265. Schinnerer, Otto P. "Systematisches Verzeichnis der Werke von Arthur

Schnitzler." *Jahrbuch deutscher Bibliophilen und Literaturfreunde*, 18/19, S. 94-121. [Monumental bibliographical compilation; only the first four of nine promised sections published. Does not include criticism on AS.]

x266. Storfer, A. J. "Arthur Schnitzler und die Psychoanalyse." *Psychoanalytische Bewegung*, 4, i, Jan./Feb., S. 62-63. [Of slight value.]

x267. Wassermann, Jakob. "Erinnerung an Arthur Schnitzler." *Neue Rundschau*, 43 i, Jan., S. 5-13. [AS's impatience the key to his personality.]

x268. Werfel, Franz. "Arthur Schnitzler: Gedenkrede." *Neue Rundschau*, 43, i, Jan., S. 1-4. [AS's works more concerned with private than with public life.]

x269. Werfel, Franz. "Arthur Schnitzler." *Revue d'Allemagne*, 6, lv, 15 mai, p. 369-374. [Suzanne Clauser, tr. #x268 in French.]

x270. Whitney, Marian P. "Schnitzler the Dramatist." *Books Abroad*, 6, ii, Apr., p. 161-162. [Contemporary prose plays best.]

x271. Zweig, Stefan. "Arthur Schnitzler, narrateur." *Revue d'Allemagne*, 6, lv, 15 mai, p. 387-398. [Suzanne Clauser, tr.]

1933

x272. Kaufmann, Friedrich Wilhelm. "Zur Frage der Wertung in Schnitzlers Werk." *PMLA*, 48, i, Mar., p. 209-219. [AS's development in values (life the highest) to an anticipation of post-impressionism.]

x273. Körner, Josef. "Erinnerungen an Arthur Schnitzler." *Die Welt im Wort*, Nov. [Supplement to #x146.]

x274. Porterfield, Allen W. "Goethe and Schnitzler." *Modern Language Notes*, 48, i, Jan., p. 20-21. [Werther-influence hinted at.]

x275. Schaukal, Richard von. "Thomas Mann über Arthur Schnitzler." *Bayreuther Blätter*, 56, i, S. 35-37. [Satirical account of a speech.]

x276. Schinnerer, Otto P. "Arthur Schnitzler's 'Nachlass'." *Germanic Review*, 8, ii, Apr., p. 114-123. [On the careful cataloging and contents of the 227 folders.]

x277. Stefan, Paul. "Arthur Schnitzler." *Jahrbuch der literarischen Vereinigung Winterthur*, 14, S. 108-114. [Abridged version of a speech.]

1934

x278. Neuse, Werner. "'Erlebte Rede' und 'Innerer Monolog' in den erzählenden Schriften Arthur Schnitzlers." *PLMA*, 49, i, Mar., p. 327-355. [Stylistic study; both vehicles well-suited for expressing AS's tragic philosophy.]

x279. Zohner, Alfred. *Jahrbuch deutscher Bibliophilen und Literaturfreunde*, 20, S. 28-32. [Fr. "Bibliophiles um das 'Jung Wien;' Moderne und Symbolismus in Österreich."]

1935

x280. Ilmer, Frida. "Schnitzler's Attitudes with Regard to the Transcendental." *Germanic Review*, 10, ii, Apr., p. 114-125. [AS's views on religion and God, especially in the poems and aphorisms. He was possessed of a reverent attitude towards the whole universe.]

x281. Ilmer, Frida. "Das Thema der künstlerischen Schöpferkraft bei Schnitzler." *Monatshefte für deutschen Unterricht*, 27, iii, Mar., p. 73-80. [For AS the artist must not seek his material, but wait for it; he is under the sway of an inner necessity.]

x282. Nesbit, Louis. "Arthur Schnitzler (1862-1931)." *Medical Life*, 42, x, Oct., p. 511-550. [More popular than scholarly discussion of AS's medical background and its influence on his works. Freudian analysis of "Der blinde Geronimo und sein Bruder."]

1936

x283.   Ben-Chorin, Sch. "Der Epiker Schnitzler." *Jüdische Rundschau*, 41, S. 846.

1937

x284.   Gross, Fritz. "Arthur Schnitzler." *Contemporary Review*, 151, dccclvii, May, p. 607-612. [AS individualist and outsider. Overwritten criticism.]

x285.   Kainz, Friedrich. *Deutsch-Österreichische Literaturgeschichte: Ein Handbuch zur Geschichte der deutschen Dichtung in Österreich-Ungarn.* (Johann W. Nagl & Jakob Zeidler, eds.) Wien: Carl Fromme, Bd. IV, S. 1745-1781. [Fr. "Arthur Schnitzler und Karl Schönherr."]

1939

x286.   Bithell, Jethro. *Modern German Literature 1880-1938.* London: Methuen, p. 257-265. [1959 edition, p. 229-237. – A useful evaluative summary.]

x287.   Block, Anita. *The Changing World in Plays and Theatre.* Boston: Little, Brown, p. 64-68. [Fr. "Modern Foundations of Contemporary Drama." – AS the creator of the psychological play.]

1940

x288.   Blei, Franz. "Arthur Schnitzler." *Zeitgenössische Bildnisse.* Amsterdam: Allert de Lange, S. 92-94. ["Liebelei" and *das süsse Mädel.*]

x289.   Gassner, John Waldhorn. "Schnitzler and the Austrian Theatre." *Masters of the Drama.* New York: Random House, p. 474-477. [Also: New York: Dover, 1954, – AS a minor dramatist.]

1943

x290.   Apsler, Alfred. "A Sociological View of Arthur Schnitzler." *Germanic Review*, 18, ii, Apr., p. 90-106. [AS the "marginal man," torn between being Viennese and Jewish.]

x291.   Feuchtwanger, Lion. "Arthur Schnitzler." *The Universal Jewish Encyclopedia.* New York: Universal Jewish Encyclopedia. Vol, IX, p. 413-415.

x292.   Schnitzler, Henry. "Otto P. Schinnerer und Arthur Schnitzler: Ein Blatt der Erinnerung und des Dankes." *German Quarterly*, 16, iv, Nov., p. 202-206. [Schinnerer's friendship with AS and his critical perception.]

1944

x293.   Liptzin, Solomon. "Arthur Schnitzler." *Germany's Stepchildren.* Philadelphia: Jewish Publication Society, p. 124-138. [AS's wrestling with the Jewish question, his claim to be German, not Jewish.]

x294.   Reiss, H. S. "The Problems of Fate and of Religion in the Work of Arthur Schnitzler." *Modern Language Review*, 40, iv, Oct., p. 300-308. [AS believes in free-will, but possessed of a negative conception of life.]

x295.   Reiss, H. S. "The Significance of Arthur Schnitzler." *Hermathena*, No. 66, Nov., p. 72-84. [AS psychologist of the erotic and the abnormal, with a limited range and a decadent view of life.]

x296.   Slochower, Harry. "Arthur Schnitzler: Bohemian Ichschmerz." *No Voice Is Wholly Lost: Writers and Thinkers in War and Peace*. New York: Creative Age, p. 25-32. [Sociological shift in AS's viewpoint after World War I.]

1946

x297.   Bentley, Eric. *The Playwright as Thinker: A Study of Drama in Modern Times*. New York: Reynal & Hitchcock, p. 346-348. [Also: New York: Harcourt, Brace, 1951, p. 263-264; New York: Meridan Books, 1955, p. 293-295. – Admires AS's middle period.]

x298.   Fuchs, Albert. "Arthur Schnitzler (1862-1931)." *Moderne Österreichische Dichter: Essays*. Wien: Globus, S. 31-43. (Tagblatt-Bibliothek). [AS's social-critical works marred by negativism.]

1947

x299.   Menter, Leo. "Arthur Schnitzler." *Der Weg*, 2, vii, 14. Feb., S. 2. [Fr. "Jüdischer Anteil an der deutschen Kultur."]

x300.   Schnitzler, Henry. *A History of Modern Drama*. (Barrett H. Clark & George Freedley, eds.) New York & London: D. Appleton-Century, p. 132-137. [Survey.]

x301.   Walter, Bruno. *Thema und Variationen: Erinnerungen und Gedanken*. Stockholm: Bermann-Fischer, S. 224-225. [Recollections of AS.]

1949

x302.   Coler, Christfried. "Arthur Schnitzler und wir." *Berliner Hefte für geistiges Leben*, 4, vii, S. 82-85 (Ausgabe A). [AS more psychologist than writer.]

x303.   Maurer, K. W. "Some Reflections on Arthur Schnitzler." *German Life and Letters*, 2, iii, Apr., p. 214-221. [A fresh evaluation with a number of incisive observations.]

x304.   Reiss, H. S. "A Note on 'Der Zug der Schatten,' an Unpublished Play by Arthur Schnitzler." *German Life and Letters*, 2, iii, Apr., p. 222-224. [Work no masterpiece, belonging to AS's first period. Evidence for lack of AS's development in outlook.]

1950

x305.   Plant, Richard. "Notes on Arthur Schnitzler's Literary Technique." *Germanic Review*, 25, i, Feb., p. 13-25. [The *Umbruch* or turnabout (a reversal of character-relationships to one another) the central point in AS. Deception a recurrent theme.]

x306. Anon. "Vienna Mirage." *Times Literary Supplement*, No. 2576, June 15, p. 365-366. [Non-historical plays best.]

x307. Beharriell, Frederick J. "Arthur Schnitzler's Range of Theme." *Monatshefte für deutschen Unterricht*, 43, vii, Nov., p. 301-311. [A surprising range displayed; erotic questions especially valid in the twentieth century.]

x308. Schnitzler, Henry. "Der Nachlass meines Vaters." *Aufbau* (New York), Nov. 9, p. 9; 10. [Rescue of the archive and its contents in general terms.]

x309. Seelmann-Eggebert, Ulrich. "Arthur Schnitzler." *Welt und Wort*, 6, x, Okt., S. 380-382. [Three periods in AS; ultimate failure to achieve artistic greatness.]

x310. Lamm, Martin. *Modern Drama*. Oxford: Basil Blackwell, p. 238-244. [Karin Elliott, tr. Fr. "Austrian Drama." – AS's best work in miniature form.]

x311. Oswald, Victor A., Jr. *Germanic Review*, 27, iii, Oct., p. 190-192. [Fr. "The Old Age of Young Vienna." – AS primarily a *Naturforscher*.]

x312. Wallisch, Friedrich. "Arthur Schnitzler spricht: Persönliche Erinnerungen zum 90. Geburtstag des Dichters." *Freude an Büchern*, 3, v, S. 114-115. [An expansion of #x166.]

x313. Beharriell, Frederick J. "Schnitzler's Anticipation of Freud's Dream Theory." *Monatshefte für deutschen Unterricht*, 45, ii, Feb., p. 81-89. [Convincing case based on "Frühlingsnacht im Seziersaal."]

x314. Seidlin, Oskar. "Einleitung." *Der Briefwechsel Arthur Schnitzler – Otto Brahm* [#G5.1.], S. 19-32. [Penetrating brief treatment of AS's basic primitivism as evidenced in the magical world of fear and sadness of his characters.]

x315. Hinrichs, Else. "Arthur Schnitzler." *Das Verhältnis von Kunst und Leben in der österreichischen Dichtung von Franz Grillparzer bis Hugo von Hofmannsthal*. Uelzen (Hannover): C. Beckers, S. 79-100. [Diss., Bern, 1953. – Longing for life and disillusionment in AS.]

x316. Mann, Heinrich. "Arthur Schnitzler: Gedächtnisrede gehalten 1931." *Essays*. Berlin: Aufbau, Bd. I, S. 445-449. (Ausgewählte Werke in Einzelausgaben, Bd. XI).

x317. Schnitzler, Olga. "Der junge Hofmannsthal." *Neue Rundschau*, 65, iii/iv, S. 514-534. [Repr. in #x359. in expanded form as chapter II.]

x318. Schnitzler, Olga. "Erinnerungen an Richard Beer-Hofmann." *Almanach: Das neunundsechzigste Jahr*. Frankfurt a.M.: S. Fischer, S. 25-32. [Repr. in #x359. in expanded form as chapter V.]

x319. Bergel, Kurt. "Einleitung." *Georg Brandes und Arthur Schnitzler: Ein Brief-*

wechsel [#G8.1.], S. 11-51. [Introduction modified from its original dissertation form (#Y18.). Brandes and AS compared.]

1957

x320.   Anon. "Freud's *Doppelgänger*." *Time*, 69, ii, Jan. 14, p. 51-52. [Letter from Freud to AS cited (May 14, 1922) by Herbert I. Kupper in address to American Psychoanalytic Association.]

x321.   Fechter, Paul. *Das europäische Drama: Geist und Kultur im Spiegel des Theaters.* Mannheim: Bibliographisches Institut, Bd. II: Vom Naturalismus zum Expressionismus, S. 102-109. [Principal dramas treated.]

x322.   Lederer, Herbert. "Arthur Schnitzler: A Chronicle of Loneliness." *German Quarterly*, 30, ii, Mar., p. 82-94. [Predominant theme in AS.]

x323.   Lockemann, Fritz. *Gestalt und Wandlungen der deutschen Novelle: Geschichte einer literarischen Gattung in neunzehnten und zwanzigsten Jahrhundert.* München: Max Hueber, S. 281-289. [Principal Novellen surveyed.]

x324.   Seyler, Athene, and Stephen Haggard. *Craft of Comedy.* New York: Theatre Arts, 114 p. (Second edition). ["Anatol" used as literary model.]

1958

x325.   Kraus, Karl. "Schnitzler-Feier." *Literatur und Lüge*, München: Kösel, S. 161-172. [AS basically a feuilleton writer; highly satirical attack.]

x326.   Rath, Gernot. "Arthur Schnitzler: Der Arzt als Dichter." *Ciba Symposium*, 6, 6, v, S. 215-218.

x327.   Weiss, Robert O. "Arthur Schnitzler's Literary and Philosophical Development." *A West Virginia State College Bulletin*, Series 45, No. 5, Aug., 12 p. [A *Rettung*, emphasizing the middle and late works, the topical range, and intellectual transformations.]

1959

x328.   Garten, Hugh F. "Arthur Schnitzler." *Modern German Drama*. Fair Lawn, N. J.: Essential Books, p. 55-63. [Also: London: Methuen, 1959. – AS never transcends "Anatol."]

x329.   Kann, Robert. "Das Österreich Arthur Schnitzlers." *Forum* (Wien), 6, lxxi, Nov., S. 421-423. [AS's extreme individualism.]

x330.   Kupper, Herbert I., and Hilda S. Rollman-Branch. "Freud and Schnitzler: *Doppelgänger*." *Journal of the American Psychoanalytical Association*, 7, i, Jan., p. 109-126. [Similarities of childhood experiences and points of view.]

1960

x331.   Alewyn, Richard. "Nachwort." *Liebelei* [#K15.], S. 155-160.

x332.   Cysarz. Herbert. "Das Imaginäre in der Dichtung Arthur Schnitzlers." *Wissenschaft und Weltbild*, 13, ii, Juni, S. 102-112. [AS's transcending of reality; "Leutnant Gustl" his best.]

x333.   Drews, W. "Der verführerische Zufall: Notiz über Arthur Schnitzler." *Theater und Zeit*, 8, S. 176-178.

x334.   Fontana, Oskar Maurus. "Arthur Schnitzler (1862-1931)." *Grosse Österreicher: Neue österreichische Biographie ab 1815.* (Anon.) Zürich, Leipzig, Wien: Amalthea, Bd. XIV, S. 129-136.

x335.   Klein, Johannes. *Geschichte der deutschen Novelle von Goethe bis zur Gegenwart.*
Wiesbaden: Franz Steiner, S. 460-463. (4. Aufl.) [AS's narratives repetitious.]
x336.   Weigel, Hans. "Der Dichter als Arzt: Gezeigt am Beispiel Arthur Schnitzlers."
Ciba Symposium, 7, vi, Feb., S. 283-286. [AS portrays illnesses of his characters
and not responsible for their views; not original criticism.]

1961

x337.   Foltinek, Herbert. "Arthur Schnitzler in Amerika." *Österreich und die angel-
säschsische Welt: Kulturbegegnungen und Vergleiche.* (Otto Hietsch, ed.) Wien,
Stuttgart: Wilhelm Braumüller, S. 207-214. [Survey based on #Y5.]
x338.   Hill, Claude. "The Stature of Arthur Schnitzler." *Modern Drama,* 4, i, May,
p. 80-91. [A *Rettung* viewing AS as an urban writer.]
x339.   Holzinger, Alfred. "Sittenbild oder Weltdeutung: Das Werk Arthur Schnitzlers." *Wort in der Zeit,* 7, x, Okt., S. 33-36. [Primacy of love and dated social-
moral criticism in AS.]
x340.   Kohn, Hans. "Eros and Sorrow: Notes on the Life of Arthur Schnitzler and
Otto Weininger." *Yearbook. Publications of the Leo Baeck Institute of Jews from
Germany,* 6, p. 152-169. [Nothing original on AS.]
x341.   Lederer, Herbert. "Arthur Schnitzler before 'Anatol'." *Germanic Review,* 36,
iv, Dec., p. 269-281. [Examination of the early portion of the archive with
quotations from AS's autobiography.]
x342.   Schorske, Carl E. "Politics and the Psyche in *fin de siècle* Vienna: Schnitzler and
Hofmannsthal." *American Historical Review,* 66, iv, July, p. 930-946. [Enlighten-
ing analysis of the Viennese bourgeoisie at the turn of the century.]
x343.   Wallisch, Friedrich. "Arthur Schnitzler: Arzt und Dichter." *Ärztliche Praxis,*
13, S. 2198.
x344.   Weiss, Robert O. "The Arthur Schnitzler Archive at the University of Kentucky: A List of Microfilms Made from Arthur Schnitzler's 'Nachlass'."
JIASRA, 1, i, Nov., p. 11-29. [Repr. in *JIASRA,* 2, iv, Winter, 1963-1964,
p. 11-26. – A catalog of the archive as it is held by the University Library,
Cambridge, England, and on microfilm by the IASRA.]

1962

x345.   Anon. "Schnitzler: Freuds Doppelgänger." *Der Spiegel,* 16, xxx, 25 Juli,
S. 58-62. [Rev. of #x359.]
x346.   Anon. "Erinnerungen an Arthur Schnitzler, 1862-1931." *Therapeutische Berichte,*
34, S. 94-98.
x347.   Ahl, Herbert. "Ein Kranz aus Immortellen: Arthur Schnitzler." *Literarische
Portraits.* München, Wien: Albert Langen, Georg Müller, S. 349-356. [First
published in the *Diplomatischer Kurier,* 1962. – Journalistic.]
x348.   Alexander, Theodor W. "Ethical Problems of the Medical Profession in Arthur
Schnitzler's Works." *Homage to Charles Blaise Qualia* (Anon.) Lubbock, Texas:
Texas Tech Press, p. 75-80. [Physician faces polarity of individual versus social
good.]
x348.1   Beharriell, Frederick J. "Freud's 'Double:' Arthur Schnitzler." *Journal of the
American Psychoanalytical Association,* 10, iv, Oct., p. 722-730.
x349.   Buschbeck, Erhard. "Gedenkrede auf Arthur Schnitzler." *Mimus Austriacus.*
(L. von Tobisch, ed.) Salzburg, S. 205-211.
x350.   Duwe, Wilhelm. *Deutsche Dichtung des 20. Jahrhunderts: Vom Naturalismus zum
Surrealismus.* Zürich: Orell Füssli, Bd. I, S. 355-389; Bd. II, S. 259-262. [Nar-
ratives and dramas respectively.]
x351.   Kann, Robert A. "Schnitzler as an Austrian Writer in the World Today."

JIASRA, 1, iv/v, Autumn/Winter, p. 3-4. [AS becoming a classic in world literature.]

x352. Klarmann, Adolf D. "Die Weise von Anatol." *Forum* (Wien), 9, cii, Juni, S. 263-265. [Anatol-type and his awareness of death.]

x353. Kohn, Hans. *Karl Kraus. Arthur Schnitzler. Otto Weininger. Aus dem Jüdischen Wien der Jahrhundertwende.* Tübingen: J. C. B. Mohr, Paul Siebeck, S. 12-29. (Schriftenreihe Wissenschaftlicher Abhandlungen des Leo Baeck Institute of Jews from Germany, Nr. 6). [Comparison with and influence of the late-Ibsen; AS's greatness not localized.]

x354. Kraus, Wolfgang. "Der Meister der Nuancen: Zu Arthur Schnitzlers 100. Geburtstag am 15. Mai." *Wort in der Zeit*, 8, v, Mai, S. 35-36. ["Wer Wien je auch nur einen einzigen Augenblick lang als Lebensform erlebt hat, wird die Worte Arthur Schnitzlers nur mit Erschütterung und Heimweh hören können."]

x355. Lothar, Ernst. "Tod und Renaissance." *Forum* (Wien), 9, ci, Mai, S. 213-216. [Some objections to AS refuted.]

x356. Natan, Alex. "Ein fruchtbarer Sumpf: Das Wien Arthur Schnitzlers." *Christ und Welt*, 15, xviii, S. 18.

x357. Politzer, Heinz. "Diagnose und Dichtung." *Forum* (Wien), 9, ci, Mai, S. 217-219; cii, Juni, S. 266-270. [AS and Freud.]

x358. Reik, Theodor. *Jewish Wit.* New York: Gamut Press, 246 p. [Cites examples of AS's wit; biographical notes.]

x359. Schnitzler, Olga. *Spiegelbild der Freundschaft.* Salzburg: Residenz Verlag, 154 S. [Introductory remarks by Hans Weigel. – Memoirs of AS's wife with biographical notes on AS, his friendship with Hofmannsthal, Herzl, Bahr, and Beer-Hofmann. Excerpts from published and unpublished correspondence.]

x360. Schorske, Carl E. "Schnitzler und Hofmannsthal: Politik und Psyche im Wien des fin de siècle." *Wort und Wahrheit*, 17, v, Mai, S. 367-381. [German version of ‡x342.]

x361. Seidlin, Oskar. "Arthur Schnitzlers 'Liebelei;' Zum hundertsten Geburtstag des Dichters. Am 15. Mai 1962." *German Quarterly*, 35, iii, May, p. 250-253. [AS's concern with elemental questions.]

x362. Seidlin, Oskar. "In Memoriam Arthur Schnitzler: May 15, 1862 – Oct. 21, 1931." *American-German Review*, 28, iv, Apr./May, p. 4-6. [AS's conversational urbanity.]

x363. Spector, Robert Donald. "Schnitzler's Availability to American Readers." *JIASRA*, 1, iv/v, Autumn/Winter, p. 8-9.

x363.1 Tauschinski, Oskar Jan. "Ein Löwe – Nicht aus dem Lesebuch: Gedanken über eine noch ausständige Schnitzler-Renaissance." *Österreich in Geschichte und Literatur*, 6, iv, Apr., S. 176-183. [AS's literary antecedents and chief characteristics.]

x364. Wallisch, Friedrich. "Arthur Schnitzler, Arzt und Dichter, zu seinem 100. Geburtstag am 15. Mai 1962." *Münchener Medizinische Wochenschrift*, 104, S. 958-959.

x365. Wallisch, Friedrich. "Erinnerungen an Arthur Schnitzler." *Welt und Wort*, 17, v, Mai, S. 140-141.

x366. Weigel, Hans. "Die grosse Vergeblichkeit: Zum hundertsten Geburtstag Arthur Schnitzlers." *Neue Deutsche Hefte*, H. 88, Juli/Aug., S. 25-43. [AS will rightly come into his own again.]

x367. Zohn, Harry. "Schnitzler and the Challenge of Zionism." *JIASRA*, 1, iv/v, Autumn/Winter, p. 5-7. [AS and Herzl, based on ‡x359.]

1963

x368. Auclères, Dominique. "Arthur Schnitzler tel que je l'ai connu." *JIASRA*, 2, ii, Summer, p. 4-34. [Recollections of France's foremost Schnitzler critic and translator; pseudonym "Suzanne Clauser."]

x369.   Bergel, Kurt. "Schnitzler's Unpublished Tragicomedy 'Das Wort'. *"SiAS,*
        p. 1-24. [Peter Altenberg prototype of protagonist; excerpts from the corre-
        spondence. Excellent scholarship.]
x370.   Dayag, Joseph H. "Schnitzler's Reception in France." *SiAS,* p. 25-34. [Paucity
        of AS-studies in France.]
x371.   Foltin, Lore B. "The Meaning of Death in Schnitzler's Work." *SiAS,* p. 35-44.
        [Death linked with man's purification.]
x372.   Garland H. B. "Arthur Schnitzler." *German Men of Letters.* London: Oswald
        Wolff, Vol. II: Twelve Literary Essays (Alex Natan, ed.), p. 55-75. (German
        Men of Letters). [Sound evaluative discussion with high praise for "Professor
        Bernhardi" and "Der Weg ins Freie."]
x373.   Kann, Robert A. "The Image of the Austrian in Arthur Schnitzler's Writings."
        SiAS, p. 45-70. [Best expression in "Der junge Medardus."]
x374.   Klarmann, Adolf D. "Arthur Schnitzler und der Existentialismus." *JIASRA,*
        2, ii, Summer, p. 35-37.
x375.   Lederer, Herbert. "Arthur Schnitzler's Typology: An Excursion into Philo-
        sophy." *PMLA,* 78, iv, Sept., p. 394-406. [Exegesis of "Der Geist im Wort
        und der Geist in der Tat."]
x376.   Perl, Walter H. "Arthur Schnitzler und das Theater von heute." *JIASRA,* 2,
        iii, Autumn, p. 28-31.
x377.   Perl, Walter H. "Arthur Schnitzler and Young Hofmannsthal." *SiAS,* p. 79-94.
        [Growth of their friendship; excerpts from the correspondence.]
x378.   Politzer, Heinz. "Arthur Schnitzler: Poetry of Psychology." *Modern Language
        Notes,* 78, iv, Oct., p. 353-372. [AS as a *doctor poeta.*]
x379.   Reichert, Herbert W. "Arthur Schnitzler and Modern Ethics." *JIASRA,*
        2, i, Spring, p. 21-24.
x380.   Reichert, Herbert W. "Nietzsche and Schnitzler." *SiAS,* p. 95-107. [Sug-
        gesting a link between them.]
x381.   Spector, Robert Donald. "Observations on Schnitzler's Narrative Technique
        in the Short Novel." *SiAS,* p. 109-116. [AS's mastery of narrative form.]
x382.   Vogelsang, Hans. *Österreichische Dramatik des 20. Jahrhunderts.* Wien, Stutt-
        gart: Braumüller. (Untersuchungen zur Österreichischen Literatur des 20.
        Jahrhunderts, Bd. I).
x383.   Weiss, Robert O. "Arthur Schnitzler's Literary and Philosophical Develop-
        ment." *JIASRA,* 2, i, Spring, p. 4-20. [Reworking of #x327.]
x384.   Weiss, Robert O. "Arthur Schnitzler's Notes on Journalistic Criticism."
        Germanic Review, 38, iii, May, p. 226-237. [Report on a fragmentary critical
        work in the archive.]
x385.   Zohn, Harry. "The World of Arthur Schnitzler." *Jewish Quarterly,* 10, i, Spring,
        p. 25-29. [First appeared as "Arthur Schnitzler and the Great Age of Vienna
        Jewry" in the *Jewish Advocate,* Apr. 4, 1963, p. 1A-2A.]

                                    1964

x386.   Alexander, Theodor W. "Aspects of Imagery in Schnitzler: Color and Light."
        JIASRA, 3, ii, Autumn, p. 4-15. [Color as a stylistic device in eight works.]
x387.   Beharriell, Frederick J. *German Quarterly,* 37, ii, March, p. 170-172. [Rev. of
        #J10. and #J11.]
x388.   Rey, William H. "Beiträge zur amerikanischen Schnitzlerforschung." *German
        Quarterly,* 37, iii, May, p. 282-289. [Discussion of *SiAS* (1963). "Es scheint
        auch wirklich an der Zeit, mit allem Nachdruck zu betonen, dass der Schlüssel
        zum Verständnis des Schnitzlerschen Werkes nicht bei Freud, nicht bei Mach
        und nicht bei Nietzsche zu finden ist – sondern bei Arthur Schnitzler selbst."]
x389.   Rey, William H. "War Schnitzler Impressionist? Eine Analyse seines un-
        veröffentlichten Jugendwerks 'Aegidius'." *JIASRA,* 3, ii, Autumn, p. 16-32.

x390.   Zohn, Harry. "Arthur Schnitzler und das Judentum." *Wiener Juden in der deutschen Literatur: Essays.* Tel-Aviv: Olamenu, S. 9-18. [Biographical-critical survey, first appearing in *Das jüdische Echo* (Wien), 12, i, Sept. 1963, S. 25-27.]

1965

x391.   Anon. "M. L. A. Conference 26, December 28, 1964." *JIASRA*, 4, i, Spring, p. 16-22. [Reports and summaries of presentations on the theme "Arthur Schnitzler's Influence on Modern Letters" by Herbert Lederer, Herman Salinger, Vincent LoCicero, Lore Foltin, Richard Plant, and Herbert W. Reichert.]

x391.1   Alexander, Theodor W. "The Author's Debt to the Physician: Aphonia in the Works of Arthur Schnitzler." *JIASRA*, 4, iv, Winter, p. 4-15. [Literary manifestations of #H13.]

x392.   Baumann, Gerhart. *Arthur Schnitzler: Die Welt von Gestern eines Dichters von Morgen.* Frankfurt a.M.: Athenäum, 43 S. [Expanded version of a lecture delivered Jan. 29, 1965, in Vienna. AS's characters as expressive of the collective unconscious.]

x393.   LoCicero, Donald. "Arthur Schnitzler und Eugene O'Neill: Masks, Pipe-Dreams, and Reality." *JIASRA*, 4, iii, Fall, p. 27-42. [Plato's cave, "Der grüne Kakadu" and "The Iceman Cometh."]

x394.   LoCicero, Vincent. "Schnitzler, O'Neill, and Reality." *JIASRA*, 4, iii, Fall, p. 4-26. ["Der Schleier der Beatrice" and "The Great God Brown." as mediating between subjective and objective truth.]

x395.   Reichert, Herbert W. "Schnitzlers egoistische Künstlergestalten." *JIASRA*, 4, ii, Summer, p. 20-27. [Reply to #388.; AS's egoistic protagonists as one pole in his dialectic.]

x395.1   Rey, William H. "Arthur Schnitzler." *Deutsche Dichter der Moderne: Ihr Leben und Werk.* (Benno von Wiese, ed.) Berlin: Erich Schmidt, S. 237-257. [Suggestive of new critical approaches to AS.]

x396.   Weigel, Hans. "Vorwort." *Spiel im Morgengrauen* [#K17.], S. 7-14.

PART Y: DISSERTATIONS ON SCHNITZLER

1917

Y1.   Bere, May. *The "Motivation" in Arthur Schnitzler's Dramas.* M. A. Thesis, University of Chicago, 57 p. ["Motivation" mainly the "sex instinct," although "Reigen" not discussed.]

1927

Y2.   Salinger, Herman. *Proust and Schnitzler as Historians of Contemporary Society.* A. B. Honors Thesis, Princeton University, vi, 65 p. [Comparative-literary approach.]

1930

Y3.   Boner, Georgette, *Arthur Schnitzlers Frauengestalten.* Winterthur: G. Binkert, 118 S. [Diss., Zürich. – AS as psychologist; rôle of women in his literary universe.]

1931

Y4.   Gemeinhart, Lawrence E. *The Reception of Arthur Schnitzler in Berlin, 1895-1914.* M. A. Thesis, Columbia University, 56 p. [Limited to periodical literature. Reception more favorable in Berlin than in Vienna.]

Y5.   Schrumpf, Beatrice M. *The Reception of Arthur Schnitzler in the United States.* M. A. Thesis, Columbia University, 48; 53 p. (Text and bibliography respectively). [Translations, stage history, and reviews of the individual works. Lists of American productions, chief critics, and chief translators.]

1932

Y6.   Wiedenbrüg, Hans. *Die literarischen Motive in der erzählenden Kunst Arthur Schnitzlers.* Frankfurt a.M.: Osterrieth, 1934, 49 S. ["Teildruck" of the 1932 diss., Frankfurt. – Literary background, motifs and male characters. No summary.]

1933

Y7.   Funt, Dorothy. *Arthur Schnitzler's Attitude toward the Ethical Problems of Love and Marriage, as Shown in His Dramatic Works.* M. A. Thesis, New York University, 59 p. [For AS marriage an empty formality; only love a true bond.]

Y8.   Ilmer, Frida. *Die Gestalt des Künstlers bei Schnitzler.* Ph. D. Diss., Johns Hopkins University, 208 p. [Division of the artist-types into "creative" and "reproducing;" centrality of art in the AS-corpus.]

Y9.   Minar, Hildegarde Maria. *Die lyrischen Elemente im Wiener Drama um 1900.*
        Diss., Wien, xiii, 136 S. [Treats AS, Hofmannsthal and Wildgans.]
Y10.   Neumaier, Paul Georg. *Der Typus des Abenteurers in der neuen deutschen Dichtung.*
        Limburg a.d Lahn: Vereinsdruck, 109 S. [Diss., Frankfurt. – AS to Gerhart
        Hauptmann.]

1934

Y11.   Burton, Elizabeth R. *Irony in the Short Stories of Thomas Mann and Schnitzler,*
        M. A. Thesis, University of Toronto, 76 p. [Chapters IV and V: Irony of human
        insufficiency and irony of fate in AS.]

1935

Y12.   Blume, Bernhard. *Das nihilistische Weltbild Arthur Schnitzlers.* Stuttgart: Knöller,
        1936, 79 S. [Diss., Technische Hochschule Stuttgart, 1935. – For AS life only
        the process of dying; the escape into pure form (art) total turning away from
        life, hence disappointing. Perceptive analysis.]
Y13.   Plaut, Richard. *Arthur Schnitzler als Erzähler.* Frankfurt a.M.: Kornsand, 119 S.
        [Diss., Basel. – AS as philosopher of love; his use of of the *Umbruch* or turn-
        about in human relationships. A new critical point of view.]

1937

Y14.   Ball, Esther Hudson. *Emotional Life in Schnitzler's Early Works.* M. A. Thesis,
        Duke University, 98 p.
Y14.1   Nussbaum, Georg. *Die Aufnahme Schnitzlers bei Kritik und Publikum.* Diss.,
        Wien, 132 S. [No longer in the University of Vienna Library; destroyed?]

1939

Y15.   McKay, Llewelyn Riggs. *The Problem of Death in the Viennese School as Re-
        presented by Schnitzler, Rilke and Hofmannsthal.* Ph. D. Diss., Stanford University,
        346 p. [*Stanford University Abstracts of Dissertations,* 15, 1939/1940, p. 82-87. –
        AS chosen as main representative of this group. Death as a foil for life, the
        complexity of the soul and the revaluation of values.]

1940

Y16.   Warheit, Israel Albert. *Jung-Wien as a Literary School: Schnitzler, Beer-Hofmann,
        Hofmannsthal. 1890-1914.* Ph. D. Diss., University of Michigan, 307 p. [Compa-
        rative study treating environment, philosophical basis, dreams and reality,
        transitoriness, death, etc.]

1946

Y16.1   Beharriell, Frederick J. *Schnitzler and Society.* M. A. Thesis, University of
        Toronto, 101 p.

1947

Y17.   Cohn, Alice. *The Concept of Death in the Works of Arthur Schnitzler.* M. A. Thesis,
        Columbia University, 53 p. [AS's and his characters' abhorrence of the unknown
        and death.]

Y17.1   Dorlag, Arthur Henry. *Schnitzler: A Production Study*. M. A. Thesis, University of Wisconsin, 140 p.

1948

Y18.   Bergel, Kurt. *Der Briefwechsel von Georg Brandes und Arthur Schnitzler*. Ph. D. Diss., University of California, Berkeley, xxxiv, 474 p. [Published in modified form as #G8.1. Introduction and notes treat such topics as Romain Rolland and AS, the biographical background of "Professor Bernhardi."]

Y19.   Singer, Herta. *Zeit und Gesellschaft im Werk Arthur Schnitzlers*. Diss., Wien, 153 S. [AS as a social critic; discussion of the social-critical and satirical works.]

Y20.   Stöger, Dorrit. *Probleme und Gestalten der österreichischen Novelle von 1890-1914*. Diss., Wien, 143 S. [Includes AS. Useful comparative study treating historical background, Novelle-types, forms and motifs.]

1949

Y21.   Polsterer, Susanne M. *Die Darstellung der Frauen in A. Schnitzlers Dramen*. Diss., Wien, 215 S. [Feminine characters not lifelike. Index of women in AS's works. Detailed analyses of Auerlie in "Komödie der Verführung" and Leonilda in "Der Gang zum Weiher."]

1950

Y22.   Davis, Evan B. *Moral Problems in the Works of Arthur Schnitzler*. Ph. D. Diss., University of Pennsylvania, ii, 196 p. [Works treated chronologically. Contains letter to Josef Körner, Nov. 7, 1927.]

Y23.   Eisserer, Elisabeth. *Arthur Schnitzler als Seelenforscher in den Novellen*. Diss., Wien, 127 S. [Characters, central problems and motifs; AS's characters not typically Viennese.]

Y24.   Jandl, Ernst. *Die Novellen Arthur Schnitzlers*. Diss., Wien, 161 S. [Divides Novellen into four periods. Development discussed with respect to form, content, and ideas.]

1951

Y25.   Smart, Frederick D. *The Influence of Meteorological Influence on Man: A Study of Schnitzler's Novellen*. M. A. Thesis, University of Kentucky, v, 144 p.

Y26.   Weiss, Robert O. *Death in the Works of Arthur Schnitzler*. M. A. Thesis University of Missouri, 84 p. [Tables of types and frequency of death in the works.]

1952

Y27.   Mindess, Veronica P. *Unconscious Motivation of Main Characters in Arthur Schnitzler's Plays and Narratives*. M. A. Thesis, University of California. Los Angeles, 144 p. [AS one of the first writers to show psychological forces at play.]

1953

Y28.   Bissinger, Helene. *Die "erlebte Rede," der "erlebte innere Monolog," und der "innere Monolog" in den Werken von Hermann Bahr, Richard Beer-Hofmann und Arthur Schnitzler*. Diss., Köln, 260 S. [Tables of speech-forms in AS; analyses of "Leutnant Gustl" and "Fräulein Else."]

126

Y29.   Lederer, Herbert. *The Problem of Ethics in the Works of Arthur Schnitzler.* Ph. D. Diss., University of Chicago, 202 p. [AS-characters' longing for absolute values or disintegration of the ego. For AS ethics a necessary fiction.]

1954

Y30.   Müller-Freienfels, Reinhart. *Das Lebensgefühl in Arthur Schnitzlers Dramen.* Diss., Frankfurt, 197 S. [Realization of the limitations of human life and the striving to achieve an aesthetic viewpoint; the ensuing demands of reality for self-assertion. A dialectical approach.]

Y31.   Wiggins, Clarence Albin. *The Concept of Death in the Work of Arthur Schnitzler.* M. A. Thesis, New York University, 90 p. [Death and the individual; death and life. (!)]

1955

Y32.   Weiss, Robert Otto. *A Study of Arthur Schnitzler (With Special Consideration of the Problem of Psychosis in "Flight into Darkness.")* Ph. D. Diss., Stanford University, 225 p. [*Dissertation Abstracts*, 16, i, p. 124. – Thirty-two cases of psychosis in AS's works presented. AS far ahead of his time in depth psychology.]

1956

Y33.   Anderson, Anne Cavanaugh. *The Image of Landscape in the Short Stories of Arthur Schnitzler.* M. A. Thesis, Ohio State University, 74 p. [*Ohio State University Abstracts of Theses for the M. A. Degree*, No. 81, p. 3. – AS's landscapes attached to psychological stratum of his stories.]

Y34.   Schmidt-Wesle, Dorothea. *Politische und soziale Probleme im Werk Arthur Schnitzlers.* Diss., Jena, 184 S. [Development of AS's ideas and his treatment of society.]

Y35.   Seibel, Charles. *The Problem of Anti-Semitism in the Works of Arthur Schnitzler.* M. A. Thesis, Columbia University, 58 p. [For AS each Jew must make his own adjustment to the problem.]

Y36.   Wilms-Posen, H. *Das innere Drama: Zeitmorphologische Reihenuntersuchung einiger Erzählungen Arthur Schnitzlers.* Diss., Bonn, 179; 6 S. [Günther Müller's method used to examine time-sequences in seven Novellen.]

1957

Y37.   Helmke, Henry Conrad. *The Delineation of Family Relationships in the Narrative Works of Arthur Schnitzler.* M. A. Thesis, Duke University, 77 p.

1958

Y38.   Lantin, Rudolf. *Traum und Wirklichkeit in der Prosadichtung Arthur Schnitzlers.* Aachen: Selbstverlag, v, 170 S. [Diss., Köln. – Use of the dream and the dream-memory; comparison with Freudian dream analysis.]

1960

Y39.   Kammeyer, Max-Peter. *Die Dramaturgie von Tod und Liebe im Werk Arthur Schnitzlers.* Diss., Wien, 158 S. [An attempt to locate AS in German literary history. Letter to Otto Brahm, Sept. 30, 1896.]

Y40. Alter, Maria Pospischil. *The Concept of the Physician in the Writings of Hans Carossa and Arthur Schnitzler*. Ph. D. Diss., University of Maryland, 225 p. [*Dissertation Abstracts*, 22, vi, 1961, p. 1991. – AS's physician often raisonneur.]

Y41. Allen, Richard Harry. *Arthur Schnitzler's Works and their Reception: An Annotated Bibliography*. Ph. D. Diss., University of Michigan, iii, 223 p. *Dissertation Abstracts*, 25, vii, 1965, p. 4140. – History of German, English, and French reception. Basis for present work.

Y42. Friedrichsmeyer, Erhard M. *Erwartung und Erinnerung in den Werken Arthur Schnitzlers*. Ph. D. Diss., University of Minnesota, 187 p. [*Dissertation Abstracts*, 26, ii, 1965, p. 1040. – AS's characters negative and positive types; former hold to the "Augenblicksleben," latter to "continuity of the personality."]

Y43. Derré, Françoise. *L'oeuvre d'Arthur Schnitzler, Imagerie viennoise et problèmes humains*. Ph. D. Diss., Sorbonne, 600 p. [Comprehensive literary investigation of the works and the attempt to deduce AS's Weltanschuung from them. To be published in 1966, Paris: Didier.]

Y44. Just, Gottfried. *Ironie und Sentimentalität in den erzählenden Dichtungen Arthur Schnitzlers*. Diss. Tübingen. [Investigation of AS's hero-types and the linguistic means by which he is portrayed.]

Y45. Kuxdorf, Manfred. *Das Schicksal im Werk Arthur Schnitzlers*. M. A. Thesis, University of Waterloo (Ontario, Canada), 119 p.

Y46. Wiley, Marion E. *The "Einakter" as Dance of Wit ("Spiel") and Court of Justice ("Gericht"): A Structural Analysis of German One-Act Play from Goethe to Dürrenmatt*. Ph. D. Diss., Pennsylvania State University, 260 p. ["The King of Life: Schnitzler," p. 96-175.]

PART Z: RESEARCH IN PROGRESS

EDITIONS AND TRANSLATIONS

z1. Bergel, Kurt. "Das Wort" (S. Fischer Verlag).
z2. Derré, Françoise. "Der Zug der Schatten." [Critical edition and commentary.]
z3. Goldsmith, Ulrich K. "AS – Fritz von Unruh Briefwechsel."
z4. Mueller, Carl. English translations of "Liebelei" (Collier) and "Reigen" (Macmillan). Article on one of the plays. English translations of five plays (Bantam).
z5. Weiss, Robert O. "Die philosophischen Betrachtungen." (S. Fischer Verlag). "Professor Bernhardi." (School edition) (Blaisdell).

CRITICISM

zx.1 Allen, Richard. H. A History of AS's Critical Reception. A Genetic-Structura Study of "Der Weg ins Freie."
zx.2 Beharriell, Frederick J. Critical-analytical study of AS (Twayne).
zx.3 Blume, Bernhard. Extensive essay on AS.
zx.4 Chiarini, Paolo. Extensive study on the dramatic works.
zx.5 Daviau, Donald G. Book on Hermann Bahr in which the Bahr – AS Briefwechsel important.
zx.6 Friedrichsmeyer, Erhard. "Zum 'Augenblick' bei Schnitzler." (Germanisch-Romanische Monatsschrift).
zx.7 Hannum, Hunter G. Chapter on AS in book on modern German literature.
zx.8 Neuse, Werner. History of the use of "Erlebte Rede," including AS.
zx.9 Rey, William H. "Schnitzlers späte Meisterprosa" [An interpretation from "Casanovas Heimfahrt" to "Flucht in die Finsternis" with main emphasis on style and form.] Monograph on AS.
zx.10 Trahan, Elizabeth. Study of AS's literary relationship to Anton Chekhov.

DISSERTATIONS

zy.1 Böhler, Ruth. "Die Gestalt des Abenteuers im Werk AS." (Münster).
zy.2 Farese, Giuseppe. "Traum, seelische Gebrochenheit und Psychoanalyse als Elemente und Strukturen im Prosawerk ASs." (München).
zy.3 Gorlin, Lalla. "Das Problem der Einsamkeit in den Werken ASs." (Columbia).
zy.4 Hannemann, Horst. "Zeiterleben, Erinnerung und Sehnsucht in der Dichtung ASs." (Kiel).
zy.5 Kuhn, Beate. "Stil- und Sprachprobleme bei AS." (Freiburg i. Br.).
zy.6 Low, D. S. "Ausländische Einflüsse auf AS." (Glasgow).
zy7. Melchinger, Christa. "AS und die dramatische Form." (Hamburg).
zy8. Nardoff, Ernest von. "Das Thema des literarischen Symbolismus in den Werken ASs." (Columbia).

129

zy.9   Pillinger, Elfriede. "Dramatische Fragmente aus dem Nachlass ASs." (Wien).
zy.10   Schnetzer, Gaby. "Dramaturgische Probleme beim jungen AS." (Zürich).
zy.11   Schneider, Gerd. "ASs Traumdeutung im Zusammenhang mit der Psychologie Freuds, Adlers und Jungs." (Washington).
zy.12   Vacha, Brigitte – "AS auf dem Wiener Theater." (Wien).
zy.13   Vander Yacht, Douglas R. "Neo-Psychoanalytic Theories of Love as Anticipated in Schnitzler's Major Dramas." (M.A., Indiana).
zy.14   Ward, Darcy. "Problems of Characterisation in the Plays of AS." (London, King's College).
zy.15   Whiton, John. "The Dimension of Social Criticism in the Works of AS." (Minnesota).
zy.16   O'Donnell, James G. "A Study of the Artist in Schnitzler's Narrative Writings." (Indiana).
zy.17   Walton, Sarah Luverne. "The Reception of the Dramatic Works of Arthur Schnitzler on the American Stage." (Indiana).

INDEX OF SCHNITZLER TITLES

(Initial Articles have been omitted)

Vital Moments: C14e.2
Von Amsterdam nach Ymuiden: F1.
Vorspiel zu einem Drama "Der junge
  Medardus": C29.2

Wandernde Musikanten: A21.
Wedding Morning: C4e.2
Weg ins Freie: B31.
Weihnachtseinkäufe: C4.
Weissagung: B27.
Weite Land: C31.
Welch eine Melodie: B58.
Wie wir so still an einem Tische sassen:
  A2.
Wife: C10e.1

Wife of the Wise Man: B14e.4
Wildenstein: A11.
Witwer: B10.
Wohltaten, still und rein gegeben:
  B45.
Woman with the Dagger: C17e.2

Zum Abschied: A18.
Zum grossen Wurstel: C23.
Zum "Professor Bernhardi": F11.
Zur Ermutigung: D1.3
Zur Physiologie des Schaffens: F16.
Zwei Tiroler Novellen: S2.
Zwischenspiel: C25.

INDEX OF PERSONAL NAMES

(Included are translators, critics, editors of AS's works, illustrators, and composers.)

Theis, O.F.: L7.
Thorel, Jean: C5f.1
Thyriot, Hans: C40x.4
Tibal, André: x43.
Titus, E. W.: C13e.2
Tögel, Fritz: C13x.24
Törnsee, F.: C13x.10
Tonnelat, Ernest: B31x.20
Towse, J. Ranken: L4x.3
Trahan, Elizabeth: zx.10
Tree, Ronald: B38x.8
Tressler, Otto: x137.
Trog, Hans: C32x.19

Ubell, Hermann: K1x.7, K4x.2
Urzidil, J.: x232.

Vacha, Brigitte: zy.12
Valette, Gaspard: B9f.1-2, C12x.14
van der Veer, Ethel: C11e.6, C11e.8
Vander Yacht, Douglas R.: zy.13
van Doren, Carl: x237.
van Doren, Mark: C4x.32
Van Rensselaer Wyatt, Euphemia: C4x.33
Vaucaire, Maurice: C4f.2, M1.
Viereck, George Sylvester: x208.
Visser, Stella & Edmond: x138.
Vogelsang, Hans: x382.
vom Bauer, E. E.: C4x.20
von der March, Ottokar: C13x.11
von Ende, Amelia: C23x.2, x115.
Vos, B. J.: S1x.2, x237.
Vries, Louis de: x138.

Walker-Smith, Derek: C32x.34
Wallis, Keene: C13e.3, C13e.5, C13e.11
Wallisch, Friedrich: x166., x312., x343.,
    x364., x365.
Walter: x233.
Walter, Bruno: x301.
Walton, Sarah Luverne: zy.17
Walzel, Oskar: x124., x133.
Wantoch, Hans: B37x.4
Ward, Darcy: zy.14
Warheit, Israel Albert: y16.
Wassermann, Jakob: G9.1, K6x.5, x94.,
    x151., x197., x237., x267.
Weber, C. Hanns von: C12x.15
Weber, Leopold: C13x.12
Weigel, Hans: K17., x336., x359., x366.,
    x396.
Weigert, Hans: C13e.10
Weiglin, Paul: B38x.5
Weil, Robert: C13x.25

Weilen, Alexander von: C36x.6, K9x.2,
    x95.
Weingartner, Felix: x137.
Weiss, Robert O.: B44x.10, F20., x327.,
    x344., x383., x384., y26., y32.,
    z5.
Weitbrecht, Richard: B9x.2, B18x.5
Wendt, H. G.: x209.
Werfel, Franz: x151., x268., x269.
Werner, Richard Maria: B9x.3
Wertheimer, Paul: x137., x179.
Wesely, Jary: x108.
Westerich, Thomas: C13x.26
Weysz, Hans: C11e.1
White, Matthew, Jr.: C4x.21
Whitney, Marian P.: x270.
Whiton, John: zy.15
Wiedenbrüg, Hans: y6.
Wiegler, Paul: B41x.6, B42x.8, B43x.24,
    x234.
Wiese, Benno von: B15.1
Wiese, Kurt: L10.
Wiggins, Clarence Albin: y31.
Wildgans, Anton: x137.
Wiley, Marion E.: y46.
Wilhelm, Paul: K2x.10
Wilms-Posen, H.: y36.
Wilson, Edmund: x235.
Winston, Richard & Clara: B30e.4
Wisdom, J. H.: B19e.3
Witkop, Philipp: x173.
Witkowski, Georg: C28x.1, C36x.7,
    C39x.1
Wittmer, Felix: B42x.9
Wolfe, Lily: C13e.2
Woticky, Edward: C31e.1
Wright, Cuthbert: B37x.9, B38x.9
Wrobel, Ignaz: C13x.34
Wymetal, Wilhelm von: C32x.20
Wyzewa, T. de: C29x.17

York-Steiner, Heinrich: D2x.5
Young, Courtland H.: B15e.1, B15e.5
Young, Stark: C24x.18, C30x.8, x237.

Zahn, Ernst: x237.
Zeisler, Paul Bloomfield: B37e.1
Zenker, E. V.: C29x.8
Zeydel, Edwin H.: C19x.3
Zieler, Gustav: C20x.2, C21x.11-12,
    C22x.2, K2x.11, K3x.13
Zohn, Harry: x367., x385., x390.
Zohner, Alfred: x279.
Zoozmann, Richard: C12x.12

Zuckerkandl, Viktor: B43x.18, D2x.6
Zucker, A. E.: C40x.5, G5.1x6, x237.

Zweig, Stefan (Stephan): x96., x137., x151., x215., x271.

INDEX OF PERIODICALS

The Colonnade (New York): X110.
Commonweal: A Weekly Review of Literature, the Arts, and Public Affairs (New York): C4x.31
The Contemporary Review (London): x284.
Corona (München, Zürich): x240.
Cosmopolis: An International Monthly Review (London): B15.1, C8x.8, C9.1
Current Literature (New York): C10e.1, x26., x47.
Current Opinion (New York): C32x.21

Die Dame (Berlin): B41.1
Decision: A Review of Free Culture (New York): B2e.1
Das Deutsche Buch (Leipzig): B43x.10
Die Deutsche Bühne (Berlin): C13x.17, C13x.21
Deutsche Dichtung (Stuttgart): A14.1, K3x.3
Das Deutsche Drama: Vierteljahrszeitschrift für Bühne und Schriftum (Berlin): C37x.3, x166.
Das Deutsche Drama in Geschichte und Gegenwart: C40x.1, G39x.2
Die Deutsche Kritik: Zeitschrift und Sammelwerk für Theater-Interessenten (Chemnitz): C21x.17
Deutsche Literaturzeitung für Kritik der internationalen Wissenschaft (Berlin & Leipzig): G5.1x2, G8.1x2, x9.
Deutsche Medizinische Wochenschrift (Leipzig):C32x.11
Deutsche Monatshefte: C32x.4
Deutsche Monatsschrift für das gesamte Leben der Gegenwart (Berlin): C15x.10, K3x.10
Deutsche Revue: Eine Monatsschrift (Berlin): B9x.1
Deutsche Rundschau (Berlin): B31x.18, B38x.3, C4x.13, C15x.7, C21x.4, C32x.12, C36x.5, C37.1, K3x.4, x29., x69.
Deutsche Wochenschrift (Wien): B1.1, E1., E2.
Deutsche Zeitung: F7.
Deutscher Journalistenspiegel: x188.
Deutsches Schrifttum (Weimar): C13x.27
Deutsches Volkstum: Monatsschrift für das deutsche Geistesleben: C13x. 31-33, C13x.36, x263.
Deutsches Wochenblatt (Berlin): C12x.4
Deutschland: Monatsschrift für die

gesamte Kultur (Berlin): C15x.13, C21x.6
Deutschlands Erneuerung: Monatsschrift für das deutsche Volk (München): x262.
Deutschvölkische Blätter: C13x.26
The Dial (Chicago & New York): B7e.2, B18e.1, B18x.10, B23e.1, B25e.1, B26e.1, B37e.1, B37x.9, B38x.6, B41x.8, L6x.4, x119., x155., x162.
Doitsu Bungaku (Tokyo): B35x.1
Dr. Blochs Wochenschrift: B31x.4
Donauland: B37x.1, C36x.3, x132.
Drama: A Quarterly Review of Dramatic Literature (Chicago): C5e.1, x83.
Drama Magazine (Chicago): x172.
The Dramatist: A Journal of Dramatic Technology (Easton, Pa.): C4x.26, C17x.2
Dramaturgische Blätter (Berlin): K2x.5
Du: Kulturelle Monatsschrift: C25.6, G7.4

The English Review (London): B12e.1, C32x.34
L'Europe nouvelle: Revue hebdomadaire des questions extérieures, économiques et littéraires (Paris): K9x.6
Everybody's Magazine (New York): C4x.24

Die Fackel (Wien): K2x.1
Das Feuer: Monatsschrift für Kunst und künstlerische Kultur (Weimar): x135.
Feuerreiter: C32x.26
Fortnightly Review (London): B14e.2, B15e.4, C17e.2, L8x.1, x46.
Forum (München): F12.
Forum (New York): B38x.8, B43x.14
Forum (Wien): C4.21, E14., x329., x352., x355., x357.
Frankfurter Zeitung: C4.6
Freeman (New York): B37x.7, B38x.9
Freie Bühne für den Entwicklungskampf der Zeit: B6.1
Freie Deutsche Bühne (Berlin): C13x.19
Der Freie Landesbote (München): A1., F2.
Die Freie Welt (Reichenberg): B41x.2
Freistaat: Süddeutsche Wochenschrift für Politik, Literatur und Kunst (München): C13x.4, C13x.5

(Binghamton, N. Y.): B18x.11, B39x.22, C4x.34, DIx.3, G2.5x, J10x.1, x344., x351., x363., x367., x368., x374., x376., x379., x383., x386., x389., x391., x393-x395.
The Judaeans (New York): C32x.24
Das Jüdische Echo (Wien): x390.
Die Jüdische Rundschau (Berlin): B39x.16, B43x.19, B59x.1, x185., x283.
Jüdischer Almanach (Wien): B31.3, G1.1
Jugend: Münchner illustrierte Wochenschrift für Kunst und Leben: B21.1, C16.1

Kleine Schriften der Gesellschaft für Theatergeschichte: G5.2, G6.1
Komödie: Wochenrevue für Bühne und Film: C13x.18
Der Kreis: Zeitschrift für künstlerische Kultur (Hamburg): B39x.1, x229.
Kritik (Wien): C8x.12, C11x.4, C25x.1
Der Kritiker (Berlin): x158.
Kunst und Volk (Wien): C40.1
Der Kunstwart: Halbmonatsschau für Ausdruckskultur auf allen Lebensgebieten (München): B3x.14, B31x.2, B31x.15, B36x.5, B41x.4, C5x.2, C8x.3, C12x.9, C13x.12, C15x.12, C21x.2, C25x.8, C26x.4, C29x.11, C30x.4, C31.2, C31x.8, C32x.7, K2x.3, K3x.7, K6x.1, x161.

Der Lesezirkel (Zürich): x154., x176.
Life (Chicago): B36x.15, C4x.18, C4x.30
Das Literarische Deutsch-Österreich (Wien): x24.
Das Literarische Echo: Halbmonatsschrift für Literaturfreunde (Berlin): B18x.4, B22x.1, B31x.9, B36x.3, B37x.3, B37x.5, B38x.4, C5x.4, C11x.1, C12x.10, C12x.13, C13x.6, C13x.13, C15x.2, C20x.2, C21x.11, C22x.2, C23x.1, C24x.4, C25x.9, C26x.2, C29x.15, C31x.3, C32x.9, C36x.6, C36x.8, C36x.9, C37x.2, K2x.6, K2x.8, K2x.11, K3x.13, K3x.15, K4x.2, K6x.10, K7x.2, K9x.2, x13., x18., x36., x38., x55., x77., x127., x165.
Die Literarische Warte: Monatshefte für Kunst und Literatur (München): C21x.9

Die Literarische Welt (Berlin): B43x.8, B43x.15, DIx.2, x215., x234.
Literary Digest International Book Review (New York): B18x.9, B31x.21, B36x.16, B39x.12
Die Literatur: B39x.5, B39x.17, B40x.1, B42x.8, B43x.24, B44x.2, C16x.1, C38x.1, C39x.3, C40x.2, C40x.4, D2x.4, x210., x225., x238.
Living Age (Boston): B41x.9, B42x.1, B45e.1, x236.
London Mercury (London): x153.

März: Eine Wochenschrift (Berlin & München): C32x.20
Das Magazin: Monatsschrift für die Literatur des Auslandes (Berlin): C4x.2
Das Magazin für Litteratur (Berlin): C8x.6, C11x.2, C12x.11, K1x.4, K2x.9, x22.
Medical Life (New York): x282.
Medizinische Klinik (München & Berlin): G7.2
Menorah: Illustrierte Monatsschrift für die jüdische Familie (Wien & Frankfurt a.M.): B31.6, DIx.1, D2.2, D2x.5, x212.
Menorah Journal (Harrisburg, Pa.): L9x.6
Mercure de France (Paris): B38x.1, B43x.16
Der Merker: Österreichische Zeitschrift für Musik und Theater (Wien): A12.2, A13.2, A14.9, A20., C3x.5, C5.4, C11x.8, C15.2, C29x.1, C36x.1, F11., x45., x63., x65., x66., x70., x73., x76., x78-x82., x88., x90-x94., x96., x97., x122.
Metropolitan Magazine (New York): B15e.6
Mitropa Zeitung: B21.5
Modern Drama (Lawrence, Kansas): x338.
Modern Language Journal (New York): B17x.1, C19x.3, S3x.1
Modern Language Notes (Baltimore): G5.1x6, G8.1x3, x274., x378.
Modern Language Quarterly (London): G5.1x4
Modern Language Review: A Quarterly Journal Devoted to the Study of Medieval and Modern Literature and Philology (Cambridge): G5.1x5, x294.

Moderne Dichtung: Monatsschrift (Leipzig, Brünn, Wien): C4.2, C4.4
Moderne Rundschau: Halbmonatsschrift (Wien): A13.1, B5.1, C4.5, F5.
Die Moderne Welt: B39X.13, X137., X138., X140., X141., X148., X150.
Moderner Musen-Almanach auf das Jahr 1894: B8.1
Der Monat (Berlin): C13X.48
Monatshefte der deutschen Freunde (Berlin): S1X.2
Monatshefte für deutschen Unterricht (Madison & Milwaukee, Wis.): B17X.2, B17X.3, G5.1X1, G8.1X1, X198., X281., X307., X313.
Monatsschrift für neue Litteratur und Kunst (Berlin): B9X.3, C8X.7
Monatsschrift für Ohrenheilkunde und Laryngo-rhinologie (Wien): X257.
Motion Picture Classic (Brooklyn, N. Y.): C4e.8
Münchener Medizinische Wochenschrift: B44X.6, X364.
Munsey's Magazine (New York): C4X.21

Nassau Literary Magazine (Princeton, N. J.): B39X.15, B41X.15
Die Nation: Wochenschrift für Politik, Volkswirtschaft und Literatur (Berlin): B18X.3, C4X.4, C8X.4, C12X.6, C15X.1, C15X.9, C21X.5, C24X.6, C25X.4, K1X.5, K3X.6
The Nation (New York): B38X.7, B41X.16, B43X.7, C4X.32, C24X.16, C29X.9, L4X.3, L6X.3, X121., X139., X231.
Nation and Athenaeum (London): B37X.8, B39X.10
Neophilologus: A Modern Language Quarterly (Groningen & The Hague): C9X.1
Neue Bahnen (Wien): C13X.10-11
Neue Bücher: Besprechungen (Bonn): B42X.13
Neue Deutsche Hefte: X366.
Neue Deutsche Rundschau (Berlin): B9.1, B11.1, B12.1, B19.2, B19X.1, C8X.5, C11.1, C12X.7, C13X.2, C14.1, C15X.3, K1X.3, K3X.8, X3., X6.
Das Neue Deutschland (Berlin & Gotha): X142.
Neue Freie Presse (Wien): B16.1, B18.1, B22.1, B26.1, B27.1, B29.1, B34.1, B56.1, C20.1, C26.1, C29.1, C38.1, F16.
Die Neue Generation (Berlin): X103.

Das Neue Jahrhundert (Köln): X11., X12.
Die Neue Literatur (Leipzig): J7X.1, X262.
Neue Revue (Wien): B7.1
Die Neue Rundschau (Berlin): B25.1, B31.1, B31X.7, B33.1, B36.1, B38.1, B39.1, B41X.6, B43X.18, B44X.4, B47.1, B49.1, B55.1, B58.1, B60.1, C21X.7, C22.1, C24X.7, C29.2, C31X.11, D2X.6, D3.2, E9., E12., E13., F20., G2.1, G2.2, G7.1, G9.1, G12.1, K6X.5, K7X.3, X17., X52., X89., X151., X163., X250., X267., X268., X317.
Die Neue Zeit: The New Times, Wochenschrift für Politik, Kunst und Literatur (Chicago): B42X.9
Neues Frauenleben: X108.
Neues Wiener Journal: B24.1, F8., F13.
Neues Wiener Tagblatt: B44.2, B45.1
New Quarterly (London): X41.
New Republic (New York): B18X.8, B36X.9, B36X.11, B39X.8, B41X.7, B43X.9, B44X.5, C13X.44, C24X.18, C30X.8, C31X.14, L4X.2, L6X.1, L9X.2, X235.
New Statesman and Nation (London): B39X.4, B39X.18, B39X.20, C32X.33. L9X.3
New York Dramatic Mirror: C4X.15, C5X.6, C11X.5, C19X.1, C31X.15
New York Dramatic News and Dramatic Times: C4X.16
New York Times Book Review: B18X.7, B36X.13, B39X.6, B41X.3, B41X.11, B42X.6, B43X.4, B43X.13, B44X.1, C4X.10, Fe.2, L5X.1
New Yorker: B36X.12, B42X.11, B43X.1, C13X.16
New Yorker Staats-Zeitung: B19.3, C20.1
Nord und Süd: Eine deutsche Monatsschrift (Breslau): C24X.2, C26X.3, C29X.21, X7., X58.
The North American Review (Boston & New York): X72.
La nouvelle revue (Paris): C13X.14
La nouvelle revue française: Revue mensuelle de littérature et de critique (Paris): B36X.6, C13X.39, X40.

Österreich in Geschichte und Literatur: X363.1
Österreichische Rundschau (Wien): B30.1, B31X.13, B31X.19, C24X.9,

C24X.12, C25X.6, C29X.4, C31.1, C31X.7, C37X.1, E5., K6X.4, X95.
Ost und West: Illustrierte Monatsschrift für das gesamte Judentum (Berlin): B31X.3, K5X.2, X30., X31.
Outlook and Independent (New York): B37X.12, B41X.10, B44X.3, C4X.29, L9X.5

Pan (Berlin): C4X.5, X86., X87.
Die Persönlichkeit: X113.
La petite illustration (Paris): C5f.2
Philological Quarterly: A Journal Devoted to Scholarly Investigation in the Classical and Modern Languages (Iowa City): C32X.32
Phöbus (München): C5X.8
Pictorial Review (New York): B17e.5
Plain Talk Magazine (New York): B43X.5, D1e.1
Poet Lore (Philadelphia & Boston): C11e.1, C12e.1, C14e.1, C17e.1, C22e.2, C23X.2, C31e.1, X71., X193.
Polybiblion: Revue bibliographique universelle (Paris): C13X.15, M1X.1
Prager Tagblatt: A17., A21.2, B41.2
Preussische Jahrbücher (Berlin): C5X.3, C12X.1, C15X.4, C17X.1, K3X.9, X15., X189.
Psychoanalytische Bewegung (Wien): X266.
Publications of the Modern Language Association of America: C13X.38, C31X.17, X272., X278., X375.
Publisher's Weekly (New York): B38X.10, C13X.37, X214.

Die Quelle (Wien): A14.7, B20.4, K7X.4

Das Recht (Wien): C32X.2
Red Book Magazine (Chicago): C4X.23
Der Regisseur: Fachblatt für Theater, Musik und Kunst: C21X.1
Reuch (Petersburg): B34.2
Revue d'Allemagne et des pays de langue allemande (Paris): C18f.1, X202., X221., X239., X244., X246., X251., X261., X269., X271.
Revue d'art dramatique et musical (Paris): C4f.1
La revue de France (Paris): B44f.1
Revue de l'enseignement des langues: B36X.17

La revue de Paris: B31X.20, C5X.10, C13X.40, X43.
Revue des deux mondes (Paris): B43X.20, C29X.17
Revue hebdomadaire (Paris): B19f.1
Revue mondiale (Paris): B38X.12, M2X.2, X241., C4.7
Die Rheinlande: X64.
Rigasche Zeitung: B29.4
Die Roman-Rundschau (Wien): B37.5
Die Romanwelt: Zeitschrift für die erzählende Litteratur aller Völker (Stuttgart & Berlin): B13.1

Saturday Review (London): C3X.4, X100.
The Saturday Review of Literature (New York): B18X.6, B36X.14, B37X.11, B38X.11, B39X.9, B41X.12, B42X.4, B43X.11, B43X.12, B44X.7, C30X.7, D2X.3, X258.
Die Scene: Blätter für die Bühnenkunst (Berlin): X157.
Die Schaubühne (Berlin): B37X.4, C21X.14, C24X.3, C24X.13, C25X.2, C25X.5, C29X.5, C29X.14, C29X.19, C30X.1, C32X.1, C36X.2, K5X.1, X67.
Die Schöne Literatur: Beilage zur Literarischen Zentralblatt für Deutschland (Leipzig): B18X.5, B39X.3, B41X.14, C21X.12, C25X.7, C29X.7, C31X.6, C32X.14, C38X.2, C39X.5, C40X.3, K9X.1
Semaine littéraire: B9f.1, C12X.14
Die Sendung (Berlin): X247.
Simplicissimus: Illustrierte Wochenschrift (München): C6.1
Smart Set: A Magazine of Cleverness (New York): B15e.2, C32X.15
Der Spiegel (Hamburg): C13X.43, X345.
The Spur (New York): X204.
Stratford Journal (Boston): C14e.5
Der Strom (Wien & Berlin): B13.4
Süddeutsche Monatshefte (München): B31X.8, B35.1, C32X.16
Survey (New York): B43X.23

Der Tag (Wien): A21.1
Das Tagebuch (Berlin): X143., X187., X217., X223.
Texas Review (Austin & Dallas): X134.
Das Theater: Illustrierte Halbmonatsschrift für internationale Bühnenkunst (Berlin): C29X.2, C29X.13, C31X.5, X75.

149

UNIVERSITY OF NORTH CAROLINA
STUDIES IN THE GERMANIC LANGUAGES
AND LITERATURES